# CHILDREN OF COMMUNISM

STUDIES IN HUNGARIAN HISTORY

*László Borhi, editor*

# CHILDREN OF COMMUNISM

## Politicizing Youth Revolt in Communist Budapest in the 1960s

SÁNDOR HORVÁTH

TRANSLATED BY
THOMAS COOPER

INDIANA UNIVERSITY PRESS

This book is a publication of

Indiana University Press
Office of Scholarly Publishing
Herman B Wells Library 350
1320 East 10th Street
Bloomington, Indiana 47405 USA

iupress.org

This book was produced under the auspices of the Research Center for the Humanities of the Hungarian Academy of Sciences and with the support of the National Bank of Hungary.



Manufactured in the United States of America

First printing 2022

Cataloging information is available from the Library of Congress.

ISBN 978-0-253-05973-4 (hardback)
ISBN 978-0-253-05972-7 (paperback)
ISBN 978-0-253-05970-3 (web PDF)

*To my children, Sanyi, Julcsi, and Ferkó*

And cold hopes swarm like worms within our living clay.

PERCY BYSSHE SHELLEY, *ADONAIS: AN ELEGY ON THE DEATH OF JOHN KEATS*, READ BY MICK JAGGER, HYDE PARK, 1969

Everyone must be made to understand, especially the young people,
that the most beautiful human goal is socialism, communism.

JÁNOS KÁDÁR IN THE LÁNG MACHINE FACTORY, BUDAPEST, 1969

# CONTENTS

# ACKNOWLEDGMENTS

A RESEARCHER WITH AN INTEREST in contemporary history sometimes must grapple with complex challenges when looking for interview partners for a story. For this book, I did not have to beg the time of famous or politically influential people and entreat them to share details about their pasts. Rather, I had to importune everyday individuals who had never played prominent roles in public events and in many cases had never taken any great interest in politics, but who had still been very exposed, in their everyday lives, to the changes wrought by political regimes. I would like to express my sincerest thanks first and foremost to my interview partners, without whom I never would have been able to write this book. These individuals include, among others, Big Kennedy, Éva Bedecs, Hobo, Indian, Jimmy, Mária, Midget, and, last but not least, Pharaoh, who provided considerable help finding the others. The conversations I had with them not only brought the information I had found in the archives to life but also called my attention to new issues and questions that further shaped my research.

I also would not have been able to write this book without the help of archivists in the Historical Archives of the Hungarian State Security, who gave me invaluable assistance obtaining and interpreting the secret police files, and in the Budapest City Archives (where I was among the first to have the opportunity to research police files), the Political History and Trade Union Archives, and the Hungarian National Archives.

I would also like to express my gratitude to László Borhi, the editor of the series Studies in Hungarian History at Indiana University Press. Borhi gave me the encouragement I needed to undertake the at times daunting task of writing this book. I also owe a debt of thanks to Pál Fodor, who was instrumental in promoting the idea of publishing this book. I also benefited immensely from conversations with my colleagues, who shared their insights as I was writing and revising the book. I am grateful to Mónika Baár, Gábor Gyáni, Gábor Klaniczay, János Mátyás Kovács, Rolf Müller, Gábor Kresalek, János M. Rainer, Áron Nagy-Csere, Marci Shore, Tibor Takács, and all of my colleagues at the Institute of History of the Hungarian Academy of Sciences.

I would also like to express my gratitude to the institutions that provided the necessary support during the years I spent working on this book. I would mention, first, the Institute of History of the Hungarian Academy of Sciences (which was recently made a part of the Eötvös Loránd Research Network), which ensured the necessary conditions for focused and sustained research. Many other institutions provided financial and/or in-kind support: the Hungarian Scientific Research Fund (OTKA), the School of International and Public Affairs at Columbia University in New York, the Mellon Foundation, the Institute of Human Sciences (IWM) in Vienna, the Center for Advanced Studies at Ludwig Maximilian University (LMU) in Munich, the Institute for East European Studies at the Free University in Berlin, the Imre Kertész Kolleg (IKK) at Friedrich Schiller University in Jena, the Gerda Henkel Foundation, and, last but not least, the Research Center for the Humanities of the Hungarian Academy of Sciences with the support of the National Bank of Hungary. I am grateful to these institutions for their generous support.

I would also like to thank Thomas Cooper, the translator and proofreader of the text, who took the trouble to understand what I was trying to say in each and every sentence and always tried to keep me on target to get the manuscript done.

It has been a pleasure, as always, to work with Indiana University Press and its staff, whose professionalism and kindness contributed immensely to the final manuscript. My work benefited significantly from the readings of the two anonymous reviewers, whose questions and suggestions helped me make the manuscript more reflective, clearer, and more coherent. I would like to express particular thanks to Jennika Baines, Sophia Hebert, and Rachel Erin Rosolina, and also to Nancy Lila Lightfoot, who ensured that the production process went smoothly, and to Julia Turner, who did an outstanding job copyediting the manuscript. I am also grateful for the wonderful book cover designed by Nancy Smith.

Finally, I would like to thank my family for their patience during the time I spent writing the book. Many thanks to you, Gabriella, my wife, for helping me focus on writing, and to you, Sanyi, Julcsi and Ferkó, my children, for your patience and love. I dedicate this book to you in the hopes that, for you and for later generations, it will offer some understanding of the trials and traumas suffered by the main characters of this story, trials and traumas which, I similarly hope, you and later generations will be spared.

# CHILDREN OF COMMUNISM

# INTRODUCTION

ON A HILL BY THE southern wall of the Buda Castle stands a stately Japanese pagoda tree (*Sophora japonica*), one of the oldest trees in Budapest. Toward the end of the 1960s, young people in Budapest started referring to the tree, which was planted as an exotic imported specimen roughly two hundred years ago, as the "Great Tree." It was the largest tree on the southern side of the castle wall above the so-called Youth Park, a site created by the Communist Youth League for concerts and socializing. It proved a good hiding place. If one walks down the hill from the castle toward Gellért Hill or the site of the former Youth Park, the Great Tree is difficult to notice, particularly in the summer, when the foliage on the boughs of the other trees hides it. From the shade under its branches, one can see the buildings of Pest, with the cupola of St. Stephen's Basilica in the middle, the largest church building in Budapest. Gellért Hill, the bridges leading to Pest, and Margaret Island to the north form the horizon, making something of a captivating spectacle, which is one of the reasons why the area remains popular among tourists today.[1]

It was this area that was transformed, under the communist government, into the Youth Park in 1961. The beautiful view, however, probably played no role in the way the authorities came to depict a specific group of young people who gathered there, for the most part to listen to music as their symbol of revolt, as did many members of the younger generation in 1969. The concerts held in the Youth Park could be heard from the Great Tree, so as the years passed, increasing numbers of young people gathered there to listen to music for free.

On July 5, 1969, 3,500 butterflies were released in front of an audience of almost half a million people in London's Hyde Park at a Rolling Stones concert held in memory of Brian Jones. Jones had been found two days earlier in his swimming pool, drowned at the age of twenty-seven. His death drew a great deal of attention to the concert, which had been organized weeks earlier as a chance for the band to present their new guitarist, who was going to replace Jones. Before the concert began, Mick Jagger read excerpts from *Adonais*, an elegy written by Percy Bysshe Shelley in memory of John Keats. The concert was broadcast by the BBC, so it reached audiences worldwide and dramatically increased the band's already large fan base.[2]

News of the concert even made it to the city of Budapest,[3] the capital of Hungary, on the far side of the Iron Curtain, where it was heard by young people who spoke only a few words of English at best. At the time, the world was waiting and watching to see which superpower would put a man on the moon, but in Budapest, a handful of ragtag youths wanted to commemorate Jones's death just like young people in the West were doing. On July 8, the young people gathering around the Great Tree organized in Budapest a march termed the "Hippie Stroll" as a commemoration of Jones's death. This stroll, which started from the Great Tree, may seem innocuous enough in retrospect, but by the time it had come to an end, many of the participants had been arrested by the police and had accusations, for the most part of a political nature, brought against them. This is how the story of the so-called Great Tree Gang (*Nagyfa galeri*)[4] began, a story that was crafted by the state authorities, including the police, the courts, and the press.

This book centers on the arrest of a group of young people referred to by the police as the Great Tree Gang. Using this incident as a touchstone for the rest of the work, I offer chapters on the interconnected topics of Hungarian youth politics, police surveillance of youth, the tabloid press, and the construction of socialist and postsocialist identities. I explore how and why the socialist authorities in Hungary adopted the Soviet construct of hooliganism to depict certain young people, mainly consumers of rock music, as deviant and how the authorities created, specifically, the story of the Great Tree Gang. I argue that as part of its efforts to further at least the appearance of political and social consensus in post-1956 Hungary, the Kádár regime promoted the idea that youth deviants were an organized threat to society and offered itself as protection from this threat. The notion of youth deviance was a way for the regime to gain support through fear of social disorder, and through this idea, the authorities also sought to produce loyal young citizens. Although cultivating youth was an important effort of the Kádár regime, the story of the Great Tree Gang gave the state bodies a chance to present the official narrative of deviance and normalcy and to present deviance as morally suspect and a threat to society.

The narratives fashioned by the press, the administrative authorities, and the police maintained the power status of these three branches of the regime (and the regime itself). Meanwhile, the "hooligans," who had simply been enjoying youthful abandon (and committing some petty crime), were described as enemies of the people and sentenced to prison. As a result, formerly apolitical youths were transformed into staunch political opponents of the regime.

I examine how police and media figures prosecuted and portrayed nonconformist young people in Budapest, Hungary, in the 1960s and made these young people symbols of an allegedly politicized youth revolt. The intention is to further a nuanced understanding of the contradictions in communist policies regarding a new generation of young people and the competing rhetorics of state officials, the secret police, the communist youth organization, and the socialist tabloid press. Although I do not argue that repression of subcultures was more important than the constructive policies in schools or youth organizations, the story of the Great Tree Gang offers insights into and examples of the repressive steps taken against young people by the regime and the controversies to which these measures gave rise.

I also explore the ways the police and communist party devised a new strategy to legitimate their moral authority in socialist society. No longer able to avail itself of the kinds of repressive measures that had been used in the Stalinist period, the regime sought to reassure citizens that the police were vigilant in protecting public safety by portraying minor infractions carried out by wayward youths as politically motivated. The story takes place at a time when communist Budapest represented a new kind of "socialist consumerism"—not simply because of the presence, in ever larger numbers, of Western tourists, but also because of the state's efforts to present the regime to its subjects as proconsumerist. Accordingly, socialist consumerism became a major source of legitimacy and a stabilizing force for the communist regime in the 1960s and 1970s.[5] The proconsumption policy was in part a product of the regime's proconsensus policies after the 1956 anti-Soviet revolution in Hungary. As anthropologist Krisztina Fehérváry puts it, "producing citizens with high expectations for modern material world was integral to the project of creating a utopian society."[6] However, as historian Eli Rubin has observed in connection with the consumer culture of the German Democratic Republic (GDR, or East Germany), the everyday culture that emerged as a consequence, in part, of the proconsumer and proconsensus policies cannot be understood simply as the result of the efforts of the regime. Rather, this culture should be seen as a "hybrid of the wants and needs of ordinary citizens" and "the wants and needs of the powers that were in control."[7]

I also consider the broader historical context that made it possible to create the story of the Great Tree Gang. I explore in this period the everyday workings of the police and the close connection between tabloid journalism and police officers that illustrate the shift to less visibly repressive measures in the exercise of state control after 1956. Because the citizens of socialist Hungary did not subscribe to so-called socialist morals, they could react critically by adopting habits and styles prevalent in Western popular culture and also part of the consumer culture that was emerging in Hungary. Manifestations of youth culture and the consumption of rock music also served as symbols of a possible way of life, and they indicated the willingness of the state, if perhaps within limits, to make accommodations for Western popular culture.

The narratives created by the authorities about the younger generations also served pedagogical aims. As Katherine Verdery has observed in connection with the end of the Ceaușescu era, "the Securitate [the Romanian secret police] increasingly became a pedagogical or didactic rather than a punitive institution."[8] Similarly, I argue that the secret police, the press, and the juvenile and children protection services cooperated closely during the socialist era in campaigns against youth culture that were characterized as part of a fight against youth violence.

This book examines the ways the official rhetoric influenced the social identities of members of the younger generation and the extent to which the younger generation was able to influence official youth policy. In the 1960s, a generation was growing up that had no experience of life before socialism. Members of this generation had been born after 1945 under a socialist regime and had only limited information concerning parts of the world where young people lived differently (i.e., the Western world). I seek to further an understanding of the ways the communist party in Hungary used mass culture to win over a new generation, the members of which were children of communism, since they had been born into and grown up in a world fashioned by the party. They were socialized in a world in which notions of a clash between capitalism and communism and the ultimate victory of socialism over capitalism as the superior system were parts of their everyday lives (for instance, in the propaganda that surrounded them and as elements of the education they were given in schools). Indeed, the story of the Great Tree Gang was created by the authorities in part because it provided a useful thread for the larger narrative of a clash between capitalism and socialism. Meanwhile, the Kádár regime's model of consumerist socialism and the fact that the authorities linked so-called hooliganism and social disorder to 1956 had a highly important role in the construction of the narrative regarding youth deviants, which was based on an antifascist ideological mobilization.

The creation of the story of the Great Tree Gang and the uses to which it was put reveal a great deal about the prevailing norms to which teenagers in Hungary in the 1960s had to adapt. Why did the authorities end up taking such an intense interest in a few dozen teenagers? Why were newspapers still reporting on the proceedings launched against some of the kids even months later? The answers to these questions lie in part in the roles that were ascribed to young people after World War II by organs of the state that were largely in the hands of members of the older generations.

Childrearing, schooling, and child welfare had become symbolical battlefields before World War II, and during the war, the reconstruction of families and childrearing norms became synonymous with the survival of civilization itself.[9] Fascism and communism both attempted to indoctrinate and mobilize children as one of their pillars of social support, even in attempts to mobilize the population for war.[10] Although political regimes of various ideological and national stripes have tried to influence and mobilize youth since the "invention of adolescence" in the nineteenth century, the very concept of youth cultures and subcultures became more visible political tools all over the world after World War II.[11] This is particularly true if we define *the youth* as a constructed socio-political category and not as an age-defined group of people. After 1945, the meaning of *youths* as a social category changed, as did prevailing ideas concerning how to raise young people properly. This was true in part because the younger generation had a seminal role in the reconstruction of societies fragmented by the war but also because this generation was cast as a new hope for Cold War Europe.[12] The notion of youths as a distinct social group provided a useful emblematic figure in larger narratives about social changes after the war—a figure, indeed, with explanatory power as both cause and effect. In other words, the troubled youth served as evidence of the alleged dangers posed by social changes and at the same time as the very threat to social institutions and continuity.

But what happened to young people in the decade after the war that made them so important (and so allegedly dire a threat to social order) in the 1950s and 1960s? The moral outrage at alleged incidents of violence among the youth in the early 1950s was given so much attention in the media that in 1955 even the United Nations placed the "prevention of juvenile delinquency" on its agenda.[13] Hardly a decade had passed since the end of the war, and the fear of new eruptions of violence was putting young people in headlines all over the world. The younger generation was used by the press in the Eastern Bloc to craft images of the West and images of a new, internal enemy. This was often done by citing voices of moral outrage in the West. The 1960 United Nations report titled

"New Forms of Juvenile Delinquency" described the new youth cultures as the main problems faced by postwar societies, and it found a new form of juvenile delinquency in the violent gang cultures in several countries, such as the Halbstarke (Germany), the teddy boys (UK), the blousons noirs (France), the hooligans (the Soviet Union), the vitelloni (Italy), and similar groups.[14]

Beginning in the late 1950s, in tandem with increasingly conspicuous depictions of youth groups as violent and the sense of moral panic that was provoked by these depictions, a growing body of scholars and journalists began to examine the lifestyles and habits of groups of young people who were characterized as nonconformists as elements of distinctive youth subcultures.[15] The images of "young people today" and moments of moral panic concerning the dangers posed by (allegedly) rebellious youths played an important role in the creation of myths of consensus across Cold War Europe as governments sought to promote conformity by creating a threat to social values (and cohesion) in the form of supposedly dissolute youths.[16]

The term *moral panic* was coined by Stanley Cohen in his book *Folk Devils and Moral Panics* (1972), a classic sociological study of the mods and rockers phenomenon of the mid-1960s. Confrontations between mods and rockers (two British youth subcultures) were happening regularly at England's seasides, usually on bank holiday weekends. The public representation of rockers was centered on motorcycling, black leather jackets and boots, pompadour hairstyles (the Elvis cut), and the influence by Marlon Brando in *The Wild One,* while the mods were represented usually with their scooters, suits, and clean-cut outfits. In addition to differences in their visual style, these two groups had favorite music genres that were distinct: rockers listened to rock and roll, while mods preferred genres like soul, rhythm and blues, and ska. The fights between them became daily news in the United Kingdom in 1964, and accordingly, the newspapers represented them as violent troublemakers. Cohen, via analysis of their representations, offers the following definition of the term *moral panics*: "a condition, episode, person or group of persons [that] emerges to become defined as a threat to societal values and interests; its nature is presented in a stylized and stereotypical fashion by the mass media; the moral barricades are manned by editors, bishops, politicians and other right-thinking people; socially accredited experts pronounce their diagnoses and solutions; ways of coping are evolved or (more often) resorted to; the condition then disappears, submerges or deteriorates and becomes more visible."[17] In this context, *moral panic* implied a periodic tendency toward the identification and scapegoating of folk devils (for Cohen, the mods and rockers) whose habits and pastimes were regarded by hegemonic groups as indicative of imminent social breakdown.

According to this model, panics function as an ideological safety valve that restores social equilibrium.[18]

The mythology of a classless society in the discourse of Soviet bloc countries, however, ensured that the images of folk devils crafted there took on a distinctive character, as socialist states saw youths as the perfect candidates for the embodiment of ideological norms and an ideal means with which to illustrate the differences between socialist and Western modes of behavior—at least, as far as socialist states defined those terms. I argue that while in Cohen's analysis media fearmongering creates social panic that prompts official responses, in the Soviet bloc countries, the media and the police were working in close cooperation. Together, they strove to create a quasi–moral panic regarding youth violence. If we adopt and modify Cohen's model to make it fit the Eastern European context, we have to consider how the police were using the press and why the police sought to light the fuses of these quasi–moral panics. In the case of Hungary, the most important force behind the quasi-panic concerning youth gangs was the police, because the press in an Eastern Bloc country had only limited influence compared to the press in the West. Although the socialist tabloid press played a very important role regarding new social identities among young people (and prevailing perceptions of these identities), party control over the press prevented journalists from crafting, unencumbered, narratives of youth crime. As I go on to discuss, in the case of Hungary, the press reports were subordinated to the police proceedings, not vice versa. The moral campaign against youth culture and so-called hooligans was led primarily by the police, not the press, which is why it is more accurately characterized as a quasi–moral panic. It is hard to confirm, in retrospect, what the public perception of the alleged deviancy of youth culture was, but as the depictions of the youth gangs came from the police themselves, they may well have not sparked any real panic among the readers of the newspapers.

Meanwhile, in the West and the East consumerism became the identifier for young people at the turn of the 1950s and 1960s.[19] For young people in socialist countries, the West represented a land of promise and plenty, although their knowledge of the Western other was highly limited and controlled by the socialist state.[20] They drew on a repertoire of images of allegedly Western practices. As historian Eleonory Gilburd argues, the import of Western culture created a Soviet West that was as Soviet as it was Western.[21] For example, "Soviet hippies drew from the practices and symbols of the Pioneers and Komsomol [communist youth organizations] as well as symbols, music, and fashions from San Francisco."[22] At the same time, however, the ways young people made use of this symbolic language (the language of dress, music, lifestyle, etc.) in turn influenced the narratives crafted by the regimes in Central Europe in their efforts to fashion alleged threats to the social order and justify the measures they took against these purported threats. This book examines both the ways the official rhetoric influenced the social identities of the young people and the extent to which members of the younger generation were able to influence official youth policy.

The analysis devotes considerable attention to the impacts of the 1956 Hungarian anti-Soviet uprising and the 1968 youth movements, as both played strong roles in the emergence of youth policies and youth identities.[23] Thousands of young people participated in the 1956 revolution in Hungary as freedom fighters on the streets of Budapest, so in the wake of the revolution, the reestablished communist regime had to confront the serious possibility that it enjoyed less favor among members of the younger generation. I contend that the regime's efforts to cast 1956 as a series of criminal acts committed by hooligans trivialized the demands of the revolution. But if the revolution of 1956 was a turning point in communist policies as well as in youth policy, then the year 1968 was a critical moment in the image of potential political participation as the first year after World War II that offered new opportunities for political participation for the generation born after the war.[24] Participants in the Western youth revolts of 1968 at first resembled potential allies for the communist party because they were critical of the consumer capitalist system. Not surprisingly, these revolts were widely covered in the official press in Hungary. The propaganda machine of the socialist state used these youth revolts as an element in its attempts to buttress its claim that socialism was more humane than capitalism. This propaganda backfired, however, for in Hungary, knowledge of and interest in the Western youth cultures started to symbolize a revolt against the socialist state.

The state institutions strove at all levels to win over the younger generation by observing, shaping, and controlling the processes through which it was socialized. Accordingly, the construction of Eastern European nonofficial youth cultures as countercultures helped bolster the practice of conjuring images of the West and fashioning ideological and military anti-Western (also anti-American) and antimodernist discourses. It also furthered the emergence of more rigid generational and social identities. These new identities were not necessarily political. Indeed, at times they were very apolitical; however, the politicizing of youth revolts gave these identities a political dimension, and they also came to be seen as part of a dropout culture. The campaign involving the younger generation also enabled the main antagonists of the public discourse on the younger generation (the police, the socialist press, and the organs of the state in charge of youth policy) to win legitimacy for their goals and the goals of the communist party. This regime kept this campaign very much in the public eye and used it to curry the favor of wider Hungarian society by casting some members of the younger generation as criminals and others as youths in need of the state's protection if they were to be saved from the temptations of a criminal lifestyle. The fact that the official campaigns against youth deviancy painted a distorted picture did not mean that young people never committed any violent acts. Disruptive behavior happened on a sporadic basis. However, the authorities and the socialist media took sporadic incidents and cast them as coordinated acts committed by members of deviant subcultures.

This approach to youth policy was driven in no small part by the desire to prove to the citizenry that socialism was a better system than capitalism, since in a socialist system the state takes care of the younger generation, while in the West (according to the socialist propaganda machine), young people were rebelling against consumer culture. This book suggests that the conceptual borders between the East and the West were not merely a kind of ideological Iron Curtain but also elements of a cultural practice that created social identities that mirrored the official opposition between East and West.[25]

The responses of the authorities to alleged Western influence (e.g., films, literature, music, clothing, or haircuts) helped shape new social identities and establish new norms of behavior among young people. Accordingly, the authorities and the youth could interpret the Cold War as a cultural conflict and cultural practices (e.g., music or musical genres) as weapons. According to this interpretation, musical genres represented the most influential weapon in this war, as they were able to create not only identities for young people but also a new cultural space and new cultural preferences through which members of the younger generation could express their relative autonomies during the socialist period. Films, new music, and fashion became cornerstones of the new social identities for young people.[26] Party functionaries and journalists of the official party press all over Eastern Europe, following this logic, created imagined communities (youth cultures and gangs) that were represented as consumers of Western popular culture in general.

As Kaspar Maase writes, "'America' provided not only the material that was particularly good, tactically, for the staging of a provocation. It also provided a discourse in which the legitimacy of mass culture and the culture that aesthetically is found in it can be articulated."[27] Furthermore, in the countries of the Eastern Bloc (Hungary among them), the public discourse on an imagined mass culture, or, in the case of young people, on the imagined youth of America, made it possible for the state to (1) use this discourse to strengthen its own legitimacy and (2) allow young people to express their views on politics within a sphere that the authorities saw as harmless. In short, the communist system sought to reinforce its own ideology by borrowing from Western discourses on generational conflict and mass culture, since this facilitated the construction of socialist interpretations of the mass culture associated with America. *Longhair* acquired a political meaning that the police used to emphasize their own (alleged) importance. It was easier to win approval for the alleged struggle of the police against young hooligans than it was to gain acceptance for the political arrests.

Thus, the habits and lifestyles of members of the youth (sub)cultures in the Soviet bloc were documented by the organs of state authority, such as party commissions and secret police departments that were created to monitor youth activities in schools and universities, especially after 1956. Accordingly, in this book I make intense use of the documents of local party commissions regarding youth issues and the secret police archives. However, to avoid limiting my inquiry to the one-sided perspective of the secret service, I also use the documents of the local courts, municipal administration, youth organizations, party archives, and, last but not least, oral history interviews with former officers, journalists, party cadres, and members of the so-called gangs. It is admittedly difficult to reconstruct popular opinion regarding youth cultures on the basis of these sources, so while it is tempting to suggest that cases like the Great Tree Gang may have had an influence on popular opinion regarding youth, however plausible this may seem, it remains an assumption.

In the first part of the book, I examine the executive and judicial bases on which the story of the Great Tree Gang (the alleged group of young fascists) and the Hippie Stroll was created. I use materials from the police investigations against the alleged gang members and the trial (chaps. 1–2). I examine the kinds of activities in which a group of young people living in Budapest in 1969 had to engage to attract the attention of the institutions that shaped the public discourses on youths, institutions that, based on allegedly moral considerations, devoted far more attention to these issues than they actually merited. In other words, I consider how the images of deviant youth or hooligans were created and how the concept of youth subculture moved away from fashion and toward violence after 1956 (chap. 3). I then consider how the public discourse on young people in Hungary in the 1960s became first and foremost a question of maintaining law and order, in which the police and the institutions dealing with minors and the protection of minors played decisive roles (chaps. 4–5).

To a large extent, this public discourse determined the social identities from which members of the younger generation could choose when making various socially relevant decisions. The range of choices was mediated by the socialist tabloid press, which reached ever larger segments of society after 1956 (chap. 6). Finally, I examine how the members of the group of youths in question presented their socially relevant decisions and their "revolt" in their own private writings (specifically, notebooks that were used by two alleged gang members almost as diaries) as well as how the official rhetoric changed their images of themselves in these notebooks (chap. 7), what roles gender relations played in the creation of the story (chap. 8), and how all of this was later remembered by some of the people involved (chap. 9). Gender roles are also worthy of special attention because the sources very rarely mention women as young people or members of a gang: it is as if the youth problem was primarily a problem for young men.

The book explores how notions of new social identities created through the construction of youth subcultures rested on representations of older intergenerational and intragenerational contrasts. I contend that the socialist state transformed this older set of contrasts to depict a difference between the older and the younger generations, between the capitalist West and the socialist East. One of the functions of this contrast was to prove that the states of the Soviet bloc had won the contest between the two competing systems (socialism and capitalism). The communist regimes borrowed headlines from the West concerning rebellious young people and used them to shape perceptions of young people and youth itself to prove that young people in the West were revolting against an unjust consumer society. Thus, this element of Cold War propaganda led to the emergence of the notion of a stark difference between young people in the West and young people in the Soviet bloc. This alleged difference became not only a cornerstone of the discourses concerning youth questions but also the bases for expressions of autonomy among young people and efforts by the regimes to legitimize state measures against the youth and assert consensus. Meanwhile, in the Soviet Union, the young communists could hold dual identities, consuming the imagined West and listening to Western music while participating in ritualistic ideological meetings without seeing any contradiction between the two.[28]

The politicization of the so-called youth question, however, had far-reaching consequences. By keeping young people under close observation and at times subjecting them to various forms of persecution, the system managed to transform members of the younger generation who were for the most part apolitical and simply took an interest in Western mass culture into political enemies. Toward the end of the 1960s, a generation came of age for which visions (and illusions) of Western consumer culture became important values and for which it was perfectly normal and natural for Western products and fashions to have political significance.

## NOTES

1. Balázs, "Az Ifipark," 137–39.
2. Wyman, *Rolling with the Stones*, 329.
3. *Esti Hírlap*, July 3, 1969, 8; July 9, 1969, 5; *Népszabadság*, July 31, 1969, 6.
4. The word *galeri* (youth gang) is singular, while *galerik* is plural (youth gangs). *Nagyfa* means Great Tree.
5. See Patterson, *Bought and Sold*, 10.
6. Fehérváry, *Politics in Color and Concrete*, 5.
7. Rubin, *Synthetic Socialism*, 12.
8. Verdery, *Secrets and Truths*, 17.
9. Zahra, *Kidnapped Souls*; Zahra, *Lost Children*.
10. Clark, *Holy Legionary Youth*; Gorsuch, *Youth in Revolutionary Russia*; Kucherenko, *Child Soldiers*.
11. Gillis, *Youth and History*; Osgerby, *Youth in Britain since 1945*.
12. Jobs, *Riding the New Wave*; Poiger, *Jazz, Rock, and Rebels*; Weiner, *Making Sense of War*.
13. *Prevention of Juvenile Delinquency*.
14. Middendorff, *New Forms of Juvenile Delinquency*.
15. See P. Cohen, *Subcultural Conflict and Working Class Community*; Hall and Jefferson, *Resistance through Rituals*; Ginzberg, *Values and Ideals of American Youth*. The interpretation of the theme in Hungary was determined by ideological reasons, especially by the representations of the participation of youngsters in the 1956 uprising. Thus, beginning in the 1960s, researchers focused more and more on why young people became "criminals" or "deviants" (Huszár, *Fiatalkorú bűnözők*; Molnár, *Galeribűnözés*).
16. S. Cohen, *Folk Devils and Moral Panics*; Lebow, "Kontra Kultura: Leisure and Youthful Rebellion in Stalinist Poland."
17. S. Cohen, *Folk Devils*, 9. For revising the theory of moral panics, see McRobbie and Thornton, "Rethinking 'Moral Panic.'"
18. For a comprehensive survey of the use of the term *moral panic* from its first use in 1972 to the present day, see Hunt, "'Moral Panic' and Moral Language in the Media."
19. Fürst, *Stalin's Last Generation*, 3.
20. The longing for the West became a generational experience. For the consequences of this experience in 1989, see Bottoni, *Long Awaited West*, 177–216.
21. Gilburd, *To See Paris and Die: The Soviet Lives of Western Culture*.
22. Risch, introduction to *Youth and Rock*, 11.

23. Kürti, *Youth and the State in Hungary*; Mark, Gildea, and Warring, *Europe's 1968*; McWilliams, *1960s Cultural Revolution*.
24. See Clifford, Gildea, and Mark, "Awakenings."
25. Cf. Junes, *Student Politics in Communist Poland*.
26. Poiger, *Jazz, Rock, and Rebels*, 67.
27. Maase, *Was macht Populärkultur politisch?*, 109.
28. Yurchak, *Everything Was Forever*, 209.

ONE

# THE HIPPIE STROLL

THE CONSTRUCTION OF THE STORY of the Great Tree Gang, the most "notorious" gang of young people in Budapest at the time, began on the evening of July 8, 1969, when police cars arrived, sirens blaring, at Liberty Square (Szabadság tér) in downtown Budapest. The police apprehended some adolescents gathered there and began to interrogate them. Both the police and the adolescents began to fashion stories of the escapade, dubbed the Hippie Stroll, which then became part of both the court documents and reports in the press.

The version of the story that became most widely known, however, was fashioned in the main building of Hungarian Television, which is on the west side of the square, less than one year after the news report had been broadcast. According to this account, the young people in question had been engaged in a "fascist demonstration." As it so happens, they had been going to the building of the American embassy on the far side of the square to hold a sort of moment of silence in memory of Brian Jones, who played guitar, sitar, xylophone, and other instruments for the Rolling Stones. For the teenagers, it was natural that the memorial meeting was held in front of the American embassy; although Jones was British, they did not care much about the nationality of the Rolling Stones members, and for them, the American embassy symbolized freedom.

What did Brian Jones have to do with the communist police or a group of Hungarian teenagers who were later characterized as fascists at the end of the 1960s? And how did this all take place in what was roughly the middle of the socialist era in Hungary, when the system seemed stable and indeed would last another two decades? This chapter explores how this group of young people became a dangerous social force in the eyes of the police, bureaucrats, and the

Figure 1.1. Budapest from the shade of the Great Tree, 1964 (Fortepan / Ferenc Sugár).

press. It also examines which institutions took part in this process and how. I focus on both the roles of the different historical agents (such as the police, institutions of youth protection, and the media) and the public discourses through which notions of "youth cultures" were constructed. I argue that the story of the Great Tree Gang was created and elaborated through the joint efforts of the police, the press, and the Communist Youth League.[1] They did this because they aimed to raise and shape members of the younger generation in a way that corresponded with notions of proper childrearing according to socialist ethics. The roots of the conflicts between the youth and police lay in neither hostile attitudes among the youth toward the police nor tensions between parents and their children. Rather, the measures used by the police against the youth were a logical consequence of policies of the police force as an institution and exigencies faced by the regime. These measures were also influenced by conflicts among the young people, in some cases over their social statuses. The violent methods used by the regime against the younger generation in the 1960s were less visible than the methods that had been used in the previous decade, but these forms of coercion were effectively used to ensure that the younger generation was cast as a threat. This was one of the ways the regime strove to secure its own legitimacy.

## WITNESSES

The person who took the first step, as it were, in casting the Hippie Stroll as a fascist action was an ordinary man, a conductor named Péter Bognár. On July 8, 1969, three days after the Rolling Stones concert in Hyde Park, Bognár was with his girlfriend, Zsuzsanna Járai, in her apartment in the center of Budapest not far from the Basilica, a large church in central Pest that today is a popular destination for tourists. The twenty-three-year-old Járai, who was eleven years younger than Bognár, worked as a stenographer and typist in the Corvina Publishing House office in Váci Street.[2] Both Péter and Zsuzsanna would later tell police that they had been getting ready to go to a concert and had left the apartment at roughly 8:30 p.m., but we know that in the end, they never arrived at the concert. The fact that they left the apartment when they did influenced the fate of several other people, as did a sudden change in the weather that day. The day before, ambulances had hit the streets of Budapest 120 times to provide care for people who had fainted because of a summer heat wave.[3] By July 8, however, the weather had gone down to about fifteen degrees centigrade, even though it was the middle of summer, and because of the cold front it had started to rain.[4]

As Bognár and Járai left the apartment, evening was falling.[5] The streets were relatively empty because of the bad weather,[6] but a strange-looking group of people was coming from the direction of St. Stephen's Basilica, perhaps some eighty people in total. They were marching in step in twos, but from time to time, they would stop marching, stand at attention, and stomp on the ground with their right feet. This march was an imitation of something they had seen in the film *Battle of the Bulge*, a color American war film that was playing in theaters in Hungary at the time, to the great delight of Hungarian audiences. The film includes scenes of German soldiers making similar shows to demonstrate their sense of camaraderie that have since become iconic.[7]

One of the heroes of *Battle of the Bulge* is Martin Hessler, a slender, blond Panzer tank commander. A critic writing for the *Szolnok Megyei Néplap* (Szolnok County people's news) claimed that Hessler was "clever, cultured, gallant, courageous, popular" and that "his soldiers loved him fanatically." According to the review, "if the Americans at times made films in which they belittled the Wehrmacht and the SS soldiers, in this production they have gone to the other extreme and have thoroughly idealized them."[8] The young people marching down the narrow street in the center of Budapest that summer evening were simply playing the roles of the German soldiers in the American war film, but as a result, they could easily be mistaken for kids with Nazi sympathies.[9]

Figure 1.2. Cinema "Bástya," Budapest, 1969 (Fortepan / *Magyar Rendőr*).

The group included a number of young men or boys with long hair and striking garb. There were only ten or fifteen girls. Some of them were singing something that, given the melody and the manner in which they were walking in step, may well have resembled a German marching song. Bognár identified it as (or, at least, believed it to be) the German military marching song "Erika," which had become popular at the beginning of World War II. This song was not the "Panzerlied" featured in the film, and none of the young people in the group knew German terribly well, although many of them may well have known an obscene Hungarian version of that song.[10] At first, Bognár had thought that they "might have been German tourists," who, toward the end of the 1960s, were coming to Budapest in ever greater numbers. But then he had heard them speaking Hungarian.[11] The group had formed a line roughly twenty meters long by the time it had caught up with Bognár and Járai, and Bognár came to the conclusion that it must be a fascist demonstration.[12]

An alarmed Bognár called the Budapest municipal police and ran to the Workers' Militia headquarters in Arany János Street, which, according to rumors circulating at the time, was linked via a secret tunnel to the Danube Palace of the Foreign Ministry a few hundred meters away.[13] Bognár asked the officers on duty to arrest the people, who were (in his assessment) disturbing the peace. By this time, the young people were walking in the direction of Liberty Square. Járai in the meantime had followed the procession—first at a distance of some ten or fifteen meters; then breaking off; and, once the group had reached Liberty Square, keeping a distance of some forty or fifty meters.[14]

The Workers' Militia had been created in 1957, in the wake of the 1956 revolution, as a kind of party army under the direct command of the communist party. It had been organized on the basis of Czechoslovak and East German (not Soviet) models, but initially the members of the militia had gotten their weapons from Soviet soldiers. It was a paramilitary organization that was used first and foremost at communist mass events and celebrations to maintain order. Its members included, alongside paid employees who worked in the center, communist party members, who frequently spent their free time in the Workers' Militia Centers.[15] The primary task of the organization was to prevent and control any and all large gatherings.[16]

On July 8, 1969, however, the militias were not sent out in droves in response to the marchers. A thirty-five-year-old mechanic and technician named Gyula Bognár (no relation to the aforementioned Péter Bognár) was on duty that day in the National Workers' Militia Headquarters.[17] According to his testimony, around seven thirty in the evening, an unfamiliar man, Péter Bognár, had come to the center and asked the members of the militia to do something about a disturbance in the street (at the beginning of July, it stays light in Budapest until roughly nine o'clock in the evening). Although the young people outside were walking right past the building, no one inside could hear them singing since the windows were closed because of the cooler weather. Had no complaint been made, the members of the militia in all likelihood would not have done anything. In any event, Péter Bognár, who was later a principal witness, told the people on duty in the militia headquarters that a large group of people outside was singing a German song, "Erika," and shouting cheers in Hitler's name. He added that he had already informed the police officers on patrol. The militia guards on duty reported this to their commander, who ordered two of them to help Péter Bognár. Gyula Bognár and one of his coworkers at the factory, who was probably not in uniform, set out for Liberty Square. They must not have

Figure 1.3. Some members of the Workers' Militia, 1968 (Fortepan / Pál Berkó).

hurried, since the police arrived at the square before they did. By the time they arrived, they saw members of the police already at work. With Péter Bognár's help, the Workers' Militia members managed to catch one (and only one) of the young people, the rest of whom were now trying to flee, and they turned him over to the police.[18]

The police came in a matter of minutes in part because the police force had been strengthened following the 1968 invasion of Czechoslovakia. In 1969 and 1970, the state set aside more money for the police force, in particular for police patrols and officers responsible for maintaining the peace in public spaces. One of the principal reasons behind this was to preclude the emergence of any kind of oppositional movements resembling the movements that had led to the Prague Spring, which had prompted the countries of the Warsaw Pact, Hungary among them, to invade Czechoslovakia.[19]

At 7:50 p.m., police lieutenant János Pusztai received orders from the political officers on duty to go to the police headquarters in the Fifth District (inner city) because an arrest had been made "for suspicion of having committed a political crime." There he learned that eleven people had been apprehended by officers working out of two patrol cars. Several of those detained had simply been watching the spectacle unfold, and they were having their papers checked by the police.[20] Even several hours after these events, the police were still apprehending some of the youths, who had fled in all directions, and checking people's papers in the nearby side streets. According to his testimony, Péter Bognár saw a group of young people being detained and said, "If only I knew where the others ran off to."[21] Some of the others—including a young man who later became infamous as a gang member known by the name "Nagy Kennedy," or "Big Kennedy"—had run toward the bank of the Danube River (which was only a few hundred meters away), jumped in, let themselves be taken downstream by the current, and climbed out once they were far enough away from the police.[22]

## THE FILE

What, then, was the police version of this event? The authorities' narrative described a show of "opposition," took violent measures against the young people involved, and transformed the event first into a secret police affair and then into a court case accompanied by a tremendous brouhaha in the press. How was the regime able to legitimize these actions?

The contemporaneous police and court documents, the articles that were published in the press, and the reports that were submitted on youth policy and the protection of minors offer a linear account of this Hippie Stroll and the group itself, which was dubbed the Nagyfa galeri, or Great Tree Gang. The fact that such an event could even take place was explained with reference, first and foremost, to the negative influence of Western and mass culture, to so-called hooliganism (which, according to the state propaganda, had been spreading ever since the 1956 revolution, an event that the communist regime always referred to as a counterrevolution), and to the carelessness of youths who had strayed down the "wrong path." If one examines the documents more closely, however, they reveal a great deal more about the organs of power that produced them than they do about the young people involved in the Hippie Stroll.

By the spring of 1969, the district police regularly made young people gathered around the Great Tree identify themselves by showing their papers.[23] The first report on them, however, was written on June 27, 1969. Police major Imre Seres played an important role in the creation of the story, since he wrote the reports that were in the dossier on the Great Tree youths. According to his report, an agent who had the code name "Lamb" had informed him one day before of youth congregating: "I was in the area above the Youth Park, where the hippie and beat young people of the inner city gather. Most of them do not

Figure 1.4. People identify themselves by showing their papers, Budapest, 1974 (Fortepan / *Magyar Rendőr*).

work, they have long hair, are disheveled and unwashed. They number between 70 and 100. They all know one another loosely. There are some girls among them, their behavior is striking, they party, and most of them are vagrants." As he would have been expected to do, the case officer who assessed the report wrote, "The members of the various youth gangs in the area above the Youth Park gather in the afternoon and evening. There, they engage in striking conduct. We already know the people listed in the report, who last year also gathered here. The young people who gather here, including several nonpolitical prisoners released from prison, are particularly interesting from the perspective of criminal affairs."[24]

This was the first time that the site itself—namely, the Great Tree—had been linked to gangs, and this served as a point of departure for the creation of the police narrative about the Great Tree Gang. The agents and informants who submitted reports on the people who gathered in the area around the Great Tree presented the site as being important because they were expected to do so by their case officers. In the secondary literature on secret police reports of the time, there is wide-ranging consensus that the authors of the reports had to meet the expectations of their case officers above all else, even in their use of language and style. Furthermore, their most important goal was to create a perception of threat of "enemy machinations" using rhetorical tools.[25]

The police version of the story of the Great Tree Gang was therefore in line with the expectations of the state security forces precisely because the state security forces wanted to create this "crime." The resulting story was thus structured more by the people who wrote the documents and the order of the documents in the file than it was by the people who wrote the reports or gave evidence. The first investigation dossier in the case was opened on October 2, 1969, long after the actual stroll had taken place. It contained the first police version of the story, which later the court, the press, and even the young people on trial retold in a number of different ways. The principal reason for this was that the events of the evening of July 8, 1969, which at the time had seemed unimportant to Major Imre Seres, had in the meantime become politically interesting to him.

Imre Seres had plenty of experience composing stories about gangs. When he was captain, the aforementioned agent, Lamb, had submitted reports to him for years on the "inner city" gang and then the "Moscow Square" gang, or "Kalef,"[26] in secret meetings in an apartment referred to by the code name "Szegedi," the very apartment where they would begin to weave the story of the Great Tree Gang. Seres had completed an earlier, larger assignment, the "Agárdi" file on the Moscow Square gang, on December 2, 1968, and submitted a summary report.[27] He had to open new files to keep the people involved in the network occupied and also to meet the expectations of his superiors, since this was one of the ways he proved to them that he was working. But he had to find a dossier in which to put the written versions of the reports, which were submitted once every two weeks.[28] In 1969, Seres was promoted to the rank of major. It was after this that he came up with the story of the Great Tree Gang, which produced six new files (each roughly 250 pages long, in accordance with the expectations of his superiors)[29] in which he could put the agents' reports and prove that the state security was doing its job. In order to open the dossier, he had to refer to an event that in some way drew on the legacy of 1956 and

Figure 1.5. A movie frame from a film made by the film studio of the Ministry of Interior used to teach methods of recruiting secret agents and related technical details, Budapest, 1962 (Fortepan / BM Filmstúdió).

alleged "fascist slogans" and some act of political opposition that had been committed in a public place. The young people strolling down the street on the evening of July 8, 1969, and the arrest in the autumn of 1969 of the young man known by the nickname Big Kennedy, who was among the people who would regularly hang out beneath the boughs of the Great Tree, gave him precisely what he needed.

In the fashioning of the story of the Great Tree Gang, a request that Seres made on October 2, 1969, was of decisive importance. Seres asked permission to open a dossier under the cover name "Tőröző," or "Stabber." He also asked that, given the political gravity of the case, he be allowed to open a separate personal dossier on Big Kennedy. He contended that it would be necessary to open a separate file because, "on the basis of the materials that have come in," the police had learned that a "gang-style group" had formed in the area around the Great Tree that consisted of young people coming from the "infected" nodes of the capital. "Among the people who have thus gathered," he claimed, "talking politics in an oppositional tone has become common, as has reviling our system and the Soviet Union, expressing fascist views, using the greetings 'Heil Hitler' and 'long live Szálasi,' making anti-Semitic statements, and disparaging the police."[30]

As a seasoned officer, Seres must have known that to compose the text and to persuade his superiors to accept the case, he would also have to make some reference to the 1956 uprising and the alleged persistence of its legacy. This was why he needed Big Kennedy, who, as someone who had become a ward of the state at age five, was perhaps the most vulnerable of the youths. As part of the story, he claimed that in 1966, Big Kennedy, who would have been sixteen years old at the time, had "organized a celebration with his peers [at the correctional institution for minors in Aszód] of the tenth anniversary of the counterrevolution." Thus, the Hippie Stroll was tied to the events of 1956. Seres also contended that "operative information suggests that they wish to continue the disturbances of the peace that were committed in July, possibly with a larger number of participants, and so they planned a gathering and disturbance of the peace on October 23, 1969." Imre Seres based all this on the testimony given by a group member identified as Márta K. and a boy with the nickname "Christ" as well as reports submitted by agents and informants.[31]

Christ's father had formerly worked in the Ministry of Interior, which oversaw the secret service. The usefulness of the testimony given to the police by Christ probably explains why, once it had been written down, he was no longer mentioned among the first suspects in the case.[32] The authorities used Christ's testimony as the keystone for their claim that the Great Tree Gang, which was first mentioned in the police documents in September 1969, was planning a disturbance of the peace on October 23, which was the day the 1956 revolution had broken out and when most of the forbidden commemorations of the revolution were held.[33] Thus, the testimony made it possible for the police to link the Great Tree Gang to 1956, and in exchange, the young man was given a short sentence and soon set free.

The link to 1956 was an important thread justifying the opening of the file. Another was the first political report on the procession of allegedly unruly (and allegedly fascist) youths, which Lieutenant János Pusztai wrote the day after the event. In this text, the contention that the young people "were singing German SS marching songs" is underlined, a charge that was used to apprehend eleven people. Only four of these eleven people were considered to have taken part in the organization of the procession, however, so the others were released.[34] The deliberate misapprehending of the obscene text of the parody of the German song probably served the goals of state security, one of which was to regularly find "fascist enemies" in the streets of Budapest. This was important in part simply because the state security forces had to justify their own existence and the violent measures used by the police.

On the basis of all this, the political police, and first and foremost Seres and his subordinates, began to compose a narrative of the events of the fateful evening so that the story could later be turned into an indictment. According to the summary report included in the file,[35] after the opening of the Youth Park, which was run by the Hungarian Communist Youth League, young people who had not been let into a concert because of their garb or because they didn't have enough money to pay the entrance fee (or because, perhaps, they had spent that money on drink) would go to the tree above the park to listen to music. Thus, the story of the Youth Park and the Great Tree Gang were closely interlinked.

## YOUTH PARK

At the suggestion of a committee of the Hungarian Communist Youth League, on August 20, 1961, the Youth Cultural Park was opened to the south of Buda Castle. This was part of a larger process in the first half of the 1960s during which Gellért Hill and the surrounding area were transformed into attractive destinations for tourists.[36] The average entrance fee into the park was five forints, and from the outset expectations regarding dress excluded many and contributed to the formation of the group of youths who gathered around the Great Tree. The entrance fee was only a problem for young people who had no income at all, since in the 1960s the average monthly income was HUF 1,600–1,800.[37] However, a lot of young people did not go to the park because of the strict stipulations concerning dress and general appearance. Boys were required to have short hair and be dressed in jackets that bordered on formal wear, a white button-down shirt, and a tie. Girls were expected to wear skirts. Instead of bothering with this dress code, many young people simply found places in the area around the park and listened to music from there. In 1968–69, the Youth Park welcomed more visitors than in any other year, and on May 27, 1969, the park celebrated the entrance of its one-millionth guest.[38]

In 1969, there was even more publicity than usual leading up to the annual opening of the Youth Park on May 1 (International Workers' Day). All spring, the events that would be held in the park were advertised on trams and buses and in newspapers, and on the day the park opened, 4,803 people bought tickets; over the course of the entire year, the park welcomed more visitors than usual. Because of this, the police introduced, for the first time and to the satisfaction of the leaders of the Hungarian Communist Youth League (which maintained oversight over the park), the "on-duty officer system, in agreement

Figure 1.6. The queue at the Youth Park, Budapest, 1969 (Fortepan).

with the police superintendent of the First District. Its purpose was to have the on-duty officer perform all the identity checks and measures necessary from the perspective of the police. The other police comrades on duty were responsible for ensuring order in the promenade—a public space—in the upper area of the park."[39] According to the Big Kennedy file, some of the police who fulfilled these functions behaved perfectly normally and did not harass the young people gathered around the Great Tree, and at the worst most of them did little more than regularly compel the young people to show their identity papers.[40]

It became a tradition that on Tuesday amateur bands would play, including the progressive rock band Sakk-Matt (Checkmate), which was one of the most popular bands among the Great Tree people. Between 1966 and 1969, more tickets were bought for performances on Tuesdays than for any other weekday.[41] This was why there were so many people at the Great Tree on July 8, 1969, a Tuesday, the day of the Hippie Stroll.

The director of the Youth Park, a man named László Rajnák (who had once been a first-class wrestler), and his men liked to stroll through the park dangling their nightsticks to encourage the young people to spend their free time in the pursuit of cultured activities with "educational purposes." Rajnák was one of the most experienced organizers of the socialist youth club system. In the early

1950s, having been commissioned by the Union of Working Youth (Dolgozó Ifjúság Szövetsége, or DISZ) Committee of the Óbuda Ship Factory, he created a club for young people in Óbuda that became known as the "teddy boy farmstead."[42] Working in cooperation with the caterers as a kind of socialist entrepreneur, the park leader managed to increase traffic and circulation in the park dramatically, and with the support and even patronage of the Hungarian Communist Youth League, he grew rich. In 1973, he was arrested for embezzlement, in all likelihood as the consequence of an internal fight for position.[43]

By 1967, the park was bringing in more than three times as much money as it had in 1962, and in 1968, earnings jumped by 35 percent, to more than HUF 1 million.[44] In 1969, the number of people who visited the park increased by 150 percent compared to the previous year, a jump that was achieved by appealing to younger teenagers (between the ages of fourteen and sixteen). As musician Lóránt Schuster recalls with a tinge of nostalgia, "this was the big meeting place. It was here that the newly arrived girls from the folksy circles who did spinning and weaving hung out, and the urban student girls from the inner city made sure, with their presence, that there was a good selection, not just in quantity but also in quality."[45] By the end of the 1960s, the average age of the people who came to the park had dropped by three or four years. Rajnák increased the number of organizers by ten or fifteen people on days when the park was particularly crowded, and he had two to four people patrol the area above the park. The police also sent two officers to provide assistance.[46] The area, which until then had gone unmentioned in the official documents, was put under close observation. The site itself and the young people who regularly gathered to listen to music became highly visible, and they were mentioned more and more frequently in police reports. The Great Tree and the area around it began to figure prominently in the police documents because the Youth Park had become increasingly popular and increasingly crowded, so the entire area was put under police observation.

Because of the growth in the number of people who came regularly to the Youth Park, the fundamental change in its image, and the fact that the area above it was put under closer observation by the authorities, the Great Tree began to be seen as a place where unkempt youths with long hair and bedraggled clothes would come and hang loose, hit up passersby for spare change, organize orgies with the girls who belonged to the gang, and fritter away their free time with useless pursuits. But, of course, this raises questions: How does a given "pastime" become "useful," and how does *idleness,* allegedly the favorite indulgence of subcultural groups, become a normative term? How did idleness figure as a crime in earlier police proceedings, and how did the uses of this term

Figure 1.7. The area above the Youth Park, Budapest, 1972 (Fortepan / Tamás Urbán).

and concept influence assessments of the young people who came to the tree overlooking the Youth Park to listen to music?[47]

At the time, Hungarian law classified anyone above the age of eighteen who could not prove that he or she had a permanent place of work as a "dangerous idler." (The Hungarian term, *közveszélyes munkakerülő*, is a bit more complex and hard to translate, but it essentially means "person who avoids work and constitutes a threat to public safety.") In most cases, someone convicted of being a dangerous idler was sentenced to thirty days in prison.[48]

"We create the impression of fevered idleness as if we were working diligently. But we must take great care to be sure this does not degenerate into work." In 1968, the police read this scribbled remark on a sheet of paper found on László P., a nineteen-year-old unskilled worker, after eleven young people

Figure 1.8. People above the Youth Park, Budapest, 1969 (Fortepan / Mona).

had been apprehended by the police because they had been strolling down Rákóczi Avenue in central Pest on an evening in May, scruffy and unkempt and wearing garb considered inappropriate (for instance fur-lined coats turned inside out).[49] In the end, the young people were released, in part because of police lieutenant Colonel Ferenc Györök's contention that "in the month of May the hippie phenomenon could not spread further in the capital."[50]

Beginning at the end of the 1960s, as police reports and newspaper articles made ever more frequent reference to the hippie movement, gang members were often identified as hippies. According to the police and the press, the "hippie gang members" were antisociety, antiwork, and antiwar.[51] This last characteristic was considered positive as long as the word *war* was thought to refer to the Vietnam conflict, but following the invasion of Czechoslovakia by the Warsaw Pact countries, an antiwar sentiment was seen as less of a virtue. The difference, compared to the early 1960s, was really simply that "in 1964, hooligans wearing ties and windbreakers over their suits" caught the attention of the police, "while in 1968, [they were replaced by] hippies wearing bell-bottoms and shirts with flowery patterns."[52] Beginning in 1968, the police wrote about the young people who gathered from time to time (usually to listen to music) as if they were hippies. Many young people took some pleasure in being referred to by this term, even some who had heard hardly anything about hippies in the West.

## THE STROLL

In the summer of 1969, in keeping with a practice that had been used for years, several editions of *Magyar Ifjúság* (Hungarian youth), the newspaper of the Communist Youth League, appeared with pictures of slender girls in bikinis on the cover page and, beneath the caption "Working Men of All Countries, Unite!,"[53] an invitation to the so-called building camps run by the league.[54] The hopes and efforts of the league notwithstanding, many of the young people living in the working-class districts preferred spending their time at the Great Tree as opposed to going to the camps. On July 7, 1969, the young people who gathered regularly at the tree hoped, with good reason, that the following evening guitarist Béla Radics (who had become something of a legend in his own time) and his first band, the aforementioned Sakk-Matt, which played progressive rock and blues (Jimi Hendrix, Cream), would hold a concert in the Youth Park. Although at the time Sakk-Matt was among the bands that were hardly favored and was even harassed by the authorities, in June 1969 it had performed in front of an audience of five thousand to six thousand young people, and in July 1969, *Magyar Ifjúság* had even published a picture of the band members.[55]

Figure 1.9. Béla Radics, the guitarist of the rock band Sakk-Matt, 1969 (Fortepan / István Péterffy).

In all probability, the young people who gathered around the Great Tree did not regularly read the communist party daily *Népszabadság* (People's liberty), which at the time had offered an account of János Kádár's trip to Bulgaria and had forecast the impending cold front that ended up being the reason organizers canceled the concert scheduled for the afternoon of July 8 (a Tuesday). Duck (a nickname, originally Kacsa), who was an influential figure in the Great Tree group, encouraged everyone to go stroll the streets of the central part of the city and to go to the American embassy to commemorate the death of Brian Jones, the member of the Rolling Stones, who in their minds embodied the American hippie, even if he was himself English (he was still part of Western culture and his music was a Western cultural import). They set out, walking in two lines, on the Hippie Stroll in the direction of Erzsébet Bridge, which had been opened some five years earlier and was a symbol of modernization in Hungary in the 1960s. They had heard the phrase *hippie stroll* from a Swedish girl who was the daughter of parents who had immigrated to Sweden and who spent her summers in Hungary, presumably with relatives. At the time, she was Big Kennedy's girlfriend.[56]

The group of between eighty and one hundred young people strolling across the bridge in unusual clothes (usually including jeans), most of them with long hair, sang Hungarian children's songs in chorus, specifically one song that begins "Lánc-lánc eszterlánc" and another that begins "Sétálunk, sétálunk." (Both songs would be familiar to most Hungarian school children today. In the first, children hold hands and sing about a thread of reed or yarn. The second is a short walking song the text of which in English would be "We stroll, we stroll, we sit down on a little hillock, plonk.") The police later noted in their report that when the young people reached the part of the second song that goes "We sit down on a little hillock, plonk," they often crouched down.[57]

They continued on to Váci Street, which was the mecca of "consumer socialism" in the 1960s (it was full of window displays, neon signs, and Western tourists). There, one of them bought a loaf of bread. The others surrounded him and started chanting in chorus, "We want bread, we want work," which—despite the obvious irony—the police later characterized as incitement against the system. The youths, most of whom were unemployed, had previously invented the Dangerous Idlers' Works so that they would have a "permanent place of employment." Lord Szőke (Lord Blondie), who had the letters *ÉSZ* ("reason" or "mind") tattooed on his forehead, was named director of the Works. According to others in the group, Lord Blondie often ate what the girls who had fallen in love with him brought him when they gathered around the Great Tree, even though it was said of him that if he had to choose between making love to a girl

Figure 1.10. Váci Street, a street full of shop window displays, 1970 (Fortepan / Zoltán Szalay).

or robbing her, he would pick the latter. Thus, it is not entirely surprising that as they strolled down Váci Street, the young people started chanting "bread without work!" The police later interpreted this as a call for support for the unemployed. Of course, in socialist Hungary (and the other socialist countries of the Eastern Bloc), officially there was no such thing as unemployment, so a call for support for the unemployed constituted a crime.[58]

When they came to the end of Váci Street, Duck steered the group in the direction of the basilica so that they could commemorate the death of Brian Jones with a "beat mass." Although Jones had had high levels of drugs and alcohol in his blood when his body had been found in his swimming pool in Cotchford Farm, East Sussex,[59] his fans nonetheless suspected that he had been murdered, and masses for the dead were organized all over the world in his honor. On the occasion of his funeral on July 10, girls wearing miniskirts had inundated the St. Mary's Parish Church in Cheltenham (Jones's hometown).[60] News of beat masses spread through Budapest in 1968 in no small part because, like the Communist Youth League, the church had realized that it could use lighter shades of rock music to appeal to members of the younger generation. In May 1968, *Népszabadság* had reported with dismay "girls wearing Coca-Cola buttons and swaying to blues melodies" in Mátyás Church (the church on castle hill in Buda overlooking the Danube).[61] The door to the basilica, however, was locked, so the young people sat down on the steps for a while to chat with passersby.

They then set off in the direction of Liberty Square. Many of them, emboldened perhaps by the fact that so far nothing had happened to them, wanted to go to the American embassy to commemorate Jones. On the way, according to police reports that were drafted after the fact, a few of them were singing the SS marching song "Erika."[62] This was when Péter Bognár and his girlfriend had seen them and called the police. Had Bognár not made that call, the event probably never would have attracted the attention of the police or the press, nor would it have become a fateful moment in the lives of the young people involved.

When Duck and the others made it to Liberty Square, the police cars appeared on the scene. The young people ran in all directions, but the police managed to nab four of them. The members of the workers' militia went to the square, but by the time they arrived, there was little left for them to do.[63] The Budapest police headquarters launched proceedings against the four youths who had been apprehended, and the case was taken over by group III/b of the Political Division, which decided to put an end to the Great Tree Gang. Almost one hundred so-called gang members were put on file, and more than a dozen informants and agents were asked to submit reports on the gang. On February 16, 1970, the Pest Central District Court handed down sentences, ranging from eight months to two years in prison, to ten of the gang members for incitement against the state.[64] Several of the condemned were kept under observation after their release by agents who had infiltrated the group or group members who had been recruited by agents. Several of the individuals who were regarded as more prominent members of the group were kept under police observation up until 1989, which meant that from time to time they had to report to the police.[65] Articles were published in the newspapers about them and about how their "idleness" had evolved into "incitement against the state." Later, two pulp novels were written about them with the goal of "educating" the hypothetical reader, who was supposed to learn from their bad example.[66]

## CONCLUSION

In the summer of 1970, by which time several members of the group of people who regularly gathered around the Great Tree had already been imprisoned, a young man who went by the name Indian was featured in the police television show *Blue Light* (*Kék fény*). Indian claimed on the show that he wanted to speak openly to reveal the "naked truth" about the hippie movement. The case became known across the country because of the reporting in newspaper. Indian contended that he had been the leader of the group, which pleased both the other members of the group and the police.

The police were relieved because there were several other ongoing proceedings against him because of accusations of rape, so if he were to emerge as the leader of the Great Tree Gang, it would be easy to cast the whole group as criminals and a threat to public safety. The other members of the group were relieved because, by casting himself as the leader of the group, Indian "took some of the heat" off them. In the course of the television show, Indian said that while the years begin to show early on hippies, he himself was ageless and always would be. According to him, the members of the group even made amateur films to show them on *Blue Light*, and these films would show the world what a hippie party and free love were really like. Indian thus played a prominent part in the case of the Great Tree Gang, though in fact he had not even been with the group on the evening of the Hippie Stroll.[67]

The members of the various groups, which were usually tied to certain events (for instance, the youths who hung out at the Great Tree were tied to the Hippie Stroll), only identified themselves as gang members as a result of the various police proceedings. Their "idleness" was portrayed in the drafted responses they gave to carefully constructed questions of the police as part of a very deliberate and purposeful series of acts. The Great Tree people had the most intense relationship not with the Communist Youth League but rather with the police, and the game of cat and mouse that they played with the police determined the narrative that the police ended up fashioning about them. In this narrative, the police figured as the essential body of social control, the primary goal of which was to appear to be acting to bring an end to the various groups, and this included criminalizing the ways the members of the groups spent their time. The goal was merely to appear to be doing this because the overall images of the groups had been constructed by the police themselves.

Informally, one of the tasks of the police was to craft images of the different groups, which would justify taking forceful measures against them. By using informants and agents, the police created work for themselves by fashioning narratives about gangs in their reports. Accordingly, a linear story was established that characterized the young people who gathered at the Great Tree as hooligan fascists linked to the official narrative of the 1956 revolution. The police tried to portray the pastimes and deeds of the groups of coevals as a sort of linear progression of events that were leading to some kind of goal. They needed to do this to depict the groups themselves, which were casual, incidental, and always shifting, as stable, permanent and, therefore potentially dangerous politically.

But how were the protagonists of the story selected to justify the steps taken by the police and meet the needs of the regime? In the next chapter, I analyze the process according to which the figures whose life stories determined the overall image of the Great Tree Gang were selected by the authorities.

## NOTES

1. The Communist Youth League (Kommunista Ifjúsági Szövetség, KISZ) was founded in 1957 as a successor organization of the Union of Working Youth (Dolgozó Ifjúság Szövetsége, DISZ). It followed the pattern of the Komsomol (Комсомол), the official Soviet communist youth organization. KISZ served as an organization of the ruling communist party. The youngest members were fourteen years old and the oldest about twenty-five, but the functionaries could be older. Younger children could join the Pioneers (Úttörő). The main task of KISZ was to teach the values of communism and help raise the next generation of party functionaries.

2. Állambiztonsági Szolgálatok Történeti Levéltára (ÁSZTL) [Historical Archives of the Hungarian State Security), 3.1.9, file V-158094/1, Sz. Gyula és társai [Gyula Sz. and his associates], minutes of the hearing of witnesses Zsuzsanna Járai and Péter Bognár, July 11, 1969, 33, 37.

3. *Népszabadság*, July 8, 1969, 9.

4. *Esti Hírlap*, July 8, 1969, 12.

5. The sun set at 7:40 that evening, but the testimony of other witnesses suggests that the two of them left their home thirty minutes earlier (ÁSZTL, 3.1.9, file V-158094/1, Sz. Gyula és társai [Gyula Sz. and his associates]).

6. Hearing of witnesses Járai and Bognár, 34.

7. *Battle of the Bulge*, dir. Ken Annakin (1965). The film was shown in Hungary in 1968–69. The title in Hungarian is "A halál ötven órája," or "Fifty hours of death."

8. "'Tiszai,' Szélesvásznú hamisságok: A halál 50 órája—avagy az igazság halála ["Tiszai," Falsehoods on the widescreen: Battle of the bulge—or the death of truth]," *Szolnok Megyei Néplap*, June 23, 1968, 7.

9. Hearing of witnesses Járai and Bognár, 34.

10. In *Battle of the Bulge*, the German soldiers sing "Panzerlied," which was written by Kurt Wiehle, a lieutenant officer in the German army, in 1935. Herms Niel wrote "Erika" before the war, specifically for the Waffen-SS (See Berszinski, "Modernisierung im Nationalsozialismus?," 54). There was also a Hungarian version of the song entitled "Rózsika" (*Horthy Miklós táborában*).

11. Hearing of witnesses Járai and Bognár, 37.

12. Budapest Főváros Levéltára (BFL) [Budapest City Archives], f. XXV-44-b, Pesti Központi Kerületi Bíróság Iratai (PKKB) [Central Pest District Court], Büntetőperes Iratok (BI) [Criminal Trial Documents], b. 640, 9. B. 23598/1969, Sz. Gyula Sz. and his associates, minutes of the hearing of witnesses Zsuzsanna Járai and Péter Bognár, hearing of the first instance, testimony of Péter Bognár, February 5, 1970.

13. ÁSZTL, 3.1.9, file V-158094/1, Sz. Gyula és társai [Gyula Sz. and his associates], minutes of the continued hearing of witness Péter Bognár, September 25, 1969, 37.

14. BFL, f. XXV-44-b, PKKB, BI, b. 640, 9. B. 23598/1969, Gyula Sz. and his associates, testimony of Zsuzsanna Járai, February 6, 1970, 10–11.

15. Kiss, *A munkásőrség megalakítása*, 239–47.

16. Germuska, *Odacsap a munkásökől?*

17. ÁSZTL, 3.1.9, file V-158094/1, Sz. Gyula és társai [Gyula Sz. and his associates], minutes of the continued hearing of witness Péter Bognár, 35.

18. According to the testimony he gave to the police, his associate was wearing civilian clothes when he left to deal with the situation, although in the court he said that both of them were wearing their uniforms (ÁSZTL, 3.1.9, file V-158094/1, Sz. Gyula és társai [Gyula Sz. and his associates], minutes of the hearing of witness Gyula Bognár, July 11, 1969; BFL, f. XXV-44-b, PKKB, BI, b. 640, 9. B. 23598/1969, Gyula Sz. and his associates, testimony of Péter Bognár, 9–10).

19. Magyar Nemzeti Levéltár Országos Levéltára (MNL OL) [Hungarian National Archives], f. XIX-B-1-Z, Belügyminisztérium (BM) Kollégium [Panel of the Ministry of Interior], b. 39, report on the circumstances of individual violent crimes of a riotous nature, June 11, 1970; MNL OL, f. XIX-B-14, Országos Rendőr Főkapitányság (ORFK) [National Police Headquarters], b. 164, 50-362-1970.

20. ÁSZTL, 3.1.5, O-13575, "Tőröző" [Foiler], report submitted by police lieutenant János Pusztai, July 9, 1969.

21. ÁSZTL, 3.1.9, file V-158094/1, Sz. Gyula és társai [Gyula Sz. and his associates], minutes of the hearing of witness Gyula Bognár, 38.

22. Interview with Gyula Sz., nickname "Big Kennedy," March 24, 2009.

23. ÁSZTL, 3.1.5, O-13575, "Tőröző" [Foiler], report submitted by police major Imre Seres on the people whose identities were checked in and around the Youth Park, July 9, 1969, 13.

24. Ibid., report submitted by police major Imre Seres on the hooligans gathering in the area around the Youth Park, June 27, 1969, 21–22.

25. See Rainer and Sereda, *Jelentések hálójában*, 16–18; Verdery, *Secrets and Truths*, 50–53, 60–65; Gieseke, *History of the Stasi*, 92–95.

26. Moscow Square, or Moszkva tér, was a square in Buda to the north of the castle. In 1929, the area, which at the time did not have a name, was given the

name Széll Kálmán tér after Kálmán Széll, who had served as prime minister for a few years at the turn of the century. In 1951, under the Stalinist regime of Mátyás Rákosi, it was given the name Moscow Square. In 2011, the original name was restored. The name Kalef, a slang term for the square that then became the name of the gang, comes from the name Kálmán.

27. Markó, *Egy zendülő a kalefről*, 105.

28. For a detailed overview of the methods used by the state security forces, see Tabajdi and Ungváry, *Elhallgatott múlt*, 144–92; Rainer and Sereda, *Jelentések hálójában*, 70–77. The length of the files (roughly 250 pages) was typical in other cases as well (Tabajdi and Ungváry, *Elhallgatott múlt*, 412).

29. ÁSZTL, 3.1.5, O-13575, "Tőröző" [Foiler]; 3.1.5, O-13708, "Májusiak" [Mayers]; 3.1.5, O-14729, "Dunai" [Danubian]; 3.1.9, file V-158094/1–3-3, Sz. Gyula és társai [Gyula Sz. and his associates].

30. ÁSZTL, 3.1.5, O-13575, "Tőröző" [Foiler], proposal made by Imre Seres to open a personal dossier, October 2, 1969, 5–6.

31. Ibid., 6.

32. BFL, f. XXV-44-b, PKKB, BI, b. 640, 9. B. 23598/1969, sentence, February 16, 1970.

33. ÁSZTL, 3.1.5, O-13575, "Tőröző" [Foiler], summary report in connection with the Great Tree Gang, September 26, 1969, 46–53.

34. Ibid., report submitted by János Pusztai, July 9, 1969.

35. Ibid., summary report on the case of Gyula Sz. and his associates, December 5, 1969, 178–90.

36. BFL, f. XXIII-102-a, Budapest Főváros Tanácsa Végrehajtó Bizottsága üléseinek jegyzőkönyvei [Minutes of the meetings of the Budapest City Council's Executive Committee], April 6, 1960, A Fővárosi Idegenforgalmi Hivatal munkája és a budapesti idegenforgalom fejlesztése [Work of the Budapest Tourism Office and the development of tourism in Budapest], 4.

37. Központi Statisztikai Hivatal, *Gazdaságilag aktívak bruttó átlagkeresete* [The average gross earnings of economically active people].

38. Mária Hegedűs, "Az Ifjúsági Parkban" [In the Youth Park], *Magyar Ifjúság*, September 6, 1968, 9; Balázs, "Az Ifipark."

39. Politikatörténeti és Szakszervezeti Levéltár (PSZL) [Political History and Trade Union Archives], f. 35, Az MSZMP Budapesti Bizottsága Archívuma (BBA) [Archive of the Budapest Committee of the Hungarian Socialist Workers' Party], dossier 1968/12, ő.e. 836, report of the Hungarian Communist Youth League Budapest Committee on the operation of the Youth Park in 1969, 5.

40. Interview with Gyula Sz., nickname "Big Kennedy," March 24, 2009.

41. PSZL, f. 35, BBA, dossier 1968/12, ő.e. 836, report of the Hungarian Communist Youth League Budapest Committee on the operation of the Youth Park in 1969, 30.

42. The term *teddy boy,* which refers to a style of dress and behavior prevalent in a subculture in Britain in the early and mid-1950s, is being used here as a translation (a rough cultural analogy) for the term *jampec* in Hungarian. As is the case with all cultural analogies, the similarities between the jampec and the teddy boy are approximate only, but both styles constituted a form of counterculture in their respective contexts, and both the teddy boy and the jampec were sometimes cast by the authorities as threats to law and order.

43. Sebők, *Volt egyszer egy Ifipark,* 48–50; *Magyar Ifjúság,* June 7, 1974, 12–13.

44. The incomes for those three years were as follows: 1962, HUF 330,000; 1967, HUF 867,000; 1968, HUF 1,172,000 (PSZL, f. 35, BBA, dossier 1962/5, 52–53; A KISZ Budapesti Bizottság Agit.prop. osztályának tájékoztatója az Ifjúsági Park 1962, évi működéséről a KISZ Budapesti Bizottságának [Memorandum of the Agitprop Division of the Hungarian Communist Youth League Budapest Committee on the operation of the Youth Park in 1962, submitted to the Hungarian Communist Youth League Budapest Committee], October 31, 1962, 52–53; PSZL, f. 35, BBA, dossier, 1968/12, ő.e. 836, report of the Hungarian Communist Youth League Budapest Committee on the operation of the Youth Park in 1969, 32).

45. Recollections of Lóránt Schuster in Sebők, *Volt egyszer egy Ifipark,* 100.

46. PSZL, f. 35, BBA, dossier, 1969/21, ő.e., 2–5.

47. Rácz, "Semmittevés."

48. MNL OL, f. 288, ő.e. 5/908, Magyar Szocialista Munkáspárt (MSZMP) [Hungarian Socialist Workers' Party], Politikai Bizottság (PB) [Political Committee], April 25, 1984, 3, Increase in the effectiveness of the legal measures taken against criminal idleness.

49. BFL, f. XXV-60-b, Fővárosi Főügyészség [Budapest Municipal Public Prosecutor's Office], Titkos ügykezelésű (TÜK) igazgatási iratok [Administrative documents of classified cases], 00223/1968, briefing on manifestations of the beat-hippie phenomenon in the month of May, 8. For excerpts from the prosecutorial text, see Kenyeres (2002).

50. Ibid., 9.

51. For instance, Júlia Székely, "Hippisors" [Hippie fate], *Ifjúsági Magazin,* December 27–28, 1968; "Hippyk" [Hippies], *Ifjúsági Magazin,* March 10–13, 1968.

52. Markó, *Egy zendülő a kelefről,* 105.

53. This is the English version of the appeal from the 1888 translation of the *Communist Manifesto* by Samuel Moore, done in cooperation with Frederick Engels and considered the standard English version. The original German (the final phrase of the manifesto) is "Proletarier aller Länder, vereinigt euch," which might more accurately be translated as "Proletarians of all countries, unite!"

54. For instance *Magyar Ifjúság,* July 11, 1969; July 25, 1969; August 1, 1969.

55. *Magyar Ifjúság*, July 18, 1969, 10. On Béla Radics, see Sebők, *Volt egyszer egy Ifipark*, 190–95; Ómolnár, *R. B. kapitány avagy pengék és halak*; Szőnyei, *Nyilvántartottak*.

56. Interview with Gyula Sz., nickname "Big Kennedy," March 24, 2009; interview with Imre M, nickname "Jimmy," May 26, 2006.

57. ÁSZTL, 3.1.9, file V-158094/1-3, Sz. Gyula és társai [Gyula Sz. and his associates], summary report of the Juvenile and Children's Social Services Probative Subdivision of the Budapest Police Headquarters, August 1, 1969, 6. This summary report was the primary source on which the police description of the events was based, along with the following summary reports on the Great Tree Gang: ÁSZTL; 3.1.5, O-13575, "Tőröző" [Foiler]; 3.1.5, O-13708, "Májusiak" [May-ers].

58. Éva Bedecs, "A 'Nagyfák' sem nőnek az égig" [Even the "Great Trees" don't grow to reach the sky], *Magyar Ifjúság*, February 20, 1970, 4–5.

59. A. A. Milne wrote all of his Winnie-the-Pooh books in this house, which was purchased by Jones in 1968.

60. Charone, *Keith Richards*, 97.

61. Sz. F., "Beatmise" [Beat mass], *Népszabadság*, May 28, 1968, 6.

62. ÁSZTL, 3.1.9, file V-158094/1, Sz. Gyula és társai [Gyula Sz. and his associates].

63. Ibid., testimony of member of the Workers' Militia Gyula Bognár, 35.

64. PKKB, 9.B.23598/1969. 14. sz; ÁSZTL, V-158094/3, 237–68.

65. For example: ÁSZTL, 3.1.5, O-14729, "Dunai" [Danubian].

66. Tolnai, *A Mohikán-galeri*; Lőrincz, *A nagy fa árnyékában*.

67. Szabó, *Kék fény*, 2nd ed., 142–65.

TWO

# THE TRIAL

## Casting

IN THE COURSE OF THE hearing for the alleged members of the Great Tree Gang in February 1970, which was given considerable attention in the press, the trial records presented the youths on trial as if they were people who had been predestined by their life histories to become members of the gang and take part in the march, which was described as a fascist demonstration. The authorities pushed this narrative in spite of the fact that the young men in question had themselves never actually heard of the Great Tree Gang before the events of July 8, 1969. In the course of its examination of the motives for the (alleged) acts, the trial records determined that "the environment at home and in the schools had made little impression on the accused, and though it had influenced them, it had by no means captured their interests. To varying degrees and in various ways in each individual case, the lack of understanding between parents and their children contributed to this, as did the absence of a nurturing, emotional relationship, which, given the ages of the accused, would have had a decisive influence at this initial stage of their integration into society."[1]

This chapter explores how the narrative created by the police was developed during the trial and how and why the alleged ringleaders were particularly targeted. I argue that the trial records tried to represent the conflicts between the parents and children involved as being about dire issues that were among the essential concerns of the young people and, thus, were essential causes of their alleged deviance. The trial records did this in spite of the fact that the parent-child conflicts were not actually extraordinary because it was essential to craft narratives that shared the responsibility for the alleged misdeeds of the young people with their parents and thus broaden the implications of the legal cases.

The show trial had to teach the importance of proper socialization—according to the socialist ethos—not only for the young people but also their parents. I also contend that a close link had to be established during the proceedings between the commemorations of the 1956 revolution and the nonpolitical crimes of the teens. This allowed the authorities to depict themselves as morally righteous and justified in their use of power; it was essential to present the case as a political incident, although most of the young people were indifferent when it came to politics.

This narrative determined the selection of the accused and also the level of charges raised against them. The accused in a case like this could be the charged in the first, second, or third degree, which is similar to the difference between being accused as a primary suspect and being accused as an accessory, and the sentences ultimately meted out by the court depended in part on where an accused fell in this hierarchy. The Hippie Stroll to commemorate Brian Jones was represented as a crime, but the trial records had to construct other political or common-law crimes to justify the sentences it sought to pass. Representations of the story in the press were in no small part a tool in this process.

## BIG KENNEDY

Big Kennedy was born in Budapest in 1950—so he was nineteen years old when the group took the Hippie Stroll, making him one of the oldest members—and his parents separated when he was young. The prosecution emphasized aspects of Big Kennedy's life that would have made him more likely to engage in "deviant behaviors," at least according to the stereotypes at the time, and suggested that everything that had happened to him as a child predestined him to someday become a gang leader. The prosecution determined that after his parents separated, he had lived for a time with his father, who was considered a drunk and who forbade him to see his mother. In 1956, after Kennedy had lived in a variety of temporary settings (which were not considered unusual, even then), he became a ward of the state. He was first put in an institution in the town of Szőlősgyörök and then in Szob. He regularly escaped, perhaps because he was punished for misbehaving.[2] (At the time—the first half of the 1950s—the number of children in the care of the state who were put in state institutions jumped dramatically, creating issues with severe overcrowding, which is discussed further in chap. 4.)[3] Since he had been in an institution since he was kindergarten age, he was more independent than children who either lived with their parents or who had become wards of the state a little later in life.

In 1962, his friends gave him his nickname because, they claimed, he resembled the American president. "I had a square head, just like Kennedy," he said. Others in his peer group sometimes got nicknames that began with noble titles, like Lord, but there is no explanation for that in the proceedings. Big Kennedy did not recall, when he and I had our conversation, who had put him in the institution or how, exactly, he had ended up there. Perhaps he had simply repressed a memory that was unpleasant or even taboo, but perhaps it had seemed perfectly natural to him, at six years of age, that he lived in a large room with thirty other children and was only allowed to go home to reside with his parents occasionally. (Big Kennedy's parents did maintain a relationship with him after he became a ward of the state—he spent one weekend every month with them and four weeks every summer[4].) He found it a little bit odd and even incomprehensible that his father lived in a nice home in Óbuda on Szépvölgyi Road, but he nonetheless had to live in an institution in Hűvösvölgy. He lived in this institution until he was ten and was then sent to various facilities outside the capital. When looking back on these years, Big Kennedy said that he was eight years old the first time he escaped from detention, and after that, he would escape at least nine or ten times a year, although he never went to his mother's or father's homes.

The police recorded that Kennedy said the following in his testimony: "I then [after Szőlősgyörök] wound up in an institution on Csepel [Island, a working-class neighborhood in Budapest], and I lived in a dormitory. I saw my parents regularly. I didn't learn a trade, I bummed around. That's why I ended up in the [correctional] institution."[5] Kennedy noted in his conversation with me, however, that the text of his alleged testimony bore little resemblance to what he actually said at the time. As far as he could recall, he was put in a correctional institution because when he had been brought back to Budapest and put in an institution for boys, one night he and his friends had broken into the kitchen and stolen some of the food. They had been hungry.[6]

At sixteen, he had been taken to the correctional institution in Aszód, twenty-three miles from Budapest. Each of the two institutions (Aszód and Csepel) was closed to the public and kept under tight security; this lack of oversight and scrutiny led to pervasive abuses, including, as regular disciplinary practices, beatings, being placed in a dark cell with a stone bench (referred to as the *elkülönítő*, the rough equivalent of solitary confinement), and having one's hair shorn off.[7] Kennedy also said that one person would hold them down while another whipped them with a belt.[8]

In Aszód, Big Kennedy was given vocational instruction to learn to be a carpenter (as, indeed, were most of the children in the care of the state), but

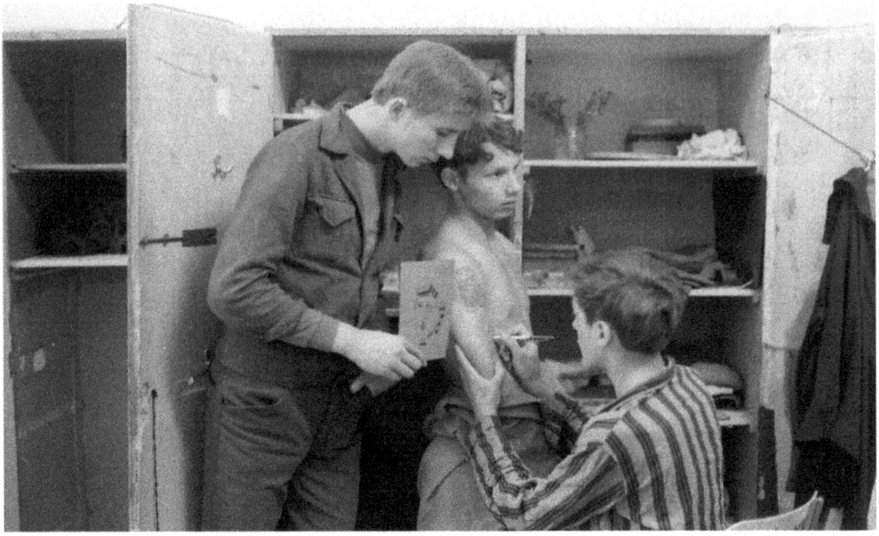

Figure 2.1. In the correctional institute in Aszód, 1974 (Fortepan / Tamás Urbán).

he gave up the trade before completing the exam that would have given him a degree. According to an assessment written in 1970 by his caregiver in the institution, "he never enjoyed love or warmth in his parents' home. He has been raised for 14 years in institutions, and he has become very disillusioned. He has no faith in anything, not even in his own life; he does not dare hope that something might go well."[9]

During the 1970 trial against the participants in the Hippie Stroll, Big Kennedy was the charged with crimes in the first degree—that is, as the primary suspect—because of his link to a commemoration of the 1956 revolution. The authorities intended to justify the measures they were taking against the young people with the claim that many of the young people had either been participants in or were the descendants of participants in the so-called 1956 counterrevolution, according to the official antifascist narrative. Big Kennedy was a convenient target for this role. One night in October 1966, an event took place that state security forces treated as a sign of Big Kennedy's attachment to the legacy of 1956: the boys at the institution shut the facility's party secretary in the large bathroom, "crowed at him," and forced him to climb up onto one of the cabinets. They got their hands on a bucket of red paint, painted his gray button-down shirts, and then fled (there were thirty of them in total). Over the course of the night, they walked to Petőfibánya, a mining town some twenty kilometers away, to tell the miners that children in the care of the state were being beaten in the nearby institution and to plead with the miners to help free them. There the police caught them and took them back to Aszód. While the wards regularly escaped from the institution, they had deliberately planned this nighttime excursion for the month of October, the ten-year anniversary of the 1956 anti-Soviet uprising, to irritate the people at the institution, according to the recollections of Big Kennedy.[10]

According to the trial records, when he turned eighteen (and thus legally became an adult), Big Kennedy was glad that he could finally "split" and go wherever he pleased. He didn't know where his mother lived, so he wanted to live with his father. His father had taken up residence with another woman, however, who was not willing to let his son move in, so Big Kennedy lived at a friend's place. When the weather was good, he often slept outside. He didn't have any official permanent address. He was most easily able to find work in light industry (for example, in a hat factory or at a company that worked in the cotton press industry), but he never worked at these places for long, although he did register for a place in the workers' hostels so that he would have a permanent address that he could show the authorities whenever they checked his identity papers. According to a workplace assessment, "his salary lasted him two days, then his coworkers gave him money, even for food."[11] In November 1968, the Sixth District Police punished him with a thirty-day prison sentence for "criminal idleness," a sentence that, as was common at the time, he served in a facility in the town of Baracska to the south of Budapest. He then found work in a warehouse, and in the summer of 1969, after the Hippie Stroll, he was again incarcerated in Baracska for a month, which is why the police didn't find him in the area around the Great Tree when they wanted to arrest him. When he was released from the facility in Baracska, he worked for two weeks as a sort of roadie for the band Bergendy (which played regularly in the Youth Park) until he was arrested. He met once with his father before he was imprisoned. He had not seen his mother for several years. According to the testimony he gave during the hearing, he had begun to hang out at the Great Tree as soon as he had left the institution in Aszód. Presumably, he frequented this spot not just because he liked to listen to music for free but also because if the weather was good he could sleep in the bushes and could got odd jobs working with the bands that played in the park (helping them carry their equipment, for instance).[12]

Big Kennedy loved the area around Great Tree. It was a symbol for him of freedom after years spent locked up in various institutions. It meant music, a circle of friends, and other people his age to hang out with, and if it also included police who sometimes beat them, much as his so-called caregivers once had, it

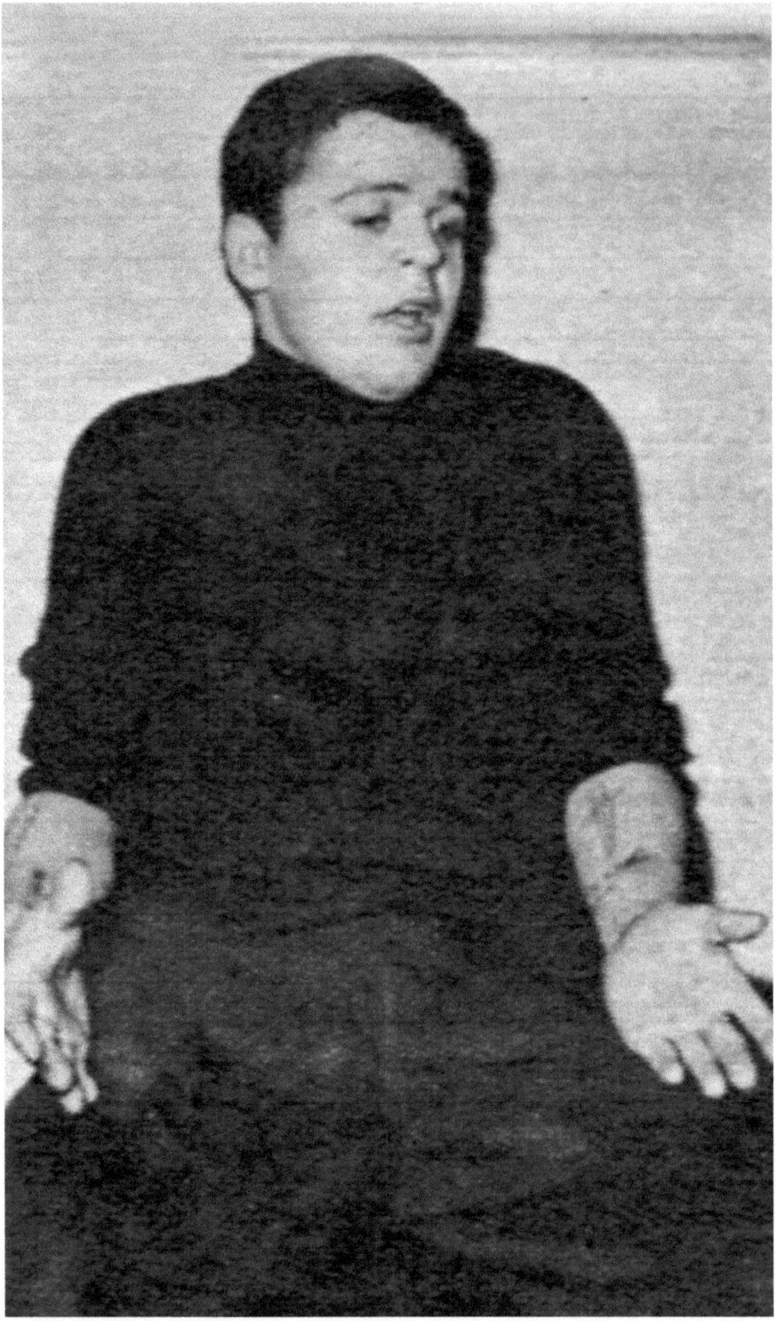

Figure 2.2. Big Kennedy in 1969.

was at least only a few times and less often than in his past experience. At the end of the 1960s, the city of Budapest itself was a symbol of freedom for him, even if the police sometimes caught up with him on its streets and treated him somewhat like the institutions where he grew up.[13]

## LORD BLONDIE

Big Kennedy and Lord Blondie had become fast friends in the correctional institution in Aszód. It is perhaps hardly surprising, in retrospect, that Lord Blondie was charged with a second degree offense in the case, even though he had not actually taken part in the Hippie Stroll. As another former ward of the state, he stood out in the group. He was only one year younger than Big Kennedy, and he was also physically strong. His parents had divorced when he was only eight years old. His father, who had worked as a bricklayer's assistant, was a recidivist and was himself serving a prison sentence when Lord Blondie was taken into custody. His mother was a typist and stenographer. He had lived with his parents until he had turned eleven, sometimes with his father but for the most part with his mother. He had then been put in an institution, positioning him at the younger end of the spectrum compared to his cohorts in the facility (the majority of the children who were in the care of the state were between ten and fourteen years of age).[14]

At the age of fourteen, he had escaped and, with others, broken into a car, so he was sent to a correctional institution. This is how he had ended up in Aszód, where he spent almost four years. He was released in the spring of 1969. That summer, he had begun to hang out with the young people at the Great Tree. Like Big Kennedy, he made money doing odd jobs and did not have a permanent place of employment, and he was convicted of "dangerous idling" twice. As he explained, he would spend his afternoons at the Great Tree. He lived with his parents, but he enjoyed the company of the others in the area above the park; he felt more at home there than at parents' home.

The police, the prosecutor's office, and the trial records all sought to demonstrate that the gang represented a subversive and potentially dangerous fascist threat, which is why, in the course of the hearing, these parties repeatedly brought up political matters and tried to compel Lord Blondie to talk about his politics, which before had been of almost no interest to him whatsoever. The testimonies depict Lord Blondie as a lazy teenager: "Sometimes we'd take or ask for food and money from the girls; we called it 'sponging.' I didn't know anything about the group's political views. I took part in the fascist salute either drunk or inebriated, never sober. I drank almost every day, using the money that I had gotten from the girls. . . . I didn't have an apartment. I 'roughed it.' . . . Sometimes I would go up to the tree in the morning, no one was there, and there was some food under the tree." According to his account, Lord Blondie claimed that he even attended a theater performance in May 1969, but he didn't enjoy it because he didn't enjoy serious dramas. When he was asked about Nazi Germany at the trial, his statement could be used as an accusation against himself in the trial records, even if he had read an antifascist novel about the Nazis for fun.

> I had a read a few books. The last book I read was *Die Jagd nach Dem Narbengesicht,* which is about World War II. Nothing really caught my attention, just the brutality. Nazi Germany can't have been a bad thing, but in the end even the people got sick of it. I also read books about Indians. I thought of myself as a hippie. My goal is not to have to work. I don't have any other goal. I was able to get by so far, I'll keep being able to get by. I lived off girls, off my mom. . . . I think about how I could change the way I live, but I'm dumb. When I get out of prison, I'll get married, I'll get a job, but then I go hang out with a gang. . . . We consider ourselves a gang, but we don't have any particular organization.[15]

The authorities were able to apprehend Lord Blondie and Big Kennedy on the basis of a report submitted by an informant with the code name "Vári" (which means, roughly, "of the castle") on October 15, 1969. The report revealed where the two suspects were residing. Vári had seen both of them the day before at the Great Tree. As previously noted, after his release from the facility in Baracska, Big Kennedy had joined the band Bergendy as a roadie for tours outside of Budapest. When István Bergendy, the head of the band, hired Big Kennedy, he noticed that his hair had been cut short, which struck Bergendy as odd, since he had seen Big Kennedy hanging around the park before with long hair. Big Kennedy's hair was short, of course, because while he had served a thirty-day sentence, it had been cut. In the testimony he gave to the police, Bergendy described Big Kennedy as a reliable worker. He also said that he had introduced him to a girl Big Kennedy wanted to marry.[16] Bergendy supported Big Kennedy, characterizing him as a young person who was in the process of growing up and improving. Though there is no mention of this in the minutes, Big Kennedy contends that Bergendy said a great deal more than this on his behalf. He said he thought it was absolutely preposterous to turn such a simple matter into a major court case.[17]

According to a report submitted on October 17 by police lieutenant Gyula Hódi, Hódi had been sent from the First District Police headquarters to the

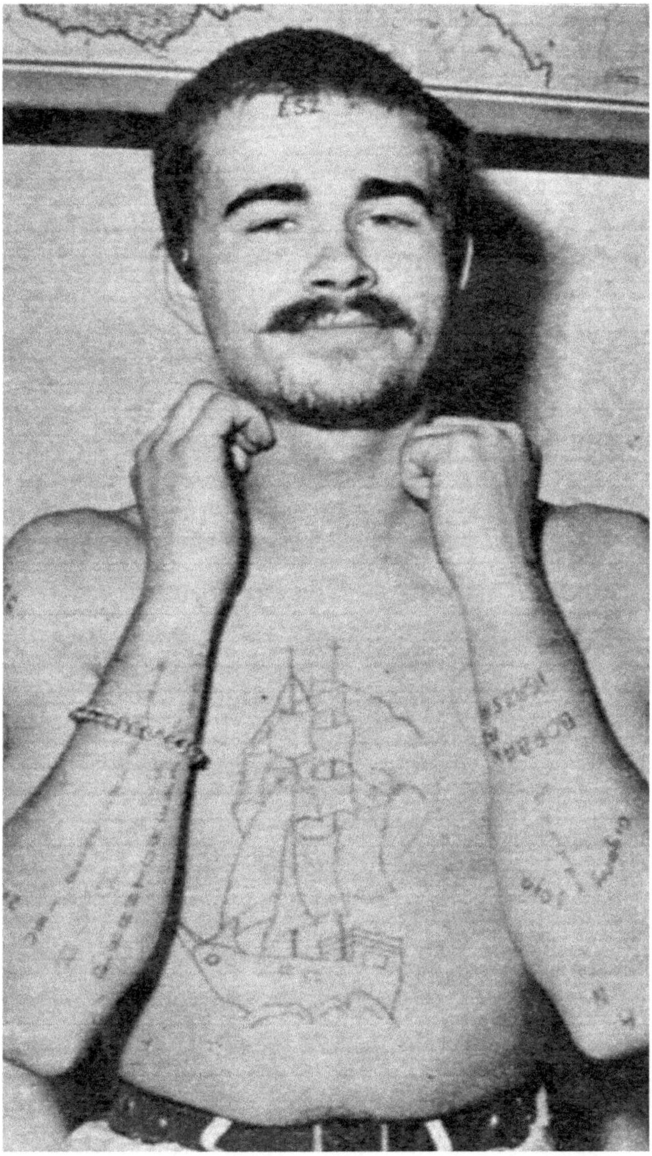

Figure 2.3. Lord Blondie in 1969.

park next to Szarvas Square (the Youth Park) because "soldiers who had been doing work there had apprehended a young man who was behaving suspiciously and had taken him to the gatehouse." Upon arrival, the policeman on patrol had recognized Lord Blondie, who informed him that he had agreed to meet with Big Kennedy at the Great Tree. When the policeman went to the Great Tree, he saw a boy (Big Kennedy) take flight. Joined by two of the soldiers, he pursued Big Kennedy, who later claimed that he had tried to run away because the authorities had taken his old identity card. He hadn't had a new one issued yet, so he knew that they would take him in if they caught him. Big Kennedy slipped while running up Gellért Hill and scraped his leg, which is how his pursuers caught up with him. The police were already looking for him, and when they found out that he had been apprehended and was being held at the First District Police headquarters, they sent someone to get him.[18] According to his account, Kennedy was immediately taken to the police headquarters in Tolnai Street, which was infamous for dealing with issues of state security. Here, his interrogation began as part of the "Great Tree case."[19] Before his arrest, police had already decided to craft the case so as to give it political meaning: the apolitical young people involved, they sought to suggest, were in fact enemies of the regime.

The police wanted to arrest the two boys (one of whom was already in custody) because they both fit the image they had of a gang leader. They had both grown up largely in reformatory institutions, and both of them had tattoos—the police found seventy-three tattoos on Lord Blondie alone.[20] At this time, toward the end of the 1960s tattoos were only just beginning to acquire a different significance as a social symbol, transforming from being the mark of having done prison time to being a sign of belonging to a youth subculture. And while *Ifjúsági Magazin* (Youth magazine), a periodical published by the Hungarian Communist Youth League, had taken note of the increasing popularity of this fashion among young people in 1967 (with a clear note of condemnation), for the police, tattoos remained the mark of people who had been in prisons or state institutions.[21] Big Kennedy and Lord Blondie were ideally suited to be used by the authorities to depict the young people around the Great Tree as both common-law criminals and teenagers guilty of political crimes. This linking of common-law crimes to political crimes was a practice that had been frequently used by the police and the trial records in the proceedings against alleged participants in the 1956 revolution as a means of portraying the regime as a righteous enforcer of morals,[22] and it is this approach that these institutions used once again in the case of the Great Tree Gang.

## "I DIDN'T FEEL GOOD AT HOME"

Lord Brown (Barna Lord), accused of crimes in the third degree, did not fit the image of a criminal and political dissident quite as persuasively, since his background was far more run-of-the-mill. In the various documents concerning the case, Lord Brown did not figure on the list of gang members for long, and he was probably charged with crimes in the third degree because of his knowledge of English (in other words, his possible ties to the West). When the others wanted to translate the text of one of their favorite songs from English, they turned to him for help. He was eighteen at the time of the Hippie Stroll. He lived with his parents in Budafok, a working-class area on the southern outskirts of Budapest. He had left grammar school after two years because his grades were poor and, instead, began attending a vocational school. His father was the head of an accounting department, and his mother was a mechanic. He offered the police the following explanation for why he joined the group: "I do not have a good relationship with my parents. I always had differences of opinion with my mother's parents. My mom treated me like she used to a long time ago because I took my grandmother's side, my father's mother. That was what caused the conflicts. I didn't feel good at home, so I joined the gang." Since he spoke good English, Lord Brown told everyone that he wasn't Hungarian.[23]

Herceg (Prince), charged with crimes in the fourth degree, had also lived in a reformatory institution. During the hearing, proceedings were already underway against Prince, who was the same age as Big Kennedy, for selling stolen goods and disturbing the peace, and he had already been found guilty of having crossed the border illegally. According to his account, his parents had had him put in an institution because he had misbehaved and had not wanted to go to school. He had six siblings, and his younger brother had also been put in the care of the state. He hung out at the underpass in Blaha Lujza Square, under a building that housed EMKE, one of the most popular catering establishments in Budapest, thus giving the underpass its popular name of "EMKE." The underpass was an infamous meeting spot for youths, and Prince was given his nickname there. Like his friends, he frequented the Youth Park until eventually they stopped letting him in. In 1969, according to the explanation he gave to the police, things had changed: "they forbade anyone with long hair from coming in," so the groups started to meet at the Great Tree. Though Prince had not been present for the Hippie Stroll, he was still sentenced to two years in prison, like Lord Blondie and Big Kennedy, his friends who were coming from correctional institutions. The fact that he had already been convicted of other infractions played a role in his sentence, as did testimony given by others that indicated Prince had used fascist greetings at the Great Tree. During the hearing, he was the first person with the courage to change the testimony he had given (probably not voluntarily) in the course of the investigation.[24]

Little Kennedy (Kis Kennedy), accused with crimes in the fifth degree, a sixteen-year-old minor, completely broke the implicit agreement with the police and retracted the testimony he had given during the investigation. Little Kennedy did not know his father at all. He lived with his mother, who worked as a gardener, until he reached adolescence. Proceedings had been launched against him for criminal idleness because he had not found employment after leaving an institution for vocational apprenticeships without completing a program of study. His mother offered the following account of this: "One day I noticed that my son's clothes were missing, and he had not come home without having let me know he wouldn't be there. Later, I discovered that the police in Szentes had incarcerated him for twenty days for dangerous idling. I was shocked, because as far as I knew, he had a job."[25]

Little Kennedy tried to escape through Yugoslavia to Italy, but he failed. He was not present for the Hippie Stroll either. His primary accusation was for having used fascist greetings and salutes at the Great Tree. When he denied the testimony he had given during the investigation two weeks before the trial, he started a chain reaction. Big Kennedy also withdrew the testimony he had given during his interrogation and the investigation and stood only by the testimony he had given to the court. He offered the following explanation: "I do not stand by the testimony I gave during the interrogation because when the investigation was underway the official working with me said that if I confessed everything that had been written down for me, I would see my fiancée sooner." When he heard this, Prince also changed his testimony. This was important, because the indictment rested to a large extent on the testimonies that were given during the police investigation. By changing or denying their testimonies, the boys made the prosecutor's job significantly harder, since he then had to rewrite the indictment in the trial, which was (as should be sufficiently clear) little more than a show trial.[26]

The next day, Christ, who was charged with crimes in the sixth degree found himself in a difficult situation, as he was one of the main witnesses for the police and his testimony provided a foundation for the accusation of political subversion. If he did not withdraw his confession, like the others, he justifies the political crime (concerning Nazi salutes). Christ was one of the accused whose family backgrounds were relatively normal. His father was a foreman and his mother a resident caretaker. Though his father drank regularly and was at the time in a detoxification program, his parents still lived together in the apartment allotted to them as the caretaker's residence. It was described as "unkempt" in the study prepared on the living conditions of the accused, but as a dwelling with one bedroom, a separate kitchen, and a bathroom, it was not significantly less comfortable than one would have expected under the circumstances. As noted in the study, "the boy's bed is in the antechamber, which has been arranged as a separate space, since the entrance to the apartment comes off the stairhall." According to the neighbors (at least as noted in the study), there were often family arguments and physical fights, primarily because of the father's drinking problem: "The father does not tolerate the presence of his children or wife, he is always rough, and when he drinks, which he often does, he argues and always provokes a fight. He regularly beats the accused boy, and he also argues with other residents in the building. Over the summer, he moved in with a female companion for several weeks, but since she is also living in rented lodgings, he couldn't remain with her. . . . The mother lives like a servant in continuous fear."[27]

Christ, who had poor vision in his right eye, finished the first eight years of school with mediocre grades. He then spent one year pursuing studies at a foodstuff trade school. He began to come home less often and lived as something of a vagabond. The squabbling between his parents played a role in this. Once, his father, who only rarely came home from the tavern, accused him of regularly having sex with his own mother. After this, Christ began to spend more time at the Great Tree. He had not been present for the Hippie Stroll, but during the trial, he repeated testimony he had given to the police concerning Nazi salutes.[28] His willingness to stand by this testimony proved decisive in the trial, since it gave the court the pretext it needed to characterize the stroll as a continuation of the revolution (or *counterrevolution*, to use the term preferred by the Kádár regime) of 1956. In his testimony, he made claims concerning the things his fellow gang members had allegedly said, statements that had important political overtones and implications: "The Czech revolution should be an example for us to follow"; "We must do what we did in 1956"; "The march was organized"; "We have to get our hands on weapons."[29]

The authorities were still only able to prove that two of the six accused had been present for the stroll, however, or what, in the accusation, was dubbed a march. What did the other four have to do with the whole thing if they had not even been present? This was why the court needed the lesser degree charges against the accused. Interestingly, in the indictment drawn up before the proceedings had been launched against Big Kennedy; the boys who were written up for seventh, eighth, ninth, and tenth degree charges in the final indictment had figured as the accused for first, second, third, and fourth degree charges. They were the four people whom the police had managed to nab on Liberty Square the night of the stroll and had not been released because the police considered it established fact that they had participated. They had been the lead suspects even though they were a few years younger (between the ages of fifteen and seventeen) than the "boys from reformatory institutions" who hung out at the Great Tree. An indictment had been drawn up against them as early as October 3, 1969. They only ended up figuring in the series of the accused in the actual trial because two weeks after these first four were apprehended, the authorities had caught Big Kennedy, an "institution boy," and had begun to envision a major trial against the Great Tree Gang based on the ideas sketched by Major Imre Seres.[30]

## THE YOUNGEST ONES

The authorities were very deliberate in their treatment of those accused of seventh, eighth, ninth, and tenth degree charges (who were also the youngest of the defendants) and exerted pressure on them to make accusations against their older cohorts. In doing so, the police and the prosecutors sought to justify the measures they had taken against the youths by conflating the Hippie Stroll with both the nonpolitical crimes and alleged (though difficult to prove) use of fascist signaling by the members of the gang. While the primary accusation against the first six accused concerned their deviant lifestyles and their use of Nazi salutes and rallying cries, the other four accused had taken an active part in the stroll.

The four people against whom the police had the strongest cases—since they had been arrested on site—were less convincing candidates as leaders of the Great Tree Gang than people like Big Kennedy, whose background as an institution boy made it easier to cast him as an enemy of the regime. From the perspective of the authorities, the biggest problem concerning the younger boys was that there was not a single mention in the accused boys' testimonies of any of the four youngest members of the group having used fascist language or gestures. In the indictment against of the boys captured at the stroll, the prosecution could offer no other explanation for their acts than their desire to commemorate Brian Jones, which even in the eyes of the communist court was not a crime. Even after their cases had been conflated with those accused of more serious charges, there was no way to produce any evidence, in the form of new testimonies, of what were described as "fascist gestures," since the investigation phase against them had already come to a close.

The youngest boys had not even been mentioned in the first indictment drawn up in December, since the order of the first six accused had followed the order of the accused in the hearing.[31] The court needed the last four and youngest accused to prove political crimes (although these four were not able to show connection to fascism). Accordingly, a verse found on an accused boy who went by the nickname "Monk" (Szerzetes—accused of crimes in the seventh degree), which he himself had composed, provided the perfect piece of evidence in support of an accusation of incitement. The most familiar of Monk's verses among the other members of the group was the poem "My Dear Homeland," especially first stanza:

My dear homeland, Hungary,
How slavery has broken you!
A red curse above our heads,
We will break it, hippie boys![32]

Monk, who was sixteen years old at the time of the stroll, was held in continuous pretrial remand after his arrest. The first time he was brought forward for questioning during the hearing, he was unable to speak because his father had died while he was in custody, and he was still in shock. He was only allowed to attend the funeral under police supervision. In the course of the investigation, the police determined that he had begun to write poetry in part because of the influence of his friend Duck, who wrote poems as well as journal-like notes in a spiral notebook that was put in the files created in the course of the investigation as evidence. Duck was the same age as Monk, and the boys were best friends. In all likelihood it was Duck who had come up with the whole idea of the Hippie Stroll, but the authorities were unable to find anything in his notes that could have been characterized as criticism of or opposition to the system.[33]

Monk's father worked odd jobs as a delivery man. His mother was a housewife. They lived in Sárvár, a small town in western Hungary, until April 1958. Monk finished grade school in Sárvár and then was enrolled in the local grammar school. According to the aforementioned report on the conditions in which the accused had grown up, "in school, he did not pay attention in class, he disturbed the class. His dress and hairstyle made him an outsider among his peers." According to his testimony, after he moved with his mother and father to Budapest, he did not want to continue attending grammar school. His mother said that, considering the family's finances, he had to find work. He got odd jobs as an unskilled worker at a truck repair company and then at the Budapest shoe factory. He also played soccer for the Vasas junior team. He wanted to be a soccer player or a mechanic, but since he had no real schooling,

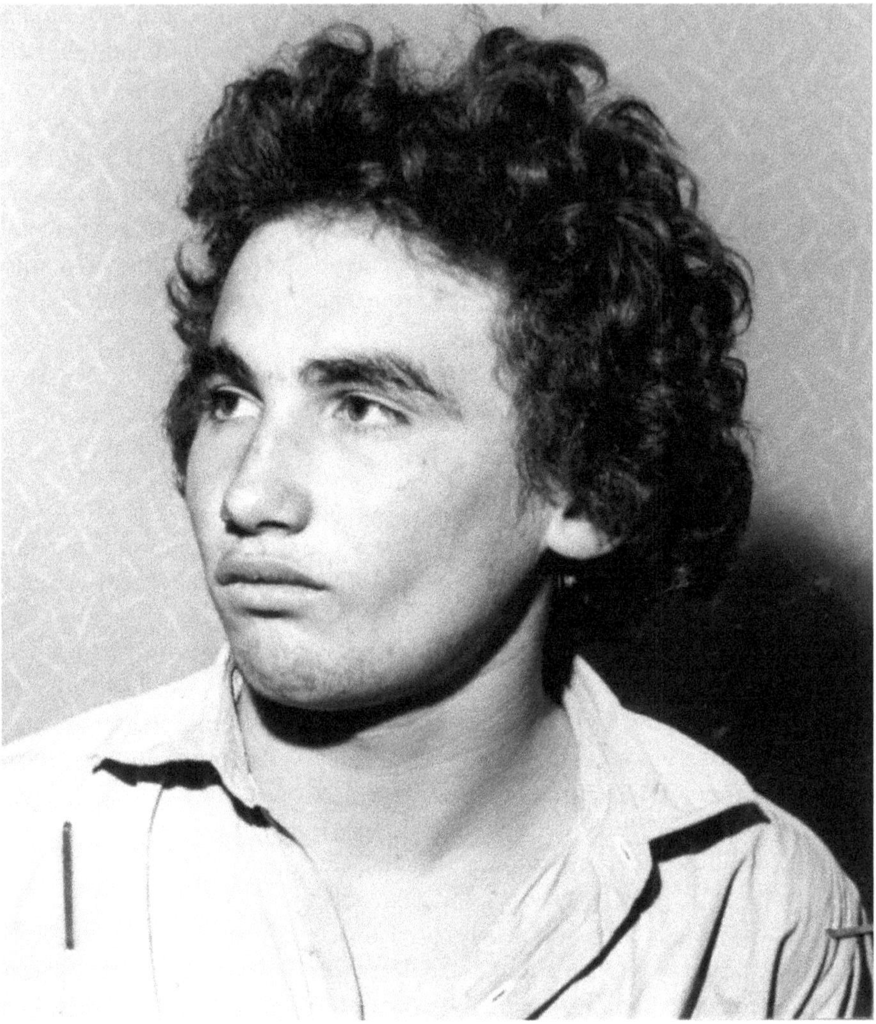

Figure 2.4. Monk, the poet of the Great Tree Gang, after his arrest, 1969 (BFL XXV-44-b 21201/1471).

like many of his friends, he found work in the ready-to-wear garment industry (which was enjoying a boom), in spite of his lack of any real qualifications. In his free time, he also went to the Youth Park. At his workplace, he was not considered the most reliable employee.[34] According to his mother, his parents had no idea that he wrote poems. True, his father had once found one of his poems, and he had been outraged and had given the boy a thorough beating.

His parents also made him promise to get a haircut.[35] Monk was sentenced to serve fourteen months in juvenile prison for having written poems that were deemed critical of the system.

Monk's friend Duck (charged with crimes in the eighth degree) had not yet turned seventeen when he suggested taking a stroll to commemorate Brian Jones to his group of friends. He was a Rolling Stones and Cream fan, and he often made references to the music of the two bands in his notebook. He had been born in Debrecen, a city in eastern Hungary. His parents had divorced five years before the hearings began, while he was still in grade school. Even as a grade school child, he was considered a bit of an extreme case. The authorities' report on Duck made mention of his fits of rage, which his companions had also noticed and presumably noted in their testimonies. During the hearing, he tried to defend his conduct by referring to a nervous disorder: "I had two stepfathers who rattled my nerves a lot; back home I only talk about things that are absolutely necessary with my mother." Presumably at the advice of others, Duck got a paper from a doctor one month before the hearing attesting to his nervous disorder. He had sought out the local doctor because of headaches (he may well have suffered migraines),[36] and the doctor had referred him to the neurological ward of the polyclinic. Because of this mitigating circumstance, he was given a "milder" sentence: fifteen months in prison. Duck was let out earlier than the other first six accused, in spite of the fact that in all probability he had been one of the most active organizers of the stroll. During the hearing, he too denied ever having heard anyone at the Great Tree use Nazi rallying cries or salutes.[37]

Pressel, who was the charged with ninth degree offenses, was probably accused and tried simply because he had not managed to flee Liberty Square in time. The instructors at the vocational school he attended had crossed his name off the roll after about six weeks because of unexcused absences. Like many of his friends, he had then taken odd jobs primarily to prevent the police from arresting him for criminal idleness. He had applied for admission to the School of the Fine Arts (he could paint and draw quite well), but his application had been rejected because of his bad grades. Presumably, he had considered the vocational school a tedious obligation. He also took an exam to become a driver. He often quarreled with his parents, who liked neither his long hair nor the clothing he wore, and although this was hardly unusual for a family with a teenage kid, the indictment nonetheless made mention of it in the section dealing with him. His father had gone into retirement by then (he had worked as a policeman), and his mother no longer worked because she was in poor health. He had two stepsiblings from his mother's first marriage.[38]

Pressel's fifty-five-year-old father made mention of his son's haircut in the testimony he gave to the court: "The kid had long hair, which I could not stand, I always nagged him about it, but he insisted on wearing his hair long."[39] The accusation against him was primarily that he had taken part in the stroll, and he was sentenced to nine months' incarceration in a workplace for juveniles serving criminal sentences. Most of the minors who were given prison sentences or sentenced to serve time in the work camp for juvenile convicts in Tököl, a small city on Csepel Island. The emphasis on conflicts between the youths and their parents over hairstyles and lifestyles was important to the police interrogators and to the court because they served to explain the kids' antiauthoritarian rebellious motives. It is worth noting that these conflicts figure prominently in the minutes of the interrogations of the adults kept by the police. The testimonies in court, however, suggest the conflicts were actually not that important to the children or their parents. Quite probably, the parents made frequent mention of how their children shocked and alarmed them with their hairstyles and their music because they knew that both the court and the prosecutor expected them to. Possibly as a result, the alleged responsibility of the parents for the acts that their children had committed was not mentioned during the trial (probably because these conflicts had no political meanings).

The boy nicknamed Hobo (Hobó), who was charged with tenth degree offenses, was the youngest member of the group, although he looked older than he was and was just as strong as the older boys. He had not yet turned fifteen when he took part in the stroll. He lived in Dohány Street in the middle of Pest, not far from Duck's mother's place, so he knew a few of the people who hung out at the Great Tree from the underpass at Blaha Lujza Square, which was infamous because it has appeared in several police news reports as the first underpass in Budapest, where many crimes were committed, especially by young people (see chap. 5 on the representation of underpasses). As a grade school student, he had mediocre grades. When he finished grade school, he enrolled in an economics vocational school, which he stopped attending after one month. As a thirteen-year-old, he had gone to the Youth Park; however, he was soon banned from the park for having gotten in a fight, so he joined the others listening to music for free under the boughs of the Great Tree. In 1969, he got a job as a loading boy at Nagyvásártelep, an enormous storage facility in southern Pest built in the 1930s. He claimed in his conversation with me to have known the song "Erika" from the film *Ordinary Fascism* (also known in English as *Triumph over Violence*) by Russian director Mikhail Romm. The 1965 documentary consists primarily of excerpts of archival film footage with annotations. Though the intention of the film was to show the rise and fall

Figure 2.5. Pressel after his arrest, 1969 (BFL XXV-44-b 21201/1471).

of fascism and, more specifically, Nazi Germany, it was also used as an anti-Western propaganda tool.[40]

During the hearing, Hobó said that he had taken part in the stroll because of a girl he had wanted to spend time with, and he had focused on her the entire time. Based on stories the others told about him, this seems entirely plausible.[41] As far as the authorities were concerned, the biggest problem with him was that in 1944 members of his family had been declared Jewish under the legal definition at the time and deported. It was thus difficult to prove or even suggest that he had used Nazi rallying cries or greetings. Nonetheless, this boy, who, according to his father, was very impressionable, was sentenced to ten months' incarceration for having taken part in the stroll.[42]

The proceedings against Little Kennedy, Christ, Pressel, and Hobo (all of whom were minors) came to an end on April 9, 1970, when the Budapest Municipal Court, a higher (appellate) court, brought them to a close.[43] The reason for this was simple: a new amnesty law applied to their sentences, which were each less than a year. In 1970, Hungary celebrated the twenty-fifth anniversary of its occupation by the Soviet army in 1945, which officially "liberated" the country from the German army and the forces of the Hungarian puppet government at the end of World War II.[44] In honor of the occasion, a general amnesty was proclaimed under decree number 7 of 1970, and this ended the incarceration of the Great Tree gang. The case continued to be described in the press as having to do with a fascist protest, however, held by youths who used Nazi rallying cries.[45]

## CONCLUSION

In the course of the trial, the authorities selected young people who fit the stereotypes furthered by the official propaganda as the main figures in the narrative they were crafting. They did this to justify violent measures taken against a group of young people who had done nothing but walk down the street in peace—even stopping at red lights![46] They chose to bring these grave accusations against marginalized youth who had been convicted of minor nonpolitical crimes, who had grown up in part in state institutions, or both. Given the age of the accused, most of whom had been born right around or a few years before 1956, it was no easy trick to link their stroll to the 1956 revolution. This was why Big Kennedy's escape from the institution in Aszód in 1966 came in so handy for the police: it could be characterized as a commemoration of 1956. And this commemoration was why Big Kennedy was charged with first degree offenses.

The trial records referred to the circumstances under which the accused had grown up and currently lived to explain their acts. It went into great detail concerning the families of the young people, as if the narrative it had crafted concerning the family environment accounted for the children's purportedly deviant behavior.

In the case of the quasi–moral panic involving the Great Tree youths, the district police headquarters was the starting point. The first condemnations in the case came not from above but from the middle, on the level of everyday police ID checks. Although the press seemed to be independent during the campaign against the youth, it was, in fact, controlled by the police and the Communist Youth League, so the stories regarding the youths in question were coming mainly from police reports. In accordance with the expectations of the police, the press found a suitable subject in the Great Tree affair to arouse a sense of moral panic and, in doing so, distract the public from everyday problems. A kind of chaotic narrative was constructed in which young people were presented as delinquents who were infected by rock music and negative elements of the Western lifestyle. According to this narrative, these influences prompted them to form gangs and respond violently to other members of society. It was not by chance that the gang was traced back to groups that allegedly had played key roles in the events of October and November 1956, since these groups had also existed in no small part as constructs of post-1956 counterrevolutionary propaganda, according to which they were well-organized and continuously active, not merely ad hoc, almost incidental clusterings.

But why did the police and the court consider this case so important, and why did the fact that a group of young people had taken a stroll through the streets of Budapest in the summer of 1969 meet with such interest in the press? Why did the police devote so much time and attention to apprehending the youths and investigating the case? Why were the young people characterized as hooligans in the texts penned by the police, and why was their ragtag group dubbed a gang? Why was the Hippie Stroll described as an oppositional (fascist) act? Which state institutions took part in the exaggeration of the events and to what ends? The answers to these questions must be sought in the mechanics and functioning of the institutions that contributed to the emergence of this narrative by adapting the Soviet discourse on hooligans to the Hungarian context and creating the term *gang*.

In the following chapters, I examine how the institutions of the Hungarian socialist state responsible for dealing with children and juveniles created a public discourse on hooligans and gangs after 1956 as well as how the stances and attitudes of the police, the socialist tabloid press, and the organs responsible for policy toward young people changed.

## NOTES

1. BFL, f. XXV-44-b, PKKB, BI, b. 640, 9. B. 23598/1969, sentence, February 16, 1970, 27.

2. When asked by the judge about his escapes, he replied, "[Because] allegedly, I misbehaved" (BFL, f. XXV-44-b, PKKB, BI, b. 640, 9. B. 23598/1969, minutes of the hearing on February 3, 1970, 3–4).

3. MNL OL, f. M-KS-288, cs. 33, ő.e. 1957/1, Javaslat a minisztertanácshoz az Országos Gyermek- és Ifjúságvédelmi Tanács felállításáról [Proposal submitted to the Council of Ministers on the establishment of a National Children and Youth Protection Council], 91.

4. Interview with Gyula Sz., nickname "Big Kennedy," March 24, 2009.

5. BFL, f. XXV-44-b, PKKB, BI, b. 640, 9. B. 23598/1969, minutes of the hearing on February 3, 1970, 3–4.

6. Interview with Gyula Sz., nickname "Big Kennedy," March 24, 2009.

7. Hanák, *Társadalom és gyermekvédelem*, 33.

8. Interview with Gyula Sz., nickname "Big Kennedy," March 24, 2009.

9. BFL, f. XXV-44-b, PKKB, BI, b. 640, 9. B. 31183, the extension of the correctional and educational work of Sz. Gyula, December 19, 1967.

10. Interview with Gyula Sz., nickname "Big Kennedy," March 24, 2009.

11. BFL, f. XXV-44-b, PKKB, BI, b. 641, 21201/1971, Gyula Sz. and his associates, assessment of Gyula Sz. by the head of the personnel department of the Cotton Press Company, October 28, 1969, 32.

12. BFL, f. XXV-44-b, PKKB, BI, b. 640, 9. B. 23598/1969, minutes of the hearing on February 3, 1970, 3–4.

13. Interview with Gyula Sz., nickname "Big Kennedy," March 24, 2009.

14. Hanák, *Társadalom és gyermekvédelem*, 37, 43.

15. BFL, f. XXV-44-b, PKKB, BI, b. 640, 9. B. 23598/1969, minutes of the hearing on February 3, 1970, 9–11. The full title of this 1962 book by Julius Mader (who went by the alias Thomas Bergner) is *Die Jagd nach Dem Narbengesicht—Ein Dokumentarbericht über Hitlers SS-Geheimdienstchef Otto Skorzeny*, or "The hunt for scarface: A documentary on Hitler's SS intelligence chief, Otto Skorzeny," published in Hungarian as *A sebhelyes gyilkos nyomában* in 1963. Skorzeny had fought in the Waffen-SS in the war and later served as a military advisor to Egyptian president Mohammed Naguib before being recruited, in 1962, by the Mossad. Mader himself worked for a time as an officer for the Stasi, the State Security Service in East Germany, and his antifascist propaganda books published in East Germany were translated into Hungarian (Wolf, *Die Entstehung des BND*, 26).

16. István Bergendy was questioned as a witness on November 13, 1969 (ÁSZTL, 3.1.9, file V-158094/1-3, Sz. Gyula és társai [Gyula Sz. and his associates], 309–11).

17. Interview with Gyula Sz., nickname "Big Kennedy," March 24, 2009.

18. BFL, f. XXV-44-b, PKKB, BI, b. 641, 21201/1971, Gyula Sz. and his associates, report submitted by Gyula Hódi on the detainment of Gyula Sz, October 17, 1969, 21.

19. Interview with Gyula Sz., nickname "Big Kennedy," March 24, 2009.
20. BFL, f. XXV-44-b, PKKB, BI, b. 641, 21201/1971, Gyula Sz. and his associates, 139.
21. Márta Zsigmond, "Bőrbe vésett vallomás" [Confession carved in skin], *Ifjúsági Magazin*, January 1967, 46–48.
22. K. Varga, "Politikai vagy köztörvényes?"
23. BFL, f. XXV-44-b, PKKB, BI, b. 640, 9. B. 23598/1969, minutes of the hearing on February 3, 1970, 12–14.
24. Ibid., 15–18.
25. BFL, f. XXV-44-b, PKKB, BI, b. 640, 9. B. 23598/1969, hearing on February 5, 1970, 2; testimony of Mrs. József N.
26. ÁSZTL, 3.1.5, O-13575, "Tőröző" [Foiler], indictment, December 17, 1969, 205–12.
27. BFL, f. XXV-44-b, PKKB, BI, b. 641, 21201/1971, Gyula Sz. and his associates, Környezettanulmány H. Imre [Study of living conditions by Imre H.], October 19, 1969, 99–101.
28. BFL, f. XXV-44-b, PKKB, BI, b. 640, 9. B. 23598/1969, minutes of the hearing on February 4, 1970, 1.
29. ÁSZTL, O-13575, "Tőröző" [Foiler]; H. Imre önvallomása [testimony of Imre H.], September 16, 1969, 109–10.
30. BFL, f. XXV-44-b, PKKB, BI, b. 640, 9. B. 23598/1969, indictment against József H. [Monk] and his associates for incitement, October 3, 1969.
31. ÁSZTL, O-13575, "Tőröző" [Foiler], indictment issued by the Budapest Municipal Prosecutor's Office, December 17, 1969, 205–12.
32. BFL, f. XXV-44-b, PKKB, BI, b. 640, 9. B. 23598/1969, Ítélet [sentence], February 16, 1970, 14. The Hungarian text of the stanza is "Édes földem Magyarország / De megtört a rabszolgaság / Fejünk fölött vörös átok / Megtörjük ezt hippi srácok."
33. See also chapter 7.
34. BFL, f. XXV-44-b, PKKB, BI, b. 640, 9. B. 23598/1969, indictment issued by the Budapest Municipal Prosecutor's Office, October 3, 1969, 3.
35. Ibid.; and Hearing on February 5, 1970, 3. H; testimony of Mrs. József H.
36. Interview with Mrs. Mária Zoltán S. (the widow of S. Zoltán, Duck), October 17, 2008.
37. BFL, f. XXV-44-b, PKKB, BI, b. 640, 9. B. 23598/1969, hearing on February 4, 1970, 5–7. For more on Duck, see chapter 8.
38. Ibid., indictment issued by the Budapest Municipal Prosecutor's Office, October 3, 1969, 3; hearing on February 4, 1970, 10.
39. Ibid., hearing on February 5, 1970, 4; testimony of Kálmán Cs.
40. The Hungarian title of the film is *Hétköznapi fasizmus*. The original Russian title is *Обыкновенный фашизм*.

41. Interview with Gyula L., nickname "Fáraó" [Pharaoh], May 25, 2006; interview with András Sz., nickname "Hobó," May 27, 2006; interview with "Törpe" [Dwarf], May 27, 2006.

42. BFL, f. XXV-44-b, PKKB, BI, b. 640, 9. B. 23598/1969, hearing on February 4, 1970, 17–19; testimony of the father of the accused; hearing on February 5, 1970, 4; testimony of András Sz.

43. According to the Soviet legal model (adopted in 1950 in Hungary), the Hungarian court system was based on regional courts and regional courts of appeal. The regional courts rendered decisions in both criminal and civil law cases (Kengyel, *Magyar polgári eljárásjog*, 51).

44. The April 9, 1970, order of the Budapest Municipal Prosecutor's Office.

45. For instance, the article by Éva Bedecs, "A 'Nagyfák' sem nőnek az égig," *Magyar Ifjúság*, February 20, 1970, 4–5; (kas), "A Nagyfa árnyékában" [In the shade of the Great Tree], *Magyar Rendőr* [Hungarian Police], December 11, 1969, 8; the *Blue Light* broadcast on them (Szabó, *Kék fény*, (1st ed.), 137–57).

46. BFL, f. XXV-44-b, PKKB, BI, b. 640, 9. B. 23598/1969, Gyula Sz. and his associates, testimony of József Spiegel, February 6, 1970, 11–12; ÁSZTL, 3.1.5, f. O-13575, "Tőröző" [Foiler], report submitted by Police Lieutenant János Pusztai on July 9, 1969; BFL. f. XXIV-1, Budapesti Rendőr-főkapitányság Központi irattára (BRFK) [Documents of the Central Archive of the Budapest Police Headquarters], Political Division, 10.

# THREE

# HOW HOOLIGANS ARE MADE

> Under communism, will there be hooligans and police who catch them?
> No, under communism there will not be hooligans anymore.
> We must free ourselves from them under socialism.
> But how do we free ourselves from the hooligans?

IN 1958, NIKITA KHRUSHCHEV, THE first secretary of the Communist Party of the Soviet Union, raised this question at the eighth congress of the All-Union Leninist Young Communist League, usually known as Komsomol.[1] In order to offer an answer to this question, however, it was first necessary to determine what the term *hooligan* actually meant. From time to time, efforts were made to do this in order to justify the measures taken by the state to pursue and apprehend alleged hooligans. It was necessary to define, redefine, and remake the image of the hooligan to convince the public that hooligans did indeed exist and did indeed constitute a threat to public safety. Even so, it is hard to determine with any measure of precision how these measures may have influenced public opinion.

In Hungary after 1956, the term *hooligan* began to be used to refer to targeted subsets of young people. This was a symptom of the general shift in the way state institutions dealt with youth in their discourses after the revolution. Groups of young people who, in the assessment of the regime, merited condemnation were given new names, and these new names (and the status they conferred on youths as peripheral and even potentially threatening members of socialist society) became elements in the formation of new identities for young people. The police played a key role in this process, since they were the ones who determined, at the instructions of the party, who among the members of the younger generation should be considered an enemy.

In this chapter, I examine how the nonviolent, fashion-oriented Hungarian teddy boys (the jampec) became violent hooligans and members of youth gangs in the eyes of the state authorities. I argue that the official narrative on the youth gangs (galerik) had its roots in the communist propaganda regarding the 1956 Hungarian uprising against Soviet occupation. The emerging societal anxiety about the threat of youth violence also had origins in the quasi-panic around the corrupting influence of comic books and films. The most important force behind this quasi-moral panic, however, was not the media but the police, who strove to politicize youth subcultures. The concept of Hungarian youth gangs emerged out of specific measures taken by the police and the narratives crafted by the police about these allegedly deviant figures after the 1956 uprising. I do not mean to suggest that youth gangs did not exist at that time, but that the meaning and uses of the term *youth gang* (galeri) in the press and in police reports were highly politicized.

In the middle of the 1950s, all over the world the identifying characteristic of the new youth folk devil became violence, not fashion.[2] The construction of hooligans was an important undertaking of historical agents who crafted discourses on youth. While many accounts of youth cultures in the former socialist countries were influenced by interpretations of similar phenomena in the West, each of these interpretations had distinctive roots in slightly different structures of power and authority, and this was especially true in Hungary because of the effects of the 1956 revolution.

## HUNGARIAN TEDDY BOYS

The term *hooligan* gained increasing familiarity in England in the 1890s as it began to be used more frequently both in comedic routines and police bulletins. In 1891, for instance, Jim O'Connor and Charles Brady performed a song entitled "The Hooligans" in the Royal Theatre in Hull (the song is about an unruly Irish family named the Hooligans). In subsequent years, the term was used in increasingly wider circles to denote "problem youths" and members of gangs. In the first decade of the twentieth century, the term was used not only in the tabloid press, but even in *The Times* by authors like Arthur Conan Doyle and H. G. Wells. As the tabloid press grew into an almost mass phenomenon in the late Victorian era, the term was used ever more frequently as a kind of alarmist technique to emphasize the importance of discipline. It was useful in various campaigns alleging a decline of social morals and for the most part targeting youths, because it could take on whatever meaning was needed in the given context. So-called hooligans, who were usually portrayed as inhabitants of working-class districts, were endowed with traits and attitudes "not worthy of an Englishman," traits and attitudes that earlier had been ascribed to workers or people living in the slums, who were allegedly a "threat to society."[3]

In the early years of the twentieth century, the term *hooligan* was already being used in the public discourse describing violence among youths in the Russian city of Saint Petersburg, most prominently in the tabloid press, which was always eager to run articles about public disorder and alcohol abuse among the youth. Writings about collective violence in 1905 and the Saint Petersburg hooligans were closely intertwined with writings about the "lower classes," and the term in Russia began to acquire the connotation of "terrorist."[4]

Under Stalin, the word *hooligan* referred to a juvenile who was disorderly in public,[5] while under Khrushchev the term *hooliganism* was coupled with the term *domestic*. This term, *domestic hooliganism*, enabled the authorities to police not only juveniles but also home lives.[6] In the Soviet Union, hooliganism was regarded by the authorities as an anti-Soviet subculture among young factory workers, and the political police devoted an increasing amount of attention to monitoring hooliganism, especially in the 1930s. The broadening of the definition of hooliganism to include juvenile crime enabled the police to treat juvenile delinquency "as a holdover from the capitalist past," and Komsomol youths began to be involved in the campaigns against hooliganism starting in 1935. In the same year, the Soviet government created a new crime, "aggravated hooliganism," and this crime became one of the most common accusations brought against defendants: every year more than 100,000 people were arrested for having committed the crime of hooliganism.[7] After 1936, as political repression in the Soviet Union got progressively worse, the police increasingly characterized hooligans as "enemies of the people," and contentions equating the two figured widely in the youth press. After World War II, the Eastern European socialist countries also started to develop their own definitions of hooliganism, drawing on the Soviet model.[8] In Poland, for instance, where the term was used mostly as a synonym for "delinquent youth" or "enemy activity," hooliganism was punishable by up to six years' imprisonment as early as the beginning of the 1950s.[9]

In Western Europe, too, the more frequently "hooligans" and "hooliganism" were mentioned in the press, the more aggressive the measures taken by the authorities and the more severe limits on free speech and the freedom of assembly for members of the younger generation became. In Nazi Germany, for instance, a public safety discourse was fashioned concerning the Edelweiss Pirates (Edelweißpiraten), a loosely organized youth group that emerged in part as a kind of protest and alternative to the Hitler Youth. The essence of this discourse was simply that young people who formed groups or gangs constituted a threat to Nazi power, which was proclaiming new principles of state organization.[10] According to this discourse, the typical hooligan lived in a working-class district, was violent, and always came on the scene when violence and American culture (for instance, swing dancing in the 1930s and 1940s) began to become palpable parts of social interaction.

In the creation of the hooligan in Hungary, the notions of both the teddy boy and the hoodlum were used, terms that before 1956 had been the most derogatory designations for the young. The image of the teddy boy (jampec) was made widely known in the first half of the 1950s in Hungarian movies, which were used as a means of spreading socialist propaganda. The word *jampec* originally meant a young man with strikingly distinctive behavior who dressed according to the latest fashions. The best-known teddy boy character was Swing Tóni (played by actor Imre Pongrácz), one of the most memorable characters of the 1950 movie *Dalolva szép az élet* (Life is lovely in song). The main characteristic of the tongue-in-the-cheek Swing Tóni is his aping of Western fashion, founded primarily in American comic strip culture, language use, and dance.[11] The teddy boy followed not so much Western trends as images of Western trends presented in the communist propaganda. In the first half of the 1950s, *Szabad Ifjúság* (Free youth) and *Esti Budapest* (Budapest evening, the forerunner of *Esti Hírlap* [Evening news]) carried numerous articles and cartoons describing the allegedly detrimental effects of American pulp fiction, comics, and movies. In general, they borrowed an argument that was used in media campaigns in the 1930s in Great Britain and the United States to justify the censoring of gangster movies.[12]

> Neon lights, whiskey, peals of wild laughter,
> A palace playing cowboy films,
> The Ku-Klux-Klan needs a black man's blood quick,
> This is Broadway, main street—in New York.
> Gangsters in the films, on the streets, in novels,
> In cars, in bars, in soft light,
> In their eyes a mad, murderous fever,
> Like their leader, in the White House.[13]

The heroes of Western comics, along with their garb and characteristic features, became symbols of American culture in the socialist propaganda, including, of course, the print media. Thus, the moral panic about Western influence was situated in an ideological context and, more specifically, in the fight against capitalism. In this narrative, youths who had strayed down the path of social deviance were the victims of pulp fiction and violent films.[14] In 1958, *Esti Hírlap* published an article borrowing from a writing on the teddy boy that had appeared in the satirical English periodical *Punch*, since the editorship regarded the teddy boy as "the English *jampec*."[15] In 1959, *Esti Hírlap*, following the lead of the English *Daily Express*, claimed that there was no difference between hooligans and Nazis.[16]

The jampec or teddy boy (to continue using the English term as a rough cultural analogy) was a recurring figure not in police bulletins in Hungary but rather in the vignettes, commentaries, and readers' letters in the newspapers in the 1950s. These genres gave the writers, journalists, and readers ample room to meet the official expectations in their characterizations of "deviant," "dangerous" young people. In these texts, the teddy boy became the embodiment not only of the pernicious effects of gangster films and Western individualism but also rudeness and the jarring slang[17] used by the younger generation. The journalists who wrote feuilletons on cultural life in the capital endowed the Hungarian teddy boy with his own distinctive garb, vocabulary, dance style, music (jazz), and favorite readings. The teddy boy generally read books "on the cover page of which a Wild West figure is holding an enormous Colt pistol," and sometimes he even had a tattoo.[18] One of the functions of the caricaturesque figure of the newspaper vignettes about street life in Budapest was to create a clear embodiment of everything that was dangerous and improper and condemned both by the authorities and anyone with good taste.

Even if the teddy boy were to try to disguise himself, he couldn't, for his clothes and his physical traits would betray him: "The person in question was a teddy boy. His hat, hair style, jacket with its dropping shoulders, drainpipe trousers stretching to his ankles, and striped socks betrayed him, not to mention the soles of his shoes. And the way he moved! Throwing his hands and legs around as if some invisible hand were yanking them on a string, like a marionette—as if this hand were yanking him around on a string all the way from America."[19] On occasion, however, people did call attention to the fact that the jampec (teddy boy) could not be defined precisely. As Martha Lampland points out, derogatory terms, like *kulák* or *class enemy* (and presumably *jampec*), could never be precisely defined because the value of these epithets was that they could be used for very different kinds of people in multiple contexts—that is, their vagueness was a tool for arbitrary abuse and repression.[20] This was possible in 1953 perhaps because of Stalin's death and the political uncertainty that followed. The teddy boy was not a self-standing social phenomenon but rather a combination of characteristics that in 1953 were already not as scandalous or outrageous as they had been a year earlier. Thus, the label *jampec* was a sort of umbrella term that could cover a fondness for jazz music as much as a fondness for womanizing.[21]

Figure 3.1. Cartoon of a jampec (teddy boy) (*Ludas Matyi,* 1950).

Figure 3.2. Kulak to the jampec [teddy boy]: "We teamed up in vain, we country folk and city folk. Looks like the storm will get us both!" (*Szabad Ifjúság*, 1950).

By 1954, the jampec was no longer a frightening enemy due to a shift in attitudes that was connected to the de-Stalinization campaign after Stalin's death. Rather, he was portrayed as part of a trend that was gradually vanishing on its own.[22] It was no longer necessary to screen films exclusively in factories and in agricultural cooperatives, and jazz was increasingly winning acceptance.[23] Police measures against the "jampec spirit" were condemned with the explanation that it was clearly not a bad thing to let the young people have their dance music.[24] The editorial board of youth newspaper *Szabad Ifjúság* emphatically rejected the idea of a decree against the jampec.[25] The figure of the jampec was decreasingly useful as a tool with which to articulate condemnation of American mass culture, but the allegedly corrupting effects of these products remained a recurring motif in the public discourses on youth.[26] The jampec still popped up from time to time for a few years in condemnations of allegedly Western lifestyles, but after 1956, the jampec-as-bogeyman was replaced by the hooligan (as the new bogyman) and, a decade later, by the hippie. Sometimes

Figure 3.3. Jampec-style clothing in 1958 (Fortepan / Károly Lipovits).

the words *jampec* and *hooligan* would be used interchangeably in a reference to an article of clothing (for instance the jampi or hooligan pullover).[27] But the term *jampec* was no longer linked to violence after the 1956 revolution. The stereotype became once again a designation for a confused youth who mimicked fashions allegedly originating in the West.[28]

The police never took the kinds of resolute measures against the jampec that they took against alleged hooligans and gangs after 1956. The jampec was a construction primarily of films and newspaper articles about young people, not a concern for law enforcement. After 1956, the violent acts committed by hooligans and youth gangs became the focus of condemnations against the younger generation, and the police played the main role in fashioning the public discourse on deviant, dangerous young people instead of the media.

## FASHIONING THE HOOLIGAN: THE POLICE AND THE COMMUNIST YOUTH LEAGUE

In early 1956, *Szabad Ifjúság*, borrowing from an article published in *Der Abend*, offered an account of jampec youths in Vienna. The main problem with these young people, according to the article, was that they were forming gangs with increasing frequency.[29] Even before the autumn of 1956, the fight against juvenile delinquency had become one of the official focuses of the institutions that dealt with minors.[30] The creation of the hooligan and the youth gang as new, violent threats to socialist society, however, came only in the wake of and as a response to the armed uprising in the late fall of 1956.

In 1963, the second edition of a book entitled *Fiúk könyve* (Boys' book) by István Harsányi (1908–2002) was published. Harsányi offered adolescent males advice on how to lead a proper life. In the first edition, which was published in 1958, there was no mention of either the jampec or the hooligan. In the second edition, however, he devoted considerable space to these two figures: over the course of the four years that had passed in the meantime, the young hooligan had popped up ever more often in the public discourses on the youth as a threat to the social order. In his 1963 work, Harsányi described the hooligan as "a rowdy slacker, usually a young adult, who has no regard for social norms or social propriety and who relishes provoking scandals. According to a new interpretation with primarily political bearing, the hooligan is a brutal, corrupted, reactionary person who can easily be influenced to commit acts of terror."[31] In contrast with the jampec, considered after the 1956 revolution to be a relatively benign cultural and fashion construction, the hooligan was depicted mostly as a male figure against whom the police were fully justified in taking steps. In the wake of the 1956 revolution, when the government was implementing repressive measures, talk of safety and security became dominant in the public discourse on the younger generation. During this period, the term *hooligan* and the term *terrorist* were used almost interchangeably.

These new terms were added to the discourses concerning juvenile delinquency, child protection, and youth policy as well. According to a work published in 1962 on the subject that identified aggressiveness as the basic feature of hooligan behavior, "In recent years, most of the articles in the press have dealt with hooliganism. Colorful reports have given accounts of shocking cases and coarse, violent acts committed by some gang or another and the gang members, the hooligans. The readership, which learned of this question primarily from these reports, for the most part nonetheless remains uninformed with regards to who a hooligan actually is and what a gang actually is."[32] Hooligans certainly existed, the work insisted, and they were the most dangerous when they formed groups or, more precisely, gangs. The hooligan allegedly acted without motive. He was utterly unscrupulous, had nothing but disdain for the rules of propriety and acceptable social interaction, and took particular delight in wreaking havoc and making a spectacle of himself.[33]

But where did the Hungarian terms *gang* (galeri) and *hooligan* (*huligán*, which is a cognate of the English *hooligan*), which were being used with increasing frequency and with an increasingly narrow meaning, come from? The origins of both terms (or, rather, the ways these terms ultimately were strategically deployed by the authorities) lay in the institutional systems through which the Kádár regime implemented repressive measures after 1956. In 1958, the police headquarters were given a collection of statutes by the National Police Department that became the foundation of the fight against gangs and the public safety discourse on the threat these gangs posed. The point of departure of this collection (which was top secret) was the following: "The disruptive ethical influence of the [1956] counterrevolution was extensive among children and juveniles. Many of them took part in the counterrevolution, and in many cases, they formed armed bands and plundered."[34]

In late 1956, the deputy minister of interior listed police measures to protect minors from corrupting influences as among the most important tasks of the authorities.[35] He offered the following justification: "The counterrevolutionary demagoguery, which came to the fore primarily with nationalist and chauvinist rallying cries, has exerted a strong influence on minors. In consequence, it has managed to use some of the young people as lackeys who support counterrevolutionary goals."[36] In accordance with instructions given by the Ministry of Interior, the National Police Department issued an order creating an independent senior official position dealing with juvenile crime in the Criminal Division, the division of the police headquarters that was charged with the task of ensuring that the officials who had been assigned to their jurisdictions dealt with the questions pertaining to juvenile delinquency. The instructions issued by the ministry also stated that the police would act in cooperation with the mass organizations (like the youth organizations), which later led to joint raids by the police and the Communist Youth League.[37]

In September 1957, less than one year after the 1956 revolution, the Kádár government issued a decree establishing the National Child and Youth Policy Council, which was responsible for coordinating the various tasks associated with protecting and providing social services for children. In creating this new council, it referred to a resolution reached at meeting of the July 11, 1957, Executive Committee of the Budapest City Council, according to which circumstances were far from satisfactory with respect to child protection. One of the primary tasks of the Youth Policy Council was to aggregate data concerning juvenile delinquency. In other words, the tasks of the body responsible for "youth policy" explicitly overlapped with law enforcement: from the outset, juveniles were approached as potential criminals. These data were then used by the police, officially mass organizations, practically political organizations

Figure 3.4. A hooligan after his arrest, picture taken by the police, 1959 (Fortepan / Budapest City Archive).

such as the Communist Youth League, and the municipal councils when they drew up explanations for their goals and policies.[38]

One clear sign of the importance of the Youth Policy Council is the fact that Ferenc Münnich served as its chair. Münnich played a prominent role in organizing the armed battalions (the armed suppression of the revolution) and the Workers' Militia (a kind of army under the direct command of the communist party, as mentioned in chap. 1) during the 1956 revolution. As chair of the Council of Ministers from 1958 to 1961, he was the second-most-powerful person in Hungary, after Kádár (indeed, in Moscow he was regarded as a possible alternative to Kádár).[39] Parallel with the creation of the Youth Policy Council, the Ministry of Interior increased expenditures at police headquarters for costs related to youth policy and quickened the pace of work in the courts dealing with (alleged) juvenile delinquents.[40] The "hooligan question" emerged as one of the most important concerns of the day at least in part because the institutions that shaped the issue as a major social problem were in Münnich's hands, and Münnich was one of the most influential politicians in Hungary.

With the increase in available funds for matters concerning youth policy and juvenile delinquency, the number of people working in the Division for the Protection of Children and Minors of the Budapest Police Department almost doubled (from twenty-eight to fifty-five), and the division began to deal with matters related specifically to law enforcement.[41] Between 1945 and 1955, work involving law enforcement was a rare exception in the Division for the Protection of Children and Minors. Before 1956, this division had dealt almost exclusively with administrative questions, and between 1955 and 1957, no law enforcement work was done in this division at all, since investigations were made the responsibility of the prosecutor's office. In the first half of 1958, after the division was given the task of pursuing youths as if they were criminals, more than 2,000 minors were apprehended, 157 of whom were turned over to the prosecutor's office for indictment. The division was headed by police captain Mrs. Andor Labányi, and 75 percent of the staff were women. This remarkably high percentage of female employees in a police institution suggests that the division reflected a pervasive and persistent stereotype that children and juveniles are the responsibility of women. Although the department has been prioritized financially and reorganized, this has not resulted in higher prestige, because it was primarily a female department prior to the buildup.[42]

In 1958, in connection with the division's report, Budapest police captain György Sós cited the case of youth protection in the Soviet Union as an example to be followed by the heads of the Budapest Police Headquarters: "There is a group of operatives (a central organ) in the Leningrad Police Headquarters, and in every police station there is a principal investigator dealing with minors, but doing only police work and investigative work. There is a children's room in every police station, where a head teacher looks after the children."[43] There was no mention in this text of the battle against hooligans and gangs, but even as early as 1958, the possible way of proceeding against both was already based on a fixed model, one that was to be used over a decade later, in 1969, against the Great Tree Gang. In the division's August 18, 1958, report, the term *hooligan* was used in the context of cases involving crimes against minors where the prosecutor's office issued overly liberal rulings against "drunkard, work-shirking hooligan parents."[44]

After the 1956 revolution, the danger posed by members of the younger generation grew in the eyes of the police, so in 1957–58, the state began to use organs of national security to keep minors under observation. It also increased the capacity of the police to deal with juvenile delinquency. Because of these changes, the police no longer concerned themselves with "preventing the ethical corruption" of minors but focused rather on methodically investigating crimes that could be traced back to circles of youths. Beginning in 1958, the post-revolutionary notion of the battle against hooligans, already official policy of the police, appeared in the press. The first bulletins portrayed the hooligan as someone who had taken an active part in the armed fighting in 1956 but who either had been released in the meantime or had never been sentenced. After his release in the summer of 1958, István Podkoniczky, who had taken part in the battles in the area around the Corvin Department Store and had been sentenced to one year in prison,[45] ended up again in the hands of the police. Borrowing from the police bulletin, *Esti Hírlap* characterized him as a "thieving hooligan." According to the article, the identifying characteristic of the hooligan was his proclivity to violence: "With his partners, who resemble him, he harassed defenseless people and in particular enjoyed hitting women."[46] The article suggested that the 1956 bandits posed a continuous threat to the peaceful residents of the city, so public and semipublic spaces had to be kept under continuous police surveillance at all costs.

Beginning in late 1957, the hooligan increasingly figured in the terminology of the authorities who dealt with domestic affairs as someone who was particularly likely to commit counterrevolutionary criminal acts. In early 1958, the network of agents opened a dossier titled "Hooligan." The dossier contained the following description of one of the people who had taken part in the fighting in Pesterzsébet (the Twenty-Sixth district of Budapest) in 1956: "Kálmán K. is a person twenty-seven years of age, of other background (hooligan), belonging to no party and unemployed. K. comes from a hooligan family: he is a musician who does not concern himself with any other form of work."[47] Over the course of 1958, the term *hooligan* became an everyday part of the vocabulary of the police and the institutions of domestic affairs, and it was used to refer to people who did not lead "honorable workingmen's lives." "One needs a great deal of data and facts to be able to say of someone that she or he is a hooligan. Prostitutes of course are included here, and certainly this category in the case of women." This citation is from a talk held by Comrade Temesi, who in March 1958 gave a long presentation on the meaning of the term *hooligan* at a consultation held for the staff of the Operative Registry Division. Temesi contended that a "hooligan" was someone who "is not willing to work," "constantly

Figure 3.5. A real sportswoman:

> "I see you've taken care of the hooligans, but why didn't you shout for help?"
> "I didn't dare let them know I was a woman."

(Cartoon in *Ludas Matyi*, 1958).

changes place of employment," "shows a lack of discipline when working," "lives an unethical private life," "lives off an illegal income," and "does not start a proper, honest working-class family."[48]

In 1959, the police and the Communist Youth League (under the control of the communist party), which had been formed only two years earlier, launched a coordinated undertaking to put an end to hooliganism. In September and October 1959, the Budapest committee of the Communist Youth League, working in close cooperation with the Budapest Police Department, "initiated efforts on eight occasions at individual sites that are increasingly frequented by hooligans." These acts were carried out by members of the so-called Young Guard, a uniformed formation consisting originally of organizers of the league. In contrast with the police, the members of the Young Guard strove to execute these measures "cunningly," without attracting any notice, as they wanted to avoid causing any affront to public sentiment.[49]

Who were these hooligans? According to the report prepared by the members of the Young Guard for the Communist Youth League,[50] it was particularly important for the authorities to deal more with the children of state and party leaders and leading figures in economic life, "because we have concrete data indicating that, among the hooligan youths, or more precisely among the people who are embarking down the path of hooliganism, we can find more than one child of these kinds of parents." At this point, the question of the gangs was raised, since some of the members of the gangs were the offspring of members of parliament or officials in one of the ministries. Later, however, the author of the report made no further mention of them. Rather, his focus shifted to young people who lived in working-class districts, perhaps because it was more in line with the official narrative.

The members of the Young Guard composed a profile of the hooligan out of the following elements: "1. lingo, 2. striking dress, 3. alcoholism, 4. rough violent sexuality, 5. rowdy behavior and scandalous fights, 6. nonpolitical crimes." They also named the places where these young people would gather most frequently, and this made it possible to speak about gangs. These places including bustling public transportation nodes such as Móricz Zsigmond Circus, parks such as the Városmajor Park, and squares next to popular hangouts, such as Almási Square, the MOM Cultural Center, and the Kerekes Dance School.

This alleged link between hooligans and violence appeared in the ever more prevalent borrowings from Western newscasts about hooligans. In the 1958 Notting Hill (London) race riots, people of color, mostly West Indian residents, were attacked by mobs of white people for several days.[51] Using the English terms of the day, *Esti Hírlap* referred to the perpetrators as hooligans and contended that "dark-skinned immigrants" had been killed (this contention was incorrect; surprisingly, there were no fatalities). The Hungarian periodical published a caricature printed in the *Daily Express* that likened the perpetrators to Nazis: "Different uniforms—same face—writes the English paper under the condemnatory sketch of the 'racist' hooligans" (a sketch of a hooligan and a Nazi in uniform).[52] In 1959, *Esti Hírlap* published an account of the moral panic that had broken out because of youth gangs in Paris. The article, entitled "Hooligan gangs," was based on an article in the *New York Herald Tribune*.[53] Thus, the creation and strategic use of the term *hooligan* in Hungary was influenced not only by Soviet terminology but also by discourses in Western Europe and in the United States.

The discourse on hooliganism played an important role in depictions of violent acts committed in the course of the uprising in 1956 as little more than nonpolitical crimes. In this interpretive framework, 1956 was not a matter of politics but rather merely the product of violent criminal elements in the populace. In propaganda pamphlets that came to be known as "White Books," the 1956 revolution was portrayed as "the violent acts of the rabble." The narrative in the pamphlets was structured not around peaceful demonstrations and political demands but rather around the alleged victims and perpetrators of acts of violence. The revolution in 1956 was presented as a moment when nonpolitical criminals filled the streets—that is, the so-called hooligans who used violence to hold the respectable denizens of the city in a state of terror.[54] The criminalization of the people who had fought in 1956, which took place via the repressive measures implemented by the regime and the show trials of the people accused, happened in parallel with the creation and increased use of the term *hooligan*. Thus, the public discourse on hooliganism enabled the regime to define anyone who sympathized with the goals of the revolution as a criminal. It also allowed the regime to present the events of 1956 to members of the younger generation as a series of violent acts.

By 1959–60, the profile of the Hungarian hooligan was official state doctrine. In the public safety discourse on youths, the hooligan was heir to the violent acts of 1956. His appearance in any public space thus constituted a threat of another "counterrevolution" in the eyes of the police and the political organizations that worked in cooperation with the police. In the press and in the police files, the alleged violent and criminal tendencies of the groups of youths who gathered in public spaces in the late '50s were directly linked to those of the armed groups that had fought the regime in 1956. It was not by chance that the characterization of alleged youth gangs closely echoed the portrayal of groups of resistors in 1956. By creating this connection, the police cast these allegedly criminal groups as well organized and continuously active rather than as ad hoc groupings. The construction of the threat of violent hooligans and youth gangs had the dual function of legitimizing the violent measures used by the police against Hungarian youth and giving credibility in the public mind to the official, counterrevolutionary propaganda.

The depiction of the Rowdytum phenomenon in the GDR was very similar to the characterization of the Hungarian youth gang (galeri). According to Thomas Lindenberger, identifying Rowdytum in the GDR in December 1956 was part of the reaction of the GDR politburo to the Soviet invasion of Hungary and the Suez crisis. In December 1956 and January 1957, in the wake of the Hungarian uprising of 1956, the GDR Politburo developed new schemes to prevent domestic uprisings in which the regular police were to play an important part. Lindenberger discerns a duplicity of discourses on Rowdytum: a military one, focused on state security, and an ideological one, in which "all products of the commercial entertainment industry, in particular pulp fiction, movies, and pop music, were perceived as part of a deliberate strategy to lure East German youths away from socialism. The categories used to characterize and to analyze these artifacts were derived from the long-standing German tradition of anti Schund und Schmutz campaigns, youth protection—Jugendschutz—and antimodernism discourses."[55]

Following the reprisals taken in the wake of 1956, hooligans figured in the parlance of the police reports as the members of society who were the most likely to commit counterrevolutionary criminal acts. In 1959, the police and the recently formed Hungarian Communist Youth League took concerted efforts to rid the country of hooliganism.[56] The most serious problem, in their assessment, was that youth crime was not declining. In the period between 1953 and 1963, the number of young people as a proportion of the group of people accused of having committed criminal acts in Budapest rose from 17 percent to 34 percent. Of course, this was primarily a consequence of the fact that after 1956, the number of people working as part of the police force—and, later, the proportion of the police focusing on youth crime—in Budapest grew.[57] According to the reports that enumerate the vaunted successes of the police force, 43 percent of the people arrested in the course of raids in 1969 were children or juveniles.[58] The images of America and the rebelliousness of its youth were useful in the war waged by the communist police against hooligans and fascist youths, particularly given the official socialist concept of culture (*kulturnost'*, imported in part from the Soviet Union), which was "the personal attributes of a 'cultured' person. *Kulturnost'* was reflected in the way one spoke, ate, dressed, made love, and went to the bathroom."[59]

Figure 3.6. The hooligan: "Alone . . . tête-à-tête . . . in a gang" (Cartoon in *Ludas Matyi*, 1958).

## GALERI: THE MAKING OF THE YOUTH GANGS

What, then, did the term *galeri*, or *youth gang*, actually mean in Hungary in the 1960s? József Molnár, a contemporary Hungarian criminologist, offered the following definition in his book about youth gangs: "It refers to groups of people where the very grouping is an expression of deviance from social average norms. Thus, an assembly of youths designated by the term 'galeri' implies, merely through this designation, a negative value judgment and the raising of a problem."[60] The "deviance from social average norms" means that there were also positive norms that the regime was trying to construct and use to influence young people positively (at least according to the regime's ideals). Molnár's book was published in 1971, and by this time, it was considered self-evident that "gangs" were a criminological issue that could be coupled with political opposition to the system.

The first major campaign against gangs was launched by the Budapest Police Department in 1960–61. Several dozen gangs that were allegedly organized on a territorial basis were broken up. This campaign created the foundation for efforts to link the term *hooliganism* and the term *gang* in the public discourse. The reports on the liquidation of the individual gangs all offered essentially the same, or at least very similar accounts, of how the gangs were originally formed. In 1960, of the various district police stations, the stations in Józsefváros and Angyalföld (working-class neighborhoods in Budapest at the time) distinguished themselves as the most diligent in this respect, since eleven gangs had been broken up in Józsefváros and thirteen in Angyalföld.[61]

The police kept highly trafficked areas and popular hangouts under observation, which indicates that they focused primarily on the areas in which young people spent their free time. In their reports, they contended that, for the most part, the gangs had been formed in 1959 (one year after the launch of the campaign to dissolve them, of course), and neither parents, nor schools, nor even the Communist Youth League could keep the unethical conduct of their members within acceptable limits.[62]

The police kept a wide array of city spaces under observation, from restaurants and tourist spots to movie theaters. In the summer of 1958, in cooperation with schoolteachers, the police launched raids of movie theaters in areas on the fringes of the city. In late 1958, several articles were published in the press on the spread of jukeboxes and their harmful effects on young people. Later, the groups of young people who gathered around jukeboxes to listen to rock and roll music were often dubbed gangs. According to these narratives, Western music drew crowds of young people (hooligans) who were easily tempted to stray from the path of proper comportment and who were even more likely to commit transgressions (and form gangs) when gathered in groups.

The story of the Gresham gang, which was one of the first gangs to be identified (or constructed) by the police, was also tied to a jukebox. According to the tale, violence, "worship of the West," and the consumption of mass culture were closely intertwined: "at the beginning of 1960, the division received warnings that a group of between 30 and 40 young boys and girls were frequenting regularly and as a group the 'Gresham' club at Roosevelt Square 5 in the fifth district." Although according to the report of the Division for the Protection of Children and Minors, the police who led the raid did not observe any unusual disturbances of the peace, the young people who had gathered were nonetheless considered a gang. The authors of the police report then offered a linear history of the group, as indeed they were expected to do, to give the clear impression that they were dealing with an important issue and potential threat: "In our assessment, the gang first formed in late 1959. The jukebox in the site helped further the creation of the gang, as it drew in young people from various districts of the city. . . . The prominence of the restaurant as a well-known spot, the presence of foreigners, the chance it gave boys and girls to meet, and the proximity of the promenade on the bank of the Danube River make the place appealing."[63] In this narrative, Western music and customs serve as means to create new identities, and its basic plot is the following: young people who listen to Western music gather in public or semipublic spaces, and since there are among them a few who are easily tempted to commit mischief (hooligans), sooner or later they form a gang. The jukebox was later replaced in this story by a space suitable for listening to concerts or music, as indeed was the case in the story of the Great Tree Gang and the Youth Park.

Figure 3.7. The jukebox in the Gresham club, 1958 (Fortepan / Sándor Bauer).

In the official discourses, the emergence en masse of gangs was always linked to the allegedly disordered states of affairs after 1956. In his aforementioned book on gangs, József Molnár contended that "the mass appearance of gangs can be dated directly to the counterrevolution and, perhaps more precisely, the years immediately following it." He then asserts that "the horde-like activity, which in the days around the counterrevolution found manifestation in numerous mass acts, has in recent times begun to wane," an assertion he supports with the contention that almost no new gangs were formed in 1965–66.[64] The explanation for this, of course, lay primarily in the fact that after 1961, the police did not begin to insist on the importance of liquidating gangs again until 1969. In 1960–61, the proliferation of cases involving gangs was a result of the repressive measures taken in the wake of 1956 and the criminalization of the younger generation—the generation made largely synonymous with the people who had taken up arms in 1956. Similarly, in 1969, the police began to deal with alleged gangs with increasing frequency because of the antireform

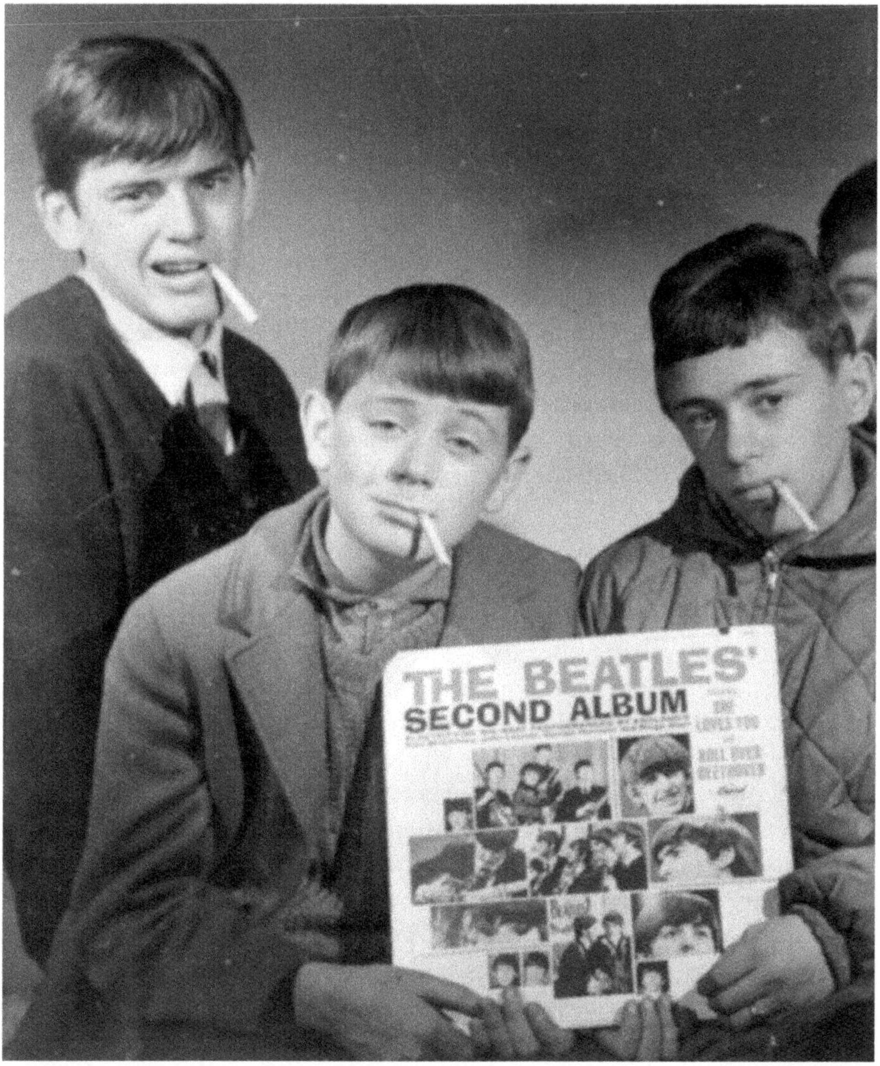


Figure 3.8. Hungarian young people and the second Beatles album, 1965 (Fortepan).

turn that came in the wake of the 1968 invasion of Czechoslovakia and subsequent additions that were made to the police force. In other words, the more the authorities feared the younger generation, the more inclined they were to see most young people as hooligans.

The police, the press, and the courts promoted the construction of gangs in the public discourse by presenting occasional and temporary gatherings of coevals as permanent, organized groups and criminalizing the consumption patterns and activities of the members of these groups. The primary transgression of gang members was that they "amused themselves completely at liberty, with no inhibitions whatsoever, according entirely to their tastes and ideas."[65] The notion that the gangs were somehow organized groups was thrown into question even in the police reports.[66] Most of them were simply incidental gatherings of young people belonging to the same generation. The strongest tie that bound the young people who gathered in similar spots was the fact that they consumed similar cultural products—primarily rock music. When the political and ideological debates of the early 1970s finally came to an end (debates in part between figures of the regime who had supported reform and figures who, especially in the wake of the invasion of Czechoslovakia, considered it a dangerous threat), the label "gang" also began to vanish. It was replaced in the official discourses by the term *csövesek,* which means "bums" or "vagrants."

## CONCLUSION

In Hungary the term *gang* has been used to denote not only violence and the tendency to ape Western trends and fashions but also, in the eyes of the socialist authorities, opposition to the regime and a serious threat to social order and ethics since the 1956 revolution. By using this label to stigmatize unauthorized gatherings of youths in public spaces, the authorities limited their freedom of assembly and made it quite clear to members of the younger generation that it was only proper to meet regularly in groups in public or semipublic spaces as part of state-organized events. The police strove to make these limitations on the use of public space by young people seem legitimate in the eyes of parents by characterizing the youths who formed groups in these spaces as deviant. The term *gang* has also gone further: it has been used to criminalize unauthorized meetings under the socialist regime. The call to maintain control over how young people spent their free time generated expansions in state funding for policing and created work for the police leading raids on what they classified as gang activity. The police and associated organizations could always find young people gathered in groups in various hangouts and thus could always find justification to keep someone under observation. The rise in the number of police raids and the regular monitoring of semipublic spaces also helped the authorities craft the discourse on gangs.

In the 1960s, according to the state authorities, hooligans and gangs constituted the greatest threat to young people in Hungary. This does not mean that the entire regime viewed all young people as a threat and only as a threat. This view, rather, reflected the needs and interests of the police. To keep young people under protective observation, the police had to craft an image of an enemy. This image of a potential threat to youth and social order then made it possible for the police to exert greater control over normative expressions of opinion concerning everyday acts.

There was also an official youth culture that strove to mold "good" young people (budding citizens of the socialist state) rather than merely preventing young people from becoming criminals, as discussed in chapter 4. The criminalization of youth represented only one part of youth policy, and youth policy was not exclusively a matter of repressive policy. Some of the contemporary authors who wrote about how to socialize young people, however, themselves acknowledged that the practice of singling out individuals among the groups of young people and branding them as negative examples rested on extremely pliable definitions of norms, definitions that always depended on the needs of the authorities at the given moment. For instance, in 1962, the authors of a comprehensive work on child services in Hungary made the following observation: "A long time ago, they used to write 'hic sunt leones' on the white spots on maps of territories in Africa that had not yet been explored or were less familiar, or 'there are lions here!' In the absence of adequate knowledge of the criteria, many are inclined to offer a summary response to the question: 'there are hooligans here!'"[67] The authors could not afford (or did not dare) to be more critical of practice and policy than this, however. Meanwhile, not all agencies within the socialist state were adopting similar tactics regarding young people or social problems. In other words, there were divisions within the government bureaucracy (and probably the party as well) about how to deal with social problems. Even the definition of social problems was different at the different levels of the administration.[68] The socialist state was not a monolith. Indeed, the fact that police felt compelled to justify their punitive measures indicates that they were unsure of their own status within the party and state.

Neither Khrushchev, who was quoted at the beginning of this chapter, nor the people responsible for the public discourse on juveniles and the social institutions that dealt with minors could say precisely what made someone a hooligan or gang member. They nonetheless had to assert with all certainty that both hooligans and gang members existed and that both posed a threat to the system and the social order. The terms also facilitated the politicization of youth revolt, a process that involved borrowing strategies from the West and, predominantly, from America.[69]

However, the Hippie Stroll that took place on July 8, 1969, initiated widespread changes in the police, the press, and the institutions that dealt with minors that went beyond consequences for the discourses that had been crafted about gangs and the dangers they posed. In the following chapters I examine how this event transformed policing in Hungary, the task of providing protection and supervision for minors, and the way public and semipublic spaces were monitored.

## NOTES

1. A Komszomol XIII. Kongresszusa. (N. Sz. Hruscsov beszéde, 1958. április 18-án.) [Thirteenth Congress of the All-Union Leninist Young Communist League (Komsomol), speech held by Nikita Khrushchev on April 19, 1958], 99, cited in Havas, Elkán, and Gayer, *Gyermek- és ifjúságvédelem*, 227.

2. See *Prevention of Juvenile Delinquency*, 1955.

3. Pearson, *Hooligan*, 74–86. Pearson traces the history of the term back to the early nineteenth century, and he links it to the stereotypes that emerged with the process of urbanization.

4. Neuberger, *Hooliganism*.

5. Shearer, *Policing Stalin's Socialism*, 219–38.

6. Bernstein, *Raised under Stalin*, 45; Solomon, *Soviet Criminal Justice under Stalin*, 224–25; LaPierre, *Hooligans in Khrushchev's Russia*, 59–95.

7. Bernstein, *Raised under Stalin*, 99–102.

8. Cf. Kotalik, *Rowdytum im Staatssozialismus*, 81–103.

9. Lebow, *Unfinished Utopia*, 138.

10. Kenkmann, *Wilde Jugend*; Kenkmann, "The Subculture of Young Urban Workers in Germany 1930–1950." For a similar phenomenon in Vienna, see Mejstrik, "Urban Youth." The Viennese *Schlurf* corresponded essentially to the Prague *potápki*, the Paris *zazou*, and the Hamburg *Swing-Heinies* (Tantner, *"Schlurfs"*).

11. Keleti, *Dalolva szép az élet*.

12. Springhall, *Youth, Popular Culture and Moral Panics*, 98–120.

13. "Amerikai kultúra" [American culture], *Szabad Ifjúság*, November 24, 1950, 9.

14. For instance, in a depiction of a gang of car thieves in California: "Together they would devour American comics (pornography), and they went to the movie theaters together to see Hollywood films. . . . They then stole a car, they crashed the stolen car into another car, which they pushed into the ditch, then they took two other cars" ("Az amerikai gyermeknevelés—és eredménye" [American childrearing: And its consequences], *Szabad Ifjúság*, March 19, 1952, 4).

15. *Esti Hírlap,* February 9, 1958, 5.
16. *Esti Hírlap,* May 24, 1959, 7.
17. Tamás Adler (a worker at the Chemical Industry Machine and Radiator Factory), "Budapesti jegyzetek: Kísértet a 26-oson" [Budapest notes: Apparition on tram 26], *Esti Budapest,* June 23, 1952, 2.
18. B. L., "Budapesti jegyzetek: 'Hát ilyen is van még?'" [Budapest notes: "So there are still types like this around?"], *Esti Budapest,* August 4, 1952, 2; L. M., "Budapesti jegyzetek: Kínai terem" [Budapest notes: Chinese Room], *Esti Budapest,* October 7, 1952, 4.
19. István Tarján, "Budapesti jegyzetek: A 'hős'" [Budapest notes: The "hero."], *Esti Budapest,* December 23, 1952, 2.
20. Lampland, *Value of Labor,* 203–16.
21. József Kopré, "Budapesti jegyzetek: A jampecnek semmi sem drága" [Budapest notes: Nothing is expensive for the jampec], *Esti Budapest,* March 27, 1956, 2.
22. Pál Szabó, "Kialakul-e önmagától az új erkölcs?" [Does morality form on its own?], *Szabad Ifjúság,* April 23, 1954, 2; Tibor Hegedűs, "Bízzuk az ifjúságra a jampec-szellem megszüntetését" [Let's entrust the youth to bring an end to the jampec spirit], *Szabad Ifjúság,* April 27, 1954, 2.
23. Ottó Kandikó, "A táncról, a zenéről és néhány műsorról" [On dance, music, and a few shows], *Szabad Ifjúság,* April 29, 1954, 2; "Véget vetünk annak a struccpolitikának, amellyel eddig a fiatalokat távol akartuk tartani ezektől a táncoktól" [We will bring an end to the policy of burying our heads in the sand with which until now we have wanted to keep young people away from these dances]; K. E., "Szalonképes lesz a szamba, a rumba, a szving és a mambo: Beszélgetés az új táncszezonról" [The samba, rumba, swing, and mambo will be suitable for the saloon: A conversation about the new dance season], *Esti Budapest,* September 27, 1956, 4.
24. For instance, János Csontos, "Adjunk a fiataloknak jó tánczenét" [Let's give the kids good dance music], *Szabad Ifjúság,* May 9, 1954, 2.
25. "Hozzanak rendeletet a jampecek ellen" [They should issue a decree against the jampec], *Szabad Ifjúság,* May 19, 1954, 2.
26. For instance, "'Ifjúsági irodalom'—Amerikában" ["Youth literature": In America], *Szabad Ifjúság,* May 11, 1954, 5.
27. András Turi, "Kihajtott ing, jampi pulóver" [Shirt with the collar turned down, jampec pullover], *Esti Hírlap,* November 27, 1959, 3.
28. "He wears a wheat blue jacket with drooping shoulders, a pair of light flannel pants cut narrow in line with the latest fashion, and pointed chocolate-brown shoes based on an Italian design" (Béla Mátrai Betegh, "Aszfaltbetyár" [Asphalt highwayman], *Esti Hírlap,* June 26, 1959, 3; Boris Palotai, "Merész divat" [Bold fashion], *Esti Hírlap,* July 15, 1959, 3).

29. "Bécsi jampecek" [Vienna teddy boys], *Szabad Ifjúság*, May 31, 1956, 5.

30. "Társadalmi összefogást a fiatalkorúak bűnözése elleni harcban! Ankét a DISZ Központi Vezetőségénél" [Social unity in the battle against juvenile delinquency! A conference at the Central Executive Board of the Union of the Working Youth], *Szabad Ifjúság*, October 3, 1956, 4.

31. Harsányi, *Fiúk könyve*, 107.

32. Havas, Elkán, and Gayer, *Gyermek- és ifjúságvédelem*, 201.

33. Ibid., 226.

34. BFL, f. XXIV-1-23-d, BRFK, 0208/1958, A gyermek- és fiatalkorúak védelmével kapcsolatos legfontosabb jogszabályok gyűjteménye: Bevezető [Collection of the most important statutes concerning the protection of children and minors: Introduction].

35. Order number 8-402 of the Deputy Minister of Interior (ibid., 5–12).

36. Ibid., 6.

37. Ibid.

38. Decree number 62/1957 (IX. 24.) of the Revolutionary Workers'–Peasants' Government of Hungary on the creation of a National Child and Youth Policy Council, *Magyar Közlöny* no. 104 (November 24, 1957). In the summer of 1957, the Ministry of Cultural Affairs issued new regulations concerning "the placement in institutions of minors who had strayed down the path of ethical depravity" (Ministry of Cultural Affairs decree number 95-30/1957, issued July 30, 1957, BFL, f. XXIV-1-23-d, BRFK, 0208/1958, A gyermek- és fiatalkorúak védelmével kapcsolatos legfontosabb jogszabályok gyűjteménye [Collection of the most important statutes concerning the protection of children and minors], 17–20).

39. Rainer and Sereda, *Döntés a Kremlben, 1956*.

40. László Lóránt, "Dr. Münnich Ferenc nyilatkozata az Esti Hírlapnak a gyermekek és az ifjúság védelméről" [Statement by Dr. Ferenc Münnich to *Esti Hírlap* on the protection of children and minors], *Esti Hírlap*, October 2, 1958, 1.

41. Szakolczai, "A fegyveres erőszakszervek restaurálása 1956–1957 fordulóján."

42. BFL, f. XXIV-1-71-d, BRFK, 1958, Budapest Police Department Division for the Protection of Children and Minors, report on the situation in Budapest from the perspective of the protection of children and minors, 091-10/1958, 9 (and the debate concerning the report).

43. Ibid., 15–16.

44. Ibid., 9.

45. Eörsi, *Corvinisták, 1956*, 309.

46. "Rendőrkézen két tolvaj huligán" [Two thieving hooligans in the hands of the police], *Esti Hírlap*, August 14, 1958, 6.

47. The word *hooligan* in the text has been crossed out and replaced in pen with the word *Gypsy*. ÁSZTL, 3.1.5, O-10431, "Huligán" [Hooligan], cited in Nagy-Csere, "Az ellenség neve: 'huligán.'"

48. Nagy-Csere, "Az ellenség neve: 'huligán,'" 4.

49. MNL OL, f. M-KS-288, cs. 21, ő.e. 15, 1959, memorandum on the Budapest measures to bring an end to hooliganism for the Central Committee of the Communist Youth League. November 30, 1959.

50. Ibid.

51. Hernon, *Riot!*, 170–184.

52. "Ugyanaz az arc . . ." [Same face], *Esti Hírlap*, May 24, 1959, 7.

53. "Huligán bandák Párizsban" [Hooligan gangs in Paris], *Esti Hírlap*, August 2, 1959, 7.

54. The communist government [the Council of Ministers] published a series of "White Books" (leaflets including propagandistic photographs) from 1957 that established the official historical account of the 1956 uprising. For instance, Minisztertanács: Tájékoztatási Hivatal, *Ellenforradalmi erők*; and Minisztertanács: Tájékoztatási Hivatal, *Nagy Imre és bűntársai*.

55. Lindenberger, *Aufklären, zersetzen, liquidieren*; Lindenberger, *Volkspolizei*; Janssen, *Halbstarke in der DDR*.

56. MNL OL, f. M-KS-288, cs. 21, ő.e. 15, 1959, notes on the elimination of hooliganism, November 30, 1959.

57. BFL, f. XXIII-102-a, Budapest Fővárosi Tanács Végrehajtó Bizottsága [Minutes of the meetings of the Budapest City Council's Executive Committee], June 23, 1965, 2.

58. MNL OL, f. XIX-B-1-Z, BM Kollégiuma [Panel of the Ministry of Interior], b. 39, report on the circumstances of individual violent crimes of a riotous nature, June 11, 1970.

59. See Lebow: "Kontra Kultura," 71–92, 83.

60. Molnár, *Galeribűnözés*, 334.

61. BFL, f. XXV-60-b, Fővárosi Főügyészség [Budapest Municipal Public Prosecutor's Office], TÜK igazgatási iratok, 0017/61, 409–10.

62. Ibid., 414–621. In the text of the summary reports, there are subchapters on the origins of the gang.

63. BFL, f. XXV-60, Tük. 0017/61, 427, Summary Report on the Liquidation of the "Gresham" Gang. Budapest Police Department Division for the Protection of Children and Minors. February 4, 1961.

64. Molnár, *Galeribűnözés*, 335–36.

65. BFL, f. XXV-60-b, Fővárosi Főügyészség [Budapest Municipal Public Prosecutor's Office], TÜK igazgatási iratok, 0017/61, 415.

66. BFL, f. XXV-60-b, Fővárosi Főügyészség [Budapest Municipal Public Prosecutor's Office], TÜK igazgatási iratok, 0017/61, 409–621.

67. Havas, Elkán, and Gayer, *Gyermek- és ifjúságvédelem*, 202–3.
68. For more on the changing definitions of social problems, see Horváth, *Két emelet boldogság*, 30–73.
69. See Poiger, *Jazz, Rock, and Rebel*, who offers a comparison of the way the question was handled in the German Democratic Republic and the Federal Republic of Germany and also examines the appearance of American mass culture.

FOUR

# YOUTH PROTECTION

THE POLICE WERE ABLE TO cast Big Kennedy as the leader of the Great Tree Gang in part because they could claim to have found an attachment in his past to the events of 1956 and in part because he had grown up in the care of the state. He believed that he was made the principal defendant simply because the police needed to identify a leader of the gang.[1]

The creation of the first file on the Great Tree Gang was tied to his arrest, and he was mentioned specifically in the first few sentences of the file, with emphasis both on his abnormal childhood, which by implication predestined him to a life of crime, and his attachment to the legacy of 1956, which enabled the police to give his alleged crimes a political relevance. State care for children and the events of 1956 were linked because after 1956, youth policy was increasingly seen as a security issue, not least because this served the interests of the state security forces. The younger generation was presented as a potentially dangerous group that had to be watched carefully and kept under strict control. Thus, Big Kennedy could be made—and, for the police, needed to be made—the leader of the gang by the court and in the documents produced over the course of the investigation, even though the occasional gatherings of Big Kennedy and his cohort bore no resemblance whatsoever to an organized criminal organization.

Although the rhetoric of socialist regimes (rhetoric that was sometimes, but not always, disingenuous) asserted that orphaned and abandoned children had the support of the state, the criminalization of orphans and children who had ended up in foster care institutions became a widespread practice in the Soviet Union and the countries of the Eastern Bloc, as did the tendency to regard their pastimes as politically motivated acts.[2] Children and young adults in the Soviet Union who had become orphans because of the war, famines, or the Great Purge of the 1930s were also often treated as likely criminals and potential enemies of the people by state authorities.[3] Some of these youths were defined as "class enemies" and were deported to the Gulag to be "educated" through work.[4] Alongside Komsomol, the People's Commissariat for Internal Affairs, or NKVD (essentially the Ministry of Interior in the Soviet Union, which included the secret police), assumed responsibility for several million orphans who became homeless after 1945, though the only salient change in the measures that were taken was that minors could be referred to as "innocents" in the texts used by the authorities.[5] Meanwhile, the childcare institutions were chronically underfunded and understaffed, so they had limited opportunities to improve the circumstances of the orphans, if they were even trying to do that. Nonetheless, this coupling of measures taken to deal with orphans and measures taken to deal with juvenile delinquency became everyday practice, so the search for solutions to the problems faced by orphans became an issue of public security.[6] The point of departure for this text, which was pedagogical in its implications, was the goal of creating productive laborers out of young criminals and hooligans using the correctional power of collective life.[7] The foster care institutions embodied this vision of collective upbringing, but children and adolescents regularly escaped from the institutions because of the mistreatment they suffered there. Since so many of their wards fled, the foster care institutions almost automatically functioned as correctional institutions, and they sought to educate and "improve" the young people in their care in the interest of realizing a communist utopia. In other words, they worked from the presumption that their wards were inclined to commit offenses from the outset.[8]

In the history of youth policy in Hungary, which after the war was increasingly shaped by the Soviet model, the 1956 revolution and the social-political measures that were taken in its wake form almost a dividing line. The precise nature and institutional forms of state foster care were among the most sensitive issues in Hungary in the 1960s, as were the processes that defined which children and adolescents needed care. Who decided a child was in need of state care and on what criteria? And what institutional tools were used to provide this care, and on the basis of what pedagogical principals?

I argue in this chapter that the police drew practically no distinction between children who were wards of the state and juvenile delinquents, largely due to the way the system, in practice, was run. After World War II the number of minors in the care of foster parents declined drastically, and during the 1950s, the foster care institutions became the predominant form of providing housing for minors in need. Because the minors in foster care institutions were intermixed with minors in correctional institutions, a child from foster parents was often taken into state care, and then, after he or she had escaped from the foster care institution, he/she was put in a correctional institution and, after reaching the age of maturity, in prison. Thus, most of the foster care homes were set up to function as correctional institutions, and accordingly, the work of pedagogy and childrearing was reduced to little more than discipline and oversight. Overcrowding and the intermixing of orphans and "delinquent youth" in foster care institutions stigmatized minors who became wards of the state, and "youth protection" thus started to be understood as a euphemism for controlling juvenile delinquency. The only difference among the Budapest foster care homes was the age of the children who were domiciled in them: in the 1960s there were homes for kindergarten children, elementary school children, minors (ages fourteen to eighteen), and youths who had already reached the age of maturity. Because they were differentiated on the basis of their ages, the children had to move regularly to new institutions. However, because of overcrowding, many of them were "overaged," which meant that sometimes for years they could not move to the next institution according to their age.[9]

I contend that state foster care and the protection of minors became political questions and questions of public safety and security in the 1950s and 1960s in Hungary because the state feared that there might well be an uprising resembling the uprising that had taken place in 1956, in which young people had played a particularly large part. One of the most prominent goals of youth policy after 1956 was to stifle any interest in politics among young people. In the eyes of the authorities, an environment that encouraged apolitical youths and where politics remained in the official framework created by the Communist Youth League (and even there was understood to be restricted to a narrow range of options) was the ideal. This shaped the ways the institutions that crafted the narrative of the Great Tree Gang functioned. I also examine how the institutions responsible for youth policy tried to influence how youths were socialized to ensure that they remained loyal to or at least neutral regarding the ideology of the system when it came to important political questions. Numerous social institutions kept any political discussions outside the official discussions in the Communist Youth League under close watch. These included the institutions responsible for the protection of minors and the foster care homes, and the need to have such surveillance meant that in addition to serving in principle to provide care, they also had political and law enforcement functions.

Figure 4.1. The wall of the correctional institute in Aszód, 1975 (Fortepan / Tamás Urbán).

## ORPHANAGES

> That wound on the body of society should be much more throbbing than it is, and there should be a greater sense of community than there is. . . . We should build foster care homes at the cost of other important investments, taking funds from them. . . . I would dare abandon the construction of schools, of store chains, hotels, even apartments, or a part of all this if this problem were to be solved. . . . With regards to the Gypsy[10] question, they also say that it needs to be solved, we need to get them apartments and jobs, but the person who holds a presentation today on how they need to be brought into the workplace will not hire a Gypsy tomorrow if he applies at the factory. If they want to put a Gypsy into the apartment where this same person lives as a co-tenant, he would be the one who would protest the most vociferously about how this would threaten the mood and mentality which has developed in the building. We do the same thing with these children. They say we need to help them, but at the same time, they regard them as social outsiders.

This excerpt is from a speech that was held in 1968 at a sitting of the Executive Committee of the Budapest City Council.[11] Why had there been no improvements made to the foster care institutions in Hungary since 1945 or 1956?

The principal reason was that the frameworks within which youth policy was formed in Budapest in the 1960s were determined by the official interpretation of the 1956 revolution. As a consequence, anyone living on the margins of society (for instance a ward of the state) was automatically considered an enemy or potential threat by the state. In 1957, the authorities drew up the following official explanation for their approach to youth policy: "Our experience indicates that a very large number of the people who took part in the counterrevolutionary events were juvenile delinquents or young people who were ethically corrupt. . . . The events of the October counterrevolution put the unsolved problems of protection of children and minors in even sharper focus."[12] The Education Division of the Executive Committee of the Budapest City Council supported this contention with the observation that 60 percent of the people who had been accused of unlawful possession of firearms in the first three months of 1957 had been under sixteen. Forty percent of the people who were convicted in April 1957 for having committed crimes against the People's Republic were minors.[13] The repressive measures that were taken in the months and weeks after the 1956 revolution disproportionately affected minors, which is why, over the course of the next decade, the question of rearing minors became a central problem. According to a report submitted by the division on July 15, 1957, "the rise in ethical decay and delinquency among minors and the participation of minors in the counterrevolutionary events prove that efforts to take effective preventative measures have failed. This stems in large part from the unresolved nature of the problems concerning the protection of children and minors."[14] The authors of the report felt that "there is an increasing desire among working parents for their children's upbringing and education to be provided within institutional frameworks."[15] In other words, according to the Budapest City Council, the solution would be for children to be decreasingly under the supervision of their parents and increasingly raised in institutions.

Youth policy was closely intertwined with the branding of youth as a potential threat and an emphasis in public discourse on habits and attitudes among young people that were labeled deviant. The construction of the youth question served primarily to enable the regime to characterize the 1956 revolution at least in part as the work of impulsive, destructive, ignorant young people. The solutions that were devised to address these problems for the most part were based on the ideas of Anton Makarenko (1888–1939), an influential Soviet pedagogue, social worker, and author who introduced the concept of productive labor into education and advocated the establishment of children's collectives in which children would be reared in part by their peers. The influence of Makarenko's theories are a significant factor for why, in Hungary, the idea of rearing children both through work and to work became one of the most important elements and tasks of children's social care and education.[16]

In the autumn of 1956, the Union of Working Youth, DISZ, which was created in 1950 on the basis of the Soviet Komsomol and was under the oversight of the party, suggested to the Budapest City Council the creation of a boarding school that "would handle children who had embarked down the path of moral decline, instead of sending them to prison. The establishment of the Aszód and Rákospalota Work Force Reserves Office Institutions,[17] a Makarenko facility for roughly 1,000–1,500 people, would help a great deal to solve the problem." The proposal met with opposition among the members of the Executive Committee, however, and it also turned out that the Budapest municipal government had little say when it came to the barracks, which were becoming available for other uses. There were no buildings in which such institutions could have been housed.[18]

The lack of space also determined the ways in which decisions were made concerning where minors would be domiciled. Because of problems with overcrowding, children and adolescents for whom there was no space available in the foster care institutions were placed in correctional institutions, which were under the oversight of the Ministry of Labor and Health. In 1957, only 500 of the minors in the correctional institutions, in which there was officially space for 1,800 people, had actually been sentenced by the courts to confinement there. The others were all there because there was no space for them in the other state institutions.[19]

The numbers offer clear examples of the perpetual problem of overcrowding. In 1962, there were 939 children at the Institution for the Protection of Children and Minors in Budapest, which had 440 spaces nominally.[20] Furthermore, because of the outbreaks of contagious diseases, the institutions were regularly put on lockdown. Given these considerations, the district councils ruled that a child should be taken into the care of the state only if the circumstances in which the child was living were truly dire or life-threatening.[21]

The intermixing of minors who, in the eyes of the state at least, were juvenile delinquents with minors who simply were in need of foster care stigmatized all of the children who were in the care of the state, as it was not clear exactly why any given minor had ended up in a correctional institution. The distinction between the two was further blurred by the fact that the foster care institutions and the correctional institutions were under the oversight of the same organs of government. The officials dealing with childcare also perceived the path from foster parents to state care and then to a correctional institution and then to prison as an ordinary trajectory.[22] The institutional system sometimes drew

Figure 4.2. Cigarette break in the correctional institute in Aszód, 1974 (Fortepan / Tamás Urbán).

little distinction between children who had been turned over to the care of the state, children who had been taken into the care of the state, and children who had been sentenced to correctional institutions.

In the period between 1956 and 1962, when the members of the Great Tree Gang who had been wards of the state were living in state institutions, the number of minors who were in the care of the state leapt from 4,623 to 8,099.[23] For roughly a decade after 1945, for the most part wards of the state had been put in the care of foster parents (as had been the case in the interwar period). Until the 1950s, two-thirds of the wards of the state were put in the care of foster parents or their own parents. It was only in the mid-1950s that the foster care institution began to become the predominant form of providing housing for minors in need. By the 1960s, the number of children in the care of the state placed in foster care or returned to their own homes dropped to between 25 and 30 percent, where it remained for more than a decade. In 1969, 24,000 children lived in state institutions in Hungary (1 percent of the population between zero and fourteen years of age).[24]

One-third of the wards of the state who were under three years of age were housed in Budapest. The reason for this was simply that children had to be given domicile in the place where they had been abandoned. Thus, many infants whose parents did not live in Budapest nonetheless were put in the care of institutions in Budapest because they had been found in the train stations, workers' hostels, and hospitals in the nation's capital. Because of the lack of space, the authorities in Budapest tried to send these children to institutions in other parts of the country, but they largely failed in these efforts because of the opposition put up by the receiving institutions, which experienced similar problems with overcrowding. In 1962, two-thirds of the children (between zero and fourteen years of age) in the care of the state were in institutions in Budapest. The number of referrals to institutions outside the city was determined not by growing demand but rather by the drop in the number of spaces. All of the children's homes were overcrowded. In 1962, the state was able to refer only about half as many children to children's homes as it had in 1957 (the number dropped from 2,095 to 1,249). The other children either lived under conditions that were deemed dangerous by the state or in the children's wards of the Budapest hospitals. Even in cases of emergency, the admission of children for reasons of health (such as outbreaks of tuberculosis) was sluggish, and sick children and infants born prematurely sometimes had to wait for months or even years for a spot in an institution.[25]

But why were foster care institutions not orphanages and why adoption wasn't their primary goal? According to studies done by Katalin Hanák in the early 1970s, roughly 90 percent of the wards of the state in the late 1960s and early 1970s had parents who had "physical occupations" (almost half of them were unskilled laborers). Only 2 percent of these children had been orphans and only 12 percent had lost one parent when they had come into the care of the state. Thus, the children's homes were not orphanages, because most of the children in them had living parents; rather, most of the children (48 percent) came from families that had fallen apart.[26] Among the official reasons for taking a child into the care of the state, the most commonly cited was teen pregnancy (or *lányanyaság*, which is gender-specific; the term refers specifically to a pregnant female minor and leaves the male out of consideration). This was the explanation (cited as a "social cause") given in 28 percent of the cases. Abandonment of a child by its parents was given as a reason in only 10 percent of the cases, as was true in the case of the "criminal parent" category. A report submitted to the Budapest City Council offers the following self-critical ascertainment in 1963: "Today, it seems that we take children who are in danger from their parents and, under the pretense of 'state protection,' we expose them to far greater danger because we are compelled to keep them in hospital wards. One also cannot underestimate the importance of the fact that the wards of the state and children waiting to be taken into the care of the state occupy between 8 and 10 percent of the children's beds in our hospitals."[27] Though the report strongly condemned the state institutions and their failure to take effective measures with regards to the provision of care for minors, it nonetheless explained the large number of minors in the care of the state as a consequence of the irresponsible conduct and attitudes of parents. The number of adopted children, furthermore, was quite low, even in comparison with the number of infants who were put in state institutions. In 1962, for instance, there were fifty-four adoptions, which was 4 percent of the total number of minors who were placed in the care of the state from 1959 1962. The report acknowledged that the primary reason for this was not that there was no interest in adoption, but rather that the process of adoption itself was complex and burdensome. No suggestions were made concerning how this might be changed, however, although the report stated that "the system of state childcare has gone bankrupt."[28]

As a consequence of this blurring of the differences among these children, children who had been taken into the care of the state because they had tumultuous home lives or their families faced difficult circumstances were often treated as potential or likely delinquents. Minors who were deemed in need of the care of the state experienced the effects of the social policy of the capital primarily in the foster care homes. One of the most important elements of this policy involved precautionary measures to prevent crime among youths, which meant that "youth protection" soon was understood as a mere euphemism for juvenile delinquency.

It was considered necessary by the authorities to profile the foster care homes to ensure that children with similar backgrounds would be placed in the same institution, and thus, children who were deemed innocent would not be placed together with children who were considered delinquent.[29] In the assessment of the Budapest City Council, the creation of an institution that was specifically correctional (or punitive) in nature would only have been possible if the institution in question had been severed entirely from the existing network of homes, which would essentially have meant giving up on the system of homes. The council also hesitated to take this step because "if we were to cut off any of the children's homes from the institutional network, we would further reduce the number of spaces for normal children." The lack of space, however, was not the only obstacle to the creation of such an institution. According to an inquiry into the matter, the creation of an institution that was more closed and self-contained would have meant separate and more costly investments (more comprehensive security measures, a school within the institution, supplies and equipment for a workshop), and "at the same time, the available spaces in the given institution would drop to half or less than half."[30]

Figure 4.3. Fight in the lavatory in the correctional institute in Aszód, 1974 (Fortepan / Tamás Urbán).

Closed institutions would have had to function as both prisons and foster care homes. Thus, their maintenance costs would have been much higher than the maintenance costs of the traditional foster care homes, which had a far simpler infrastructure (and from which it was much easier to escape). However, the fact that children sometimes fled had certain advantages for the institutions, since at least for a time they did not have to feed or clothe their wards. Furthermore, after a child had returned or been apprehended and brought back, he or she could be put, as punishment, in a significantly less costly institution, thus leading to further savings. The practice of putting juvenile delinquents in regular foster care homes thus not only served the purpose of giving the authorities a pretext for keeping closer watch over the other wards of the state but also helped cut costs. Escape was considered a crime, so most of the children who fled the crowded institutions (usually soon after being put in them) were branded criminals in the official records.[31]

Of the children placed in Budapest institutions because of overcrowding, 62 percent were technically overage (this proportion was 46 percent nationwide)—that is, according to their age they were supposed to move to another institution, but because of the pervasive overcrowding in the institution system, there were no places available for them. The primary reason for moving was that every time a child was moved to a different type of school (nursery school, kindergarten, elementary school, vocational school), accordingly, he or she was also moved to a different home. There was thus no real chance for any emotional bonds to develop between the wards and their caregivers. It was something of a great step forward when, in 1963, the authorities reached the following decision with regards to the children's home in Csatárka Street in the Third District of Budapest: "orphans and abandoned children who are wards of the state [may remain] in the framework of one institution from age three until age fourteen." These children (roughly one-tenth of the children in the care of the state) were almost the only ones regarded as innocent by the state, which is why this provision—exceptional at the time—was made for them.[32]

In the course of the debate concerning this question, one of the members of the committee cited a claim made by the commander of a prison for juvenile delinquents who stated "in his institution 70 percent of the inmates are wards of the state. We cannot turn a blind eye to the fact that there are children in Hungary who go as if predestined from foster parents to state care and then a correctional institution and then prison."[33] In other words, in his perception, for many children, the path from foster care to prison was very much a straight line. He did not add, however, that some young people with without family, education, or training avoided the foster care institutions to prison track, and instead moved to workers' hostels and then, as they aged, state homes for the elderly. From this perspective, prison, like the other social institutions, can be seen as a state-care institution, if with a larger sphere of authority and responsibility than the other closed institutions. From the perspective of inmates, prison may hardly have seemed worse than the homes in which they had been housed, except in that it was harder to escape.[34]

## JUVENILE DELINQUENCY

In 1962, 31 percent of the wards of the state lived in institutions in the jurisdiction of Budapest (the population of Budapest was around 20 percent of the population of the whole country). Juvenile delinquency rose in Budapest between 1958 and 1962, while it dropped a little bit nationwide. Changes in lifestyle that were part of the larger process of urbanization also took place for the most part in Budapest, so the authorities tended to see these changes as the explanation for why Budapest was becoming "the collection point for the country's problems with the protection of children and juveniles." The number of people working as part of the council apparatus that dealt with youth policy was, considering this, rather small, but its size also reflected the fact that the system primarily used police measures to address the problems that arose. At the beginning of the 1960s, just over one hundred officials dealt with youth policy in Budapest (including the people on the district committees).[35] Though their title somewhat obscured their actual sphere of activity, the youth policy superintendents for the most part dealt with the process of taking people into the care of the state, whether the people in question were children, the mentally incompetent, or the abandoned elderly. Officially, they were entrusted with the task of "removing children who were exposed to the danger of ethical corruption from their environments" so that "in state institutions, [these children] can become useful citizens of our society."[36]

In the 1960s, social work did not enjoy widespread official acceptance as an important profession, but for ideological reasons, the protection of children and minors did. Thus, people who were not simply looking for employment in a government office but who actually took a genuine interest in social concerns often sought these positions. For instance, in 1959 György Konrád, who later became famous as an author, began employment as a caseworker who paid visits to families beset by strife and as someone who held presentations on youth policy. His 1969 novel—*A látogató*, or *The Case Worker* (available in English translation by Paul Aston)—offers a portrayal of the Kádár era from the perspective of a council employee who regularly goes to the homes of families grappling with conflicts.

The Education Division of the Executive Committee of the Budapest City Council created a network of educational advisories in 1960. It had a similar function to the network of youth policy superintendents and was organized on an essentially ideological basis. In late 1961, the Executive Committee contended with palpable satisfaction that in part due to this network, "hooliganism" and "gangs" no longer constituted the problem they had been in 1960: "They have been eliminated. Judiciously applied preventative work stops them from forming again."[37] Of course, it didn't take long for the authorities to come up with new hooligans and gangs, since the police associated juvenile delinquency with the existence of threats often originating in the overcrowded foster care institutions.

As far as the Budapest City Council was concerned, the most serious problem was that there was no decline in juvenile delinquency in the capital, at least not as a percentage of the national total. In 1953, Budapest accounted for 17 percent of the juveniles who were accused of having committed a crime. By 1963, this number had risen to 34 percent. This shift in percentages may simply have been a consequence of the fact that after 1956 the number of people working in the security apparatuses in Budapest grew, so the number of accused also grew. Nonetheless, in 1965, when a child was taken into the care of the state, more than half of the time the state based its decision on the alleged alcoholism of the parents.[38] Year in and year out, the education division of the Budapest City Council contended that the "the failure to allocate properly the children who are put in foster care homes" was harmful. Wards of the state ended up in the same institutions as children who had been referred by law enforcement, children who had been taken into the care of the state because of social problems found themselves under one roof with "children in the advanced stages of ethical decline," and children suffering from epilepsy were housed together with overage children and children who were only in institutions during the workweek.[39]

Most of the children were moved to different homes at least once every four years, and more than half of the foster care homes had kindergartens and elementary schools. Thus, the children in the homes never met children who were being raised by their parents, and there was little time for any emotional bond to form between them and their caregivers. For a child coming out of this system (for instance Big Kennedy or Lord Blondie), the area around the Great Tree, where lots of "normal" children hung out, was something of a new experience. In three-fourths of the Budapest institutions, the children were separated by gender, and more than half of the people in the elementary school institutions were overage. In the mid-1960s, numerous suggestions were made concerning how to draw up profiles of the various foster care homes to determine which children they might be most suitable for, but only a few of these proposals were actually implemented.[40] Since the police had far more resources than the district councils, in some periods there were children who spent more time domiciled at a police station than in one of the foster care homes.[41]

As there were no playrooms or clubrooms in the institutions, in most of the homes the children's lives played out in the classrooms, the lunchroom, and the sleeping quarters. In the sleeping quarters, the space allotted for each child was less than two square meters of floor, which was similar to the dimensions of a prison cell. In general, there were no closets, tables, or chairs in the bedrooms, so the children had little to do after dinner apart from go to bed (particularly in the winter, when they could not go out into the yard).[42] They were therefore constantly being admonished and disciplined, since they didn't have any space in which to spend their free time. The teachers in the foster care homes had meagre salaries, even in comparison to the salaries of other teachers. It is thus perhaps not surprising that in some of the institutions the teaching staff changed every year.[43]

Accordingly, attempts to escape were common in all institutions.[44] There were institutions that were more closed than the average foster care home from which half of the children escaped. At a January 17, 1968, sitting of the Executive Committee of the Budapest City Council, Budapest police captain György Sós offered the example of a youth who had already escaped seventeen times: "It is tragic that one of the thirteen year-old children has already escaped seventeen times. I asked him if the home was not a good place for him, and why he would flee. He replied, 'Sir, please, I would like to go home.' And it's true, these children live under inhumane conditions, conditions so bad that an adult would not stay, an adult would flee too." Sós suggested the following solution:

> We proposed . . . that it was a sin to take children who had not committed a crime to the police. We take a three-year-old and a ten year-old who have wandered away from home or gotten lost to the police. We keep them there until the parents or the foster home take them back. This is a crime against the children. We again asked the Council to address this question. . . . At the moment, we take children who should not be dealt with by the police to the police. What are we doing? We put them into a little car used to transport prisoners and for the children there is often a certain romance to this, and there have been children who have boasted about how they had already been taken into the police station.[45]

Figure 4.4. Dance room in the correctional institute in Aszód, 1975 (Fortepan / Tamás Urbán).

Conflict emerged between the police and the council on this issue primarily because neither wanted to accept responsibility for finding and apprehending the children who had fled the institutions. The police took children who had fled and been caught to the Youth Protection Division in Rómer Flóris Street in Buda, so the council began to refer to this police station, which was entrusted (or burdened) with this particular task, as a youth protection institution. Thus, at least in practice, the police complemented the network of foster care institutions, which tended to function more as disciplinary and correctional institutions anyway.[46] Gyula Mezei, the head of the education division (which oversaw the institutions), made quite clear in one of his remarks that when it came to rearing children in the institutions, in his assessment methods similar to those used by the police were ideal: "To a certain extent, military discipline should be maintained in these homes."[47]

For the minors who were going back and forth between institutions and police custody, professional qualifications offered a chance to break out of the cycle. However, due to a regulation in the institution system, anyone housed in an institution who passed an exam to become a skilled vocational laborer would be compelled to leave the institution. This regulation discouraged minors from pursuing training, in part simply because they would not have been given lodging in a workers' hostel (which was only available to adults) after leaving the institution and would have had to rent a room or apartment, which not only would have constituted a significant expense but also, "particularly in the case of girls, not infrequently meant being exposed to ethical dangers."[48] In contrast, a young woman who worked as an unskilled laborer was given a place in one of the girls' dormitories. Given these considerations, some of the pupils pursuing training terminated the apprentice contracts they had signed to avoid being compelled to leave their dwelling places.[49] After someone left an institution as an adult, the next station was the workers' hostel. In late 1965, between one-third and one-fourth of the people who were under the oversight of the Budapest administration and were living in a workers' hostel were under the age of twenty-five. One-fourth of them were under the age of eighteen: "People who were in the care of the state and who, having reached the age of majority, have no home because of the absence of a family environment. . . . In Budapest, some of the young people who are coming out of state foster care homes end up in the temporary workers' hostels which were provided precisely to serve this purpose, but a significant number of them live scattered, in rented apartments and company workers' lodgings."[50]

## CONCLUSION

In spite of the fact that between 1963 and 1968 the Executive Committee of the Budapest City Council dealt with the questions concerning the protection of children and minors and reached forty-four resolutions on the topic, hardly any organizational or structural changes were actually made to the institutional foster care system, even though it was precisely this area of the larger welfare system that was characterized as the most important. The perennial problem of overcrowding only got worse with time. In 1967, there were 5,039 spaces for 7,247 wards of the state in Budapest.[51]

Thus, by the end of the 1960s, the police dealt with minors far more than they had at the beginning of the decade not simply for ideological reasons but because law enforcement was serving at least in part to complement the work done by foster care institutions. The increasingly widespread propaganda about gangs offers a clear illustration of this practice. Overcrowding in the foster care institutions grew in parallel with the number of police-identified gangs of children and adolescents. In 1963, according to police records, there were 6 children's gangs and 46 adolescent gangs; by 1967, these figures had grown to 102 and 473, respectively.[52] Overcrowding in foster care led to a rise in the number of escapes, and this made the provision of care and social welfare for minors increasingly an area involving the police. The expanding role of the police in issues pertaining to child welfare is shown by the reallocation of resources from child protective services to the policing of minors: in 1957, 471 officials dealt with the protection of children as their profession, over the course of the next ten years this number dropped by two-thirds.[53] This decline in numbers was the result of the high number of minors who had been condemned for political reasons after the 1956 revolution, which led, in the 1960s, to the supervision of children and minors becoming first and foremost a police issue.[54]

The young people who were apprehended at the Hippie Stroll on Liberty Square on July 8, 1969, were taken to the Youth Protection Division in Rómer Flóris Street, where children who had fled the institutions were often taken. For some of them, the police station in Rómer Flóris Street was not unfamiliar. For the minors who fled the institutions or were not even given space in them, there was little place to go other than the workers' hostels, in which, for the most part, the conditions were more atrocious than in the foster care homes. Some of the workers' hostels were characterized as hotbeds of crime during sittings of the Budapest City Council. Indeed, many of the members of the council thought that the police should be more actively drawn in to improve the situation in the workers' hostels, "for instance because over the course of the year and a half before that year [1971], there were murderers among the people coming out of three workers' hostels." At the sitting of the council during which the report on the circumstances in the worker's hostels was discussed, the most vehement debate concerned whether or not the report should be made public. In the end, the council decided not to make it public, since then "even the world outside of Hungary would receive news concerning the conditions in our workers' hostels."[55] This concern with international opinion has an interesting parallel with the representation of children's homes in the USSR of the 1920s and 1930, mentioned at the beginning of this chapter.

Given the conditions in the institutions and the workers' hostels, it is thus not terribly surprising that young people who had left the foster care homes often slept outside when the weather was good (for instance, in the area around the Great Tree, like Big Kennedy and Lord Blondie, or elsewhere), and were willing to subject themselves to the identity checks done by the police. Since several of the figures in the official narrative of the Great Tree Gang had spent years in foster care institutions, the game of cat and mouse with the police or the foster homes was not new.[56] They didn't have many choices. They could take work in a factory and live in a workers' hostel, where the police often held raids, or they could take odd jobs (for instance lending the members of a band a hand, like Big Kennedy and Lord Blondie did), sleep outside or sometimes at a friend's place, and put up with the identity checks by the police. The shift in the image of members of the young generation (from the flag-bearers of a communist utopia to rowdy hooligans) had little to do with them or their lifestyles. It was, rather, the product of the official assessment of 1956 and the needs of bureaucrats always under pressure to demonstrate the importance of their roles.

But it was not merely the official image of the younger generation that changed after 1956; the very spheres of authority of the police had altered. The police worked in ever closer cooperation with the organs of the state responsible for protecting minors, and this ended up exerting a decisive influence on the creation of narratives concerning juvenile delinquency and juvenile delinquents and, thus, the alleged gangs too. In the next chapter, I examine the ways in which the roles of the police shifted and the fateful consequences these shifts had in Hungary at the time for young people, who had to grapple with the authorities' gradual criminalization of youth itself.

## NOTES

1. Interview with Gyula Sz., nickname "Big Kennedy," March 24, 2009.

2. Cf. Lindenberger, *Volkspolizei*, 367–86. On the support provided for orphans and abandoned children and also on the official stances concerning them, see Green, "There Will Not Be Orphans among Us."

3. Kelly, *Children's World*, 238.

4. Kuhr, "Children of 'Enemies of the People,'" 210–11.

5. Zezina, "System of Social Protection for Orphaned Children in the USSR," 49–51; Kelly, *Children's World*, 243–46.

6. Bernstein, *Raised under Stalin*, 205–6.

7. Balina, "'It's Grand to Be an Orphan!'" 113–14.

8. Fürst, *Stalin's Last Generation*, 38.

9. BFL, f. XXIII-102-a, Budapest Főváros Tanácsa Végrehajtó Bizottsága üléseinek jegyzőkönyvei [Minutes of the meetings of the Budapest City Council's Executive Committee], proposal concerning the profiling of foster care homes, September 15, 1965.

10. The Hungarian text uses the Hungarian word *cigány*, not the politically correct term *Roma*, so it is deliberately translated here as "Gypsy" instead of "Roma" in order to preserve the connotations of the original text.

11. BFL, f. XXIII-102-a, Budapest Főváros Tanácsa Végrehajtó Bizottsága üléseinek jegyzőkönyvei [Minutes of the meetings of the Budapest City Council's Executive Committee], January 17, 1968, 31, 34.

12. Ibid., report of the education division on the situation in Budapest from the perspective of the protection of children and minors, July 11, 1957.

13. Ibid.
14. Ibid.
15. Ibid., July 15, 1957.
16. Although in Hungarian education Makarenko was cited extensively, the Bolshevo commune was more influential in the 1920s and 1930s, as it became "a showcase for propagating the virtues of rehabilitation in the Soviet penal system." See David-Fox, *Showcasing the Great Experiment*, 158–74.
17. Work Force Reserves Office. It was formed in 1950 to ensure training would be provided for the necessary number of skilled workers. This institution oversaw the industrial schools, including the ones that were part of the punitive and correctional institutions for minors.
18. BFL, f. XXIII-102-a, Budapest Főváros Tanácsa Végrehajtó Bizottsága üléseinek jegyzőkönyvei [Minutes of the meetings of the Budapest City Council's Executive Committee], October 4, 1956. On some of the questions concerning rearing minors, see ibid., September 29, 1956.
19. Ibid., August 16, 1957, 3.
20. BFL, f. XXIII-102-a, Budapest Főváros Tanácsa Végrehajtó Bizottsága üléseinek jegyzőkönyvei [Minutes of the meetings of the Budapest City Council's Executive Committee], October 2, 1963, 6.
21. Ibid. Some current problems concerning the protection of children and minors, June 23, 1965, 1.
22. Ibid., July 10, 1963. Report of the education division on the profiling of the foster care homes, 11.
23. In 1946, there had been far more spaces (6,617). By 1957, the number of spaces available in the children's homes that had elementary schools had dropped particularly drastically, by 1,900 (BFL, f. XXIII-102-a, Budapest Főváros Tanácsa Végrehajtó Bizottsága üléseinek jegyzőkönyvei [Minutes of the meetings of the Budapest City Council's Executive Committee], report of the education division on the situation in Budapest from the perspective of the protection of children and minors, July 15, 1957; ibid., report on the situation of state foster care in Budapest, April 12, 1957).
24. In 1947, 80 percent of the wards of the state did not live in children's homes. This proportion dropped to 54 percent by 1954 and 25 percent by 1959 (Hanák *Társadalom és gyermekvédelem*, 27–28, 37–39).
25. BFL, f. XXIII-102-a, Budapest Főváros Tanácsa Végrehajtó Bizottsága üléseinek jegyzőkönyvei [Minutes of the meetings of the Budapest City Council's Executive Committee], report on the situation of state foster care in Budapest, April 12, 1963, 3–4.
26. Hanák, *Társadalom és gyermekvédelem*, 54–55, 85–88.
27. BFL, f. XXIII-102-a, Budapest Főváros Tanácsa Végrehajtó Bizottsága üléseinek jegyzőkönyvei [Minutes of the meetings of the Budapest City

Council's Executive Committee], report on the situation of state foster care in Budapest, April 12, 1963, 3–4.

28. Ibid., 5.

29. Ibid., October 2, 1963, 5. In 1960, children who were deemed "normal" by the state and children who had special educational needs were guaranteed places in separate institutions.

30. Ibid., Report of the education division on the profiling of the foster care homes. July 10, 1963, 2.

31. Ibid.

32. Ibid., 3.

33. Ibid., 11.

34. The social programs that were introduced in prisons resembled programs in some of the foster care homes. On the theoretical background concerning this question, see Chih Lin, *Reform in the Making.*

35. BFL, f. XXIII-102-a, Budapest Főváros Tanácsa Végrehajtó Bizottsága üléseinek jegyzőkönyvei [Minutes of the meetings of the Budapest City Council's Executive Committee], October 2, 1963, 3–4.

36. BFL, f. XXXV-1-a-4, ő.e. 75, Sittings of the Budapest Executive Council of the Hungarian Socialist Workers' Party, April 25, 1960, 27.

37. BFL, f. XXXV-1-a-4, ő.e. 117, Sittings of the Budapest Executive Council of the Hungarian Socialist Workers' Party, December 22, 71.

38. Ibid., 2.

39. Ibid., 7.

40. Ibid., 5–8.

41. Ibid., debate, 27. György Sós made the following statement: "A sense of humanity wants these children not to sit in a police station every day. If the members of the Executive Committee are interested in this question, I ask them please to come to Romanelli Street and observe the situation for themselves. In other organs, 25 times as many people deal with the protection of children in the capital than do among us."

42. BFL, f. XXIII-102-a, Budapest Főváros Tanácsa Végrehajtó Bizottsága üléseinek jegyzőkönyvei [Minutes of the meetings of the Budapest City Council's Executive Committee], report on the childrearing work of the foster care homes, May 22, 1967, 6–7.

43. Ibid. 8.

44. Ibid. 9.

45. Ibid., January 17, 1968, debate, 10a–10c.

46. Ibid., 28.

47. Ibid., 30a.

48. Ibid., report on the childrearing work of the foster care homes, May 22, 1967, 10.

49. Ibid.

50. BFL, f. XXIII-115-c, 2000.196/1966, Social Political group, report on the work of the health division and the Society Political Group for the second half of 1965, February 21, 1966, 4.

51. BFL, f. XXIII-102-a, Budapest Főváros Tanácsa Végrehajtó Bizottsága üléseinek jegyzőkönyvei [Minutes of the meetings of the Budapest City Council's Executive Committee], September 11, 1968, appendix 1.

52. BFL, f. XXIII-102-a, Budapest Főváros Tanácsa Végrehajtó Bizottsága üléseinek jegyzőkönyvei [Minutes of the meetings of the Budapest City Council's Executive Committee], September 11, 1968, appendix 3.

53. Ibid., 2.

54. See the institutions established after 1956 for protecting minors in chapter 3.

55. Ibid., The situation and problems of the workers' hostels in the Seventh, Eighth, and Ninth districts of Budapest, January 20, 1971. 94.

56. For example, in the trial the accused in the first, second, and third degree: Big Kennedy, Lord Blondie, and Prince; and in the later proceedings: "Midget," Gyula L. (Pharaoh), and Doxa.

FIVE

# THE POLICE AND USES OF THE URBAN SPACE

CAPTAIN KOVÁCS, HEAD OF THE criminal division of the district police, protagonist of a 1975 Hungarian crime novel by Kálmán Tolnai entitled *A Mohikángaleri* (The Mohikan-gang), said as he wove through the crowds headed this way and that in the morning jumble of the underpass: "—I'll have a lovely old age, because I began young! . . . Then his glance fell on the little group of youths standing by one of the columns, gaudily dressed kids with grubby, matted hair who were making an earsplitting racket.—I'd love to go over and check their identity papers."[1]

The protagonist, rather than make the suspicious youths produce their papers, boards the tram and continues on his way. The novel, which was widely read in Hungary in the latter half of the decade, was partially about the Great Tree Gang, though it also borrowed from a repertoire of images of other youth gangs. In the novel, the author, who was also the director of the Pálhalmi agricultural prison (meaning a prison in which many young prisoners were effectively forced laborers who did work in agriculture), depicted the police as characters who were as important to the plot as the "corrupted" youths. The youths were suspicious to the protagonist in part simply because they violated the conventions of acceptable dress. Anyone who dared venture into public spaces wearing something that did not conform to the socialist dress code was a threat to the public order in the eyes of the police.[2]

Police captain Százados, a detective who both respected and enforced the rules of socialist society, continues to keep a mindful eye on the crowds that come and go in the underpass, but he does not once stop anyone and ask for identity papers. This is not simply a minor detail of the plot of a work of fiction. Rather, it corresponds to the actual organizational hierarchy and division of labor in the police system at the time. Kovács was not part of the division of public safety, which was in charge of monitoring city spaces first and foremost by checking people's identity papers, so he had to rein in his initial urge to make the kids show theirs. But what fed this urge in the first place? How did the attitude of the police toward urban spaces and the people who gathered in them change in the first few decades of the socialist era? This question is important in part because the ways young people are permitted to use public spaces (and the limits that are placed on their behavior in these spaces) play a significant role in the ways they are socialized and come to relate to the various rules and prohibitions they are expected to obey.

If police reports constituted expressions of the regime's normative view, then crime novels partially captured the popular view. As Jack Katz argues with regards to the crime news in New York in the 1970s, "crime is made 'news' by a modern public searching for resources to work out sensibilities routinely made problematic in everyday modern urban life."[3] It may seem a bit surprising, given that the social world of Hungary in the 1960s and 1970s was distant in many ways from the social world of New York, but this observation harmonizes with the notion that the socialist police functioned not simply as an institution responsible for safeguarding the public and maintaining security but also as a moral authority. While Katz says the "modern public" makes the news, in Hungary the discourses about the police were created mostly by the regime-affiliated media. However, the narrative structure of the police reports (and, in particular, the many narratives of specific criminal cases) offered constructions of the social spaces that resemble the portrayals of these spaces in fictional crime stories. In other words, the narratives can be interpreted as moral fables. Thus, an article in *Magyar Rendőr* in which a wise policeman does not allow drunks to transform a Budapest street into a "prairie bar" presents police oversight of the social space as a moral tale.[4] It is a story that offers a ritualistic explanation of how the social space in question, which appears chaotic, can be made comprehensible to the reader as a coherent and knowable map instead of a shifting mosaic.

The ambition to monitor and control public spaces is one of the illusory goals that has contributed to shaping the everyday work of the institutions of the modern state, the jurisdiction of which has spread to the various spaces (literal and figurative) of discipline. As part of this process, institutions have emerged that never would have managed to acquire any legitimacy with the continual reinforcement of the conviction (or delusion) that society is more chaotic than it appears to many. The mirage of control over social relations contributed in the modern era to the creation of specifically urban institutions, including the police force itself. Of the many approaches that were adopted in an attempt to keep social and urban spaces under watch and under control, the solution used by the socialist police is noteworthy in part because it furthers an understanding of how, under the socialist regime, oversight and punishment became very palpable parts of everyday life.[5]

In the secondary literature on the relationship between urban communities and the police and, more specifically, collective violence as a practice used and regulated by the state, the effects of measures used by the police on the denizens of cities for the most part are characterized as a learning process or part of the spread of disciplinary techniques that are ineluctable concomitants of modernization (or "civilization").[6] The police force figures in these documents as an important actor; however, the documents do not portray the members of this force as individuals but rather simply as parts of a larger structure. Yet the individual policemen who listlessly gazed on the spaces of the big city and who, in principle at least, were responsible for "harmonizing the mechanism of big city life" could just as easily (and just as deservingly) have been subjected to scrutiny or analysis as the members of the groups they were keeping under observation.

The police force was one of the institutions entrusted with the tasks of providing comprehensible overviews of the city in its reports and monitoring and controlling social habits related to the uses of public spaces. The reports, of course, shed considerably more light on the ideas and expectations of the *observers* (in this case the police) concerning the uses of public spaces than they do on the ideas of the observed, but this makes them no less relevant as historical sources.

Accordingly, in this chapter I explore how the police controlled the public spaces of Budapest and how they depicted the use of public spaces by members of the younger generations as well as the reactions, on the one hand, of the police to the activities in which young people engaged and, on the other, of the young people to the measures used by the police. I argue that the criminalization of some youth cultures and the urban fear[7] created by the police regarding the use of public spaces by members of the younger generations gave a special moral authority to the socialist police. Moreover, the political functions of the police made it possible to politicize the appearance of young people in public spaces, which led to a differentiation in city spaces according to social status and portrayals of the habits and conduct of the youth. By creating this politicized environment, the socialist police were not only labeling the "good young people" and the "bad young people" in the city but also drawing distinctions among the young people according to their uses of urban spaces. These

Figure 5.1. Policemen in downtown of Budapest, 1965 (Fortepan / *Magyar Rendőr*).

distinctions created new ways for young people to identify themselves with the public spaces where they gathered, listened to Western music, or, sometimes, fled at the first sign of the police. The places where youth gangs were identified in the police reports (such as pedestrian underpasses, the Youth Park, the Great Tree, and Moscow Square in the center of Buda) later became intensely personal and were invested with generational meanings. This process contributed to the production of new generational identities.

Meanwhile, with the creation of gangs—one of the threads of the narrative concerning alleged hooligans—some of the public spaces also came to be characterized and seen as "more dangerous" in the police reports and in the media, and some individual streets and squares came to function as metaphors for crime and corruption. The police reports show that the police most likely accepted the youth subcultures as reality and constructed the investigations to fit and reinforce this perception. As part of this process, some of the most crowded underpasses and poor and working-class neighborhoods of the city were portrayed as spaces that were ruled by hooligans and gangs of youthful ruffians. Officially, there was no such thing as poverty under socialism, so it was impossible to speak openly about the poor. Instead, it became common practice for socialist police to draw up reports that labeled these youths hooligans or gang members. Accordingly, instead of a public discourse regarding poverty, a new discourse was invented by the authorities regarding hooligans who hailed mostly from the working-class districts.

I also argue in this chapter that the pressure the police felt from their superiors (mostly the Ministry of Interior and the communist party) determined how they would "meet their quotas" of arrests. In other words, local authorities fabricated disputes and exercised excessive force to satisfy the expectations of their superiors in the bureaucracy and party. The numbers of arrests were predetermined by the plans or, in other words, by the ideological needs of the party. The uses of this tactic can be examined from the perspective of the shifting targets of blackmail by the police and secret police.

I also address the proconsumerism policies of the Kádár regime and the functions of tourism in remaking the image of the public spaces of Budapest (especially the inner city). These policies contributed to the stark contrast between the ways the police treated working-class areas, which they saw as gang hangouts, and how they policed parts of the city envisioned as tourist areas. They also influenced the ways the authorities and the young people who hung out by the Great Tree imagined the use of urban space of Budapest in the 1960s. These proconsumerism and protourism policies were also highly relevant to the creation of a "socialist mode of consumerism"—or what has come to be called refrigerator socialism, a reference to the high number of refrigerators sold in the 1960s and 1970s. While the fridge was not a product aimed at young people, it came to be understood as a symbol of the new consumer culture often represented by the younger generation in Hungary. This consumerist politics, I argue, rested to an important degree on the construction of teenagers as a principal target group of the policies of the Kádár era, a process visible in all postwar societies, both in the Eastern Bloc and in the West.[8] A rise in the number of tourists coming to Budapest from the West in the 1960s and the socialist modes of consumerism supported by the state shaped new consumer identities among the members of the younger generations, and this, in turn, influenced the representation of youth cultures and the policies targeting them in urban spaces. Accordingly, the authorities needed to find a foil to this image of the shiny inner city, and the areas imagined by the police as the "bad parts of the city," areas that were allegedly ruled by youth gangs, were ideally suited to this purpose. The police needed this foil not simply to justify the different policing methods used in different parts of the city but also to increase their control over public spaces.

## THE MONITORING OF URBAN SPACES

The police kept public spaces under close watch largely as part of the regime's broader efforts to attain ideological goals, which is why the police force was not clearly separate from the political secret police according to its organizational structure, its methods, or its actual function.[9] From time to time, the police were entrusted with tasks that were connected to enforcing limits on the expression of political views. This is clearly exemplified by a statement made by János Kádár in the summer of 1969 (roughly at the time as the Hippie Stroll) regarding the work of the Ministry of Interior:

> During periods of the most varied kinds of crisis, the Ministry of Interior was firm and accepted the politics of the party . . . at the time of such a crisis, if a drunk man in a tavern says down with us and our kind and long live the enemy, at other times they perhaps dump a bucket of water on him, take him home, and done. But on the day of such a crisis, he must be arrested, and perhaps he will sober up, but he will sober up at the police station. And in general, our Ministry of Interior understands this and does this. And this is no small amount of work or stress for the employees of the ministry.[10]

The process of keeping Budapest society under close observation during the socialist era was shaped in no small part by the image the police had of the denizens of the city and the ways the fragmented social spaces were depicted (within specific kinds of simplistic frameworks) in the police reports, the documents produced by the city councils (which were based on the police reports), and the local press, which was particularly fond of reporting news issued by the police. The images of the urban spaces were also influenced by what the police wrote (in clear accordance with what they were expected to write) on the given (literal) spaces in which they moved and how they envisioned the task of keeping these spaces under observation.

Notwithstanding prevalent stereotypes, which were based, for instance, on detective novels, and individuals' daily view of officers on the streets, nightsticks in hand, most members of the police force worked not on the streets but rather in the police stations. In the 1950s, the roles that were assigned to the police in the individual districts were influenced both by American westerns and the Soviet council system. Essentially—though this was never expressly admitted—in their given districts, police commissioners had to play the same role as sheriffs in films. In other words, at times they were the righteous enforcers of justice who stood above the law. Notions of the functions of the district commissioner were influenced by westerns, but in practice their jobs were shaped by the rituals of the planned economy. Thus, they spent more than 80 percent of their workday inside performing tasks of an administrative nature for the most part.[11] As the district commissioners regarded strengthening ties between the police (which in 1945 and 1956 had conducted raids in cooperation with Soviet soldiers) and the civilian population as their primary task, from time to time they sent patrols to the parts of the city that were considered infected. These campaigns led to an increase in the number of specific measures taken by the police of as much as 40 percent, but the district commissioners, who noted the importance of their administrative responsibilities, still did not often want to leave their stations.[12]

In wintertime, of course, it was always more difficult to send police units out into the city, but the weather was hardly the only factor that influenced the ways the police force kept public spaces under observation. On the basis of internal reports and checks, the police force in Hungary in the 1950s, which in narratives of political history tends to be characterized as ironfisted, seems more like a group of unruly youths than it does the firm pillar on which a dictatorship rested. The internal disciplinary routines and processes exerted a far stronger influence on the everyday work lives of the members of the police force than their ideological tasks did. The internal affairs tasks included efforts to monitor the private lives of members of the force and prevent or at least curb alcoholism. One of the reasons for this focus on alcoholism was that among the members of the police force in the Eighth District, it had become common practice for "some of the comrades to consume wine before going on duty and the supervisor would find them on patrol drunk." The effort to keep the private lives of the members of the force under close watch and control found manifestation in the practice of permitting them to marry (or rather not permitting them to marry).[13] As Edward Cohn argues, the postwar communist regime became more interested in how communists behaved in their private lives; in other words, the regime became "more intrusive."[14] Thus, the private lives of police officers became more and more controlled.[15]

The socialist police hoped to maintain control over public spaces by using three distinct methods: conducting raids, having the personnel in charge of keeping the spaces of the city under observation move more freely and rapidly within the city (for instance, by providing motorized vehicles for the patrols in charge of maintaining public safety and by establishing police patrols that could be summoned by telephone), and using volunteer police at events that drew large crowds. With regards to the final method, it is worth noting that in the 1960s the observation was made that the number of volunteer police who were available for service always jumped during soccer matches and always dropped during state celebrations and ceremonies because the volunteers received free entry to the matches.[16] The Budapest police divided the mass events into three different categories on the basis of the "political influence of public safety." International political events, the celebrations on April 4, soccer matches between the Hungarian and Soviet teams and other popular teams (such as Vasas and Dózsa), and performances by some foreign bands and orchestras belonged to the first category. The other prominent soccer matches were in the second category along with larger festive events. The third category consisted of the events that were assigned to the district police headquarters.[17] The concerts that were held in the Youth Park were in the third category and thus only qualified for a third-ranking level of security.

As a complaint that was made in 1956 makes clear, though volunteer police were only used when events that drew large crowds were being held, the authorities were still by no means satisfied with them: "At a dance that was held in Rákócziújfalu in Szolnok County, a volunteer policeman by the name of Szöke stabbed two people. In Vas County, two volunteer policemen working for the Mester district commissioner disappeared and probably fled to the West. In Győr, a volunteer policeman by the name of Simonka collected the fuel vouchers from the workers in the factory and sold them for twice the price. He also bragged about how he was an informer for the police."[18] According to a 1962 memorandum, the voluntary police "offer social assistance as a way of performing the role of the police as a force for education."[19] This may explain why, in 1959, in the Twentieth District, "two voluntary policemen detained people unlawfully because, in the vestibule of the movie theater—the film that was playing was restricted to people over the age of eighteen—they were obliging people to produce their identity papers and then taking people under the age of eighteen to the police headquarters."[20] Accordingly, the volunteer police force could have only very limited functions, and it served mostly as a demonstration of potential force at public gatherings.

## POLICE RAIDS AND PUBLIC SPACES

The police were expected to increase the number of raids continually. The question of whom they would look for and why in any given raid, however, was determined by shifts in the goals of the political campaigns and images of the enemy. Frequently, the plans specified the number of people that the individual police divisions were supposed to detain. In 1947, the vice squad of the Budapest police headquarters was charged, as part of one such plan, with the task of detaining one thousand "secret prostitutes" on average every month. The vice squad held more than fifty raids to fulfill the plan, and referring to this, the head of the branch insisted in an ever more strident tone that he be provided with a personal car and his division with a prison van.[21]

In 1950, the goals of the raids that were being conducted across the country were defined as follows: "monitoring motor vehicles, finding secret prostitutes, and monitoring other vehicles being used to traffic black-market goods."[22] In 1951, Árpád Házi, who served as minister of interior, issued an order to round up beggars, which in Budapest meant an increase in the number of extraordinary patrols.[23]

It was only possible to increase the number of people detained without actually increasing the size of the police force by focusing on members of the citizenry who were less able to put up resistance. According to a 1959 police summary, in 1956 only 1,055 people had been detained for prostitution in Budapest (in contrast with as many as 4,000 or 7,000 in previous years) because members of parliament had insisted that "we have put an end to prostitution." It was therefore not considered proper or helpful to detain prostitutes. In 1957, when the regime acknowledged that in fact it had not put an end to prostitution, the number of people detained for prostitution grew to 5,300, although even into the mid-1960s the numbers still did not reach the records set during the golden age of the early 1950s.[24]

Beginning in the late 1950s, because of the lack of unskilled industrial labor, the party and the organizations responsible for the economy made more concerted efforts to draw the Roma population into industry.[25] This included a June 20, 1961, resolution by the Political Committee of the Hungarian Socialist Workers' Party on "improving the circumstances of the Gypsy population," which led both to more vibrant research on the Roma communities in Hungary in the 1960s and a more vibrant security discourse on "Gypsy [Roma] crime." The idea of increasing the number of raids held in neighborhoods and settlements with Roma majorities came up as an additional option in the practice of keeping social spaces under police observation. Increasing emphasis was placed, furthermore, on "ensuring agents to deal with Gypsy crimes." In the wake of the passage of the aforementioned resolution, the term *Gypsy crime* (*cigánybűnözés*) began to appear ever more frequently in the police documents, and the police launched campaigns to put an end to "Gypsy crime," which meant an increase in the number of raids in the neighborhoods and settlements where Roma lived.[26]

Although it seems statistically plausible that some portion of the young people who were characterized as hooligans were Roma, it would be very difficult to estimate the percentage of Roma youth caught up in police actions against hooligans. However, the clear connection between hooliganism and wayward youth as current or former residents of state care institutions would suggest that many of the young people dubbed hooligans by the state were Roma.[27] Even if it is impossible to figure out exact numbers about the proportion of Roma among the so-called hooligans or youth gangs, there are still many other indications that the police raids against hooliganism can also be contextualized in the racialization of crime and poverty in Hungary. So-called "Gypsy crime" as a construction of the police was registered by the police as a "racial type of crime" throughout the Kádár era. As the head of the Department for Criminal Investigation of the Inner Ministry, Ferenc Györök, put it in an article in 1963, "it is an essential task to give priority to the study of 'Gypsy crime.'"[28] The term *Gypsy crime* as a clear indication of the racialization of crime was used by all authorities publicly, and beginning in 1974, even official statistics were created regarding Gypsy crime.[29] According to the statistics created by the police, the rate of criminality among the Roma youth was more than double that among non-Roma young people.[30] According to the police statistics regarding so-called Gypsy crime, Roma youth committed crime mostly in groups.[31] Nonetheless, the term was used very rarely in the press until the end of the 1970s,[32] and the Roma as hooligans or members of youth gangs (galerik) were almost invisible in the police and news reports. The traces of racialized crime and poverty can be found only in the nicknames of the members of the youth gangs, for instance a boy with the nickname "Gypsy" (Cigány) was mentioned many times as a member of a youth gang, especially in the reports regarding the youth gangs on the outskirts of Budapest.[33]

In addition to focusing their efforts on beggars, prostitutes, and Roma, the police also turned their attention to a large extent to children and adolescents who escaped institutions. In 1952, the children and youth protection police divisions (which in the meantime had been strengthened) were entrusted with the task of apprehending children and adolescents who had escaped from the institutions in which they had been placed. This made it significantly easier for the police to increase the number of people it detained.[34] According to police reports that listed the successes, in 1969 more than 43 percent of the individuals detained in the course of raids were either children or adolescents.[35] After 1956, the police were expected to detain more adolescents, because adolescents came to be seen as a more dangerous threat after the uprising. The police fulfilled this expectation.

From the perspective of the police, the function of the efforts to keep public spaces under observation was primarily to provide the heads of the various divisions with clear evidence they could use to demonstrate the indispensableness of the police force itself in the socialist state. For the most part, police reports, which emphasized the importance of keeping social spaces under open observation, made references to conflicts between social groups that in fact were resolved fairly easily and smoothly in part because public spaces in practice were already divided to a large extent based on social background and belonging. In other words, any given space tended to be frequented by people from similar social groups or with similar social backgrounds. The police constantly had to explain why they were so zealously keeping close watch over both public and private spaces, but the reports had one narrative feature in common: in the descriptions they provided, the public spaces were always thronging with people who happened to embody the proclaimed enemy of the given historical moment.

## FROM SLUMS TO URBAN SPACES CONTROLLED BY HOOLIGANS

For the most part, the police force used increases to its budget to strengthen its role and presence in the monitoring of public spaces, since this was the most visible sphere of its work. In 1968, for instance, after the Warsaw Pact invasion of Czechoslovakia, at the orders of the party, the police increased the number of raids held. This was accompanied by an intense press campaign. In the later summary reports, this was portrayed as a response to the alleged growth in the number of crimes committed by rowdy hooligan types, which, the authors of the reports explained, necessitated an increase in the budget for the police force. The budget for the police was increased in 1969 and 1970, and increases were made in particular for the members of the force who kept public spaces under observation. This explains why the police force, after having drawn emphasis to an alleged growth in the number of hooligan-style crimes, was given two new helicopters and ten motorboats as well as having its number of patrol cars doubled; the people on patrol were also given a "danger" supplement (a regular bonus to their incomes) and new clothes.[36]

After 1956, the police reports about hooligans made it possible for the regime to rewrite the image of the urban spaces by using the police bulletins about gangs of young people and articles in the press. In these narratives, hooligans—also referred to metaphorically as "the ragged"—play the part once played by the inhabitants of the slums. In other words, they burst onto the otherwise idyllic spaces of the socialist city and endangered families who were living in harmony with socialist ethics. The discourse concerning hooligans also made it possible for the authorities to reinforce a distinction between symbolically prestigious and notable sites and areas on the (similarly, though negatively) symbolic perimeter of the city. When crafting the discourse on hooliganism, the authorities made particularly effective use of the prevalent stereotypes concerning the residents of the industrial suburbs, which had been made part of Budapest administratively in 1950.

Industrial areas and districts in which most of the inhabitants were workers had been considered infected parts of the city in earlier eras too, but after the war and the rise of the communist dictatorship, it was no longer possible, given the ideology of the regime, to hold numerous raids in an area only because the area in question was populated for the most part by workers. The crafting of the narrative concerning gangs helped the police continue keeping the public and semipublic spaces of working-class districts under regular observation and holding raids in them. In other words, the regime (and more specifically, the police force) was not able to refer to poverty or social divisions as explanations for the robust presence of police in public spaces, but it could refer to hooligans and gangs. Poverty and the criminalization of youth (and youths) made it possible, after 1956, for the police to continue to keep under observation public spaces that earlier had been dubbed slums because now these spaces, allegedly, were frequented by hooligans. By the end of the 1960s, workers from small towns and villages had come to constitute a majority of the people who were moving to the capital. In 1962, the government attempted to limit, unsuccessfully, migration into the city. From the perspective of its social background, habits, and lifestyles, the population of the city had palpably changed.[37]

A description of the so-called Tripolisz gang in Angyalföld (Tripolisz is a neighborhood in the Thirteenth District that was traditionally working-class) offers an example of the way the police kept watch on an area of the city that at an earlier time had been regarded as a dangerous slum and had become an alleged meeting ground for hooligans. In this description, the prosecutor of the Thirteenth District contends that, although he had little data with which to corroborate his claim, "the group is a friendly, chummy meeting of people who live in a single street, a single area." According to the prosecutor, as was

Figure 5.2. A slum in Budapest ("Mária Valéria") in front of a new housing estate, 1961 (Fortepan / Budapest City Archives / Photographs of the Department of Urban Planning and Architecture).

typical of these kinds of gangs, most of its members were unemployed or regularly changed places of employment, and they were children of adults who had had many offspring. They also had working-class backgrounds, and they "lived under remarkably bad conditions."[38]

The police finally found something on which they could justify raids in poorer neighborhoods. The stereotypes concerning slums resurfaced in new form in the police campaigns against the (alleged) gangs. According to a stereotype that became increasingly prevalent after 1956 (and enjoyed the full support of the police), some of the public and semipublic spaces of the peripheral areas of the city and the working-class neighborhoods were controlled by gangs. The stereotype regarding the gangs and the working-class neighborhoods served as a work plan for the police officers in these neighborhoods. As noted in a 1961 police report, the police group responsible for breaking up gangs sought to identify the so-called Black Half-Moon gang, which was (allegedly) active in the Sixteenth District, in spite of the fact that, according to the district prosecutor (who was also part of the police department), no such gang existed. The police eagerly sought to find a gang active in the so-called state (*állami*) housing project, but as the report on their raid reveals, the implementation of their plan was hard because they could not find any gangs: "In the course of the elimination of it [the gang], it became clear that there was no organized gang in the state housing project, only smaller groups which were committing more trifling criminal offenses or breaches of the peace. For instance, in January 1961, József V. and his associates turned off the lights in the house of culture in Cinkota [once an independent settlement, today a neighborhood in the Sixteenth District] and groped the female caretaker."[39] The police group according to their work plan (which was writing reports regarding gangs), could not return to the central headquarters without having found a gang, since it had been charged with the task of writing reports on the liquidation of gangs. So "after the brigade in charge of liquidation had established that there were no organized, active gangs in the state housing project, it determined that there was a gang of 20 people active in Cinkota, so it began to break up this gang." This contention, however, was not entirely convincing, since no one had ever heard of any gang in Cinkota. Thus, when a new inquiry was done, it became clear, according to the report, that "one cannot speak of any organized, active gang here either." The group responsible for liquidating gangs in the end determined that "at various points in the district, individuals or groups consisting of one or two people are committing criminal offenses," so to be sure that it would be able to submit a report, the police group began to investigate the (alleged) acts of these groups (consisting of "one or two" people).[40] The summary report of the district police department essentially said that in the Sixteenth District, one gang had been liquidated.[41]

The stereotypes concerning hooligans and gangs were useful because they enabled the police to "discover" gangs in areas that earlier had been designated as slums. In a 1960 sociographical book entitled *Barakkváros* (Barrack city), Rudolf Szamos tried to identify the parts of the city that, according to him, had been infamous as slums before the war.[42] Although the book presumably did not influence the police raids, the descriptions he offers of the city shed light on what was considered a former slum in 1960. The year after the book was published, the police conducted investigations in search of gangs in each of the neighborhoods listed by Szamos.[43] Indeed, the brigades entrusted with this task found (that is, invented) gangs in almost all of the neighborhoods that had once been slums. In their search, the police went first to densely populated areas that were considered dangerous, since they had to come up with suitable findings in these neighborhoods to meet the expectations of their superiors. Essentially, they had to find or fabricate gangs. A comparison of the district- and city-level reports reveals that police leadership at the city level believed there was a great deal of organized gang activity, and its insistence that there was significant gang activity forced district-level officers to manufacture cases involving gangs and gang activity to meet the expectations of their superiors.

In 1961, the Budapest public prosecutor reproached investigators who sometimes wrote about criminal acts as if they had been committed by individuals acting alone instead of organized groups of young people—that is, gangs. The prosecutor asked the first deputy police commissioner to be sure that the reports and the documents pertaining to the investigations presented the criminal acts they described as acts committed by groups.[44] In other words, if an adolescent committed a criminal act in a part of the city where the police wanted to find or claimed to have found a gang, then the crime was ascribed to a gang allegedly active in the area. As part of this effort to magnify the presence of gangs in the city and the threat they allegedly posed, prosecutors combined cases that originally had been submitted separately in order to ensure an adequate number of proceedings concerning criminal acts allegedly committed by groups of young people.[45]

The working class was divided, in ways that drew on and reinforced prevalent stereotypes predating the rise of the socialist regimes in Eastern Europe, into two opposing poles. The worker either embodied the "ideal citizen" who was striving to claim his rights in an unjustly hierarchical society or he belonged to the *lumpenproletariat*, which, according to the propaganda, was devoid of class consciousness and easy prey to reactionary forces and ideologies. This division is discernible both in the ways the police campaigns against alleged hooligans and gangs were launched in specific neighborhoods of the city and in the narratives in the police reports, which rather consistently included the assertion that "most of the [gang members] are composed of lumpen elements, though alongside them one finds a few children of honest workers too."[46] This division clearly established an opposition between the ideal of the worker who led an honest life and was evolving into the socialist citizen and the public spaces in which this worker moved on the one hand and the "amoral" residents of the slums and their (mis)uses of public space on the other. The reports on the formation of gangs often used stereotypes concerning the so-called lumpenproletariat: "Some lumpenproletariat parents use most of their wages to purchase alcoholic beverages, so family life comes unraveled, scandalous fights become part of everyday life, and they raise their children to be heedless and coarse. The children then continue leading this lifestyle."[47]

In the documents of the Budapest police headquarters, one sees a clear and consistent difference in the ways the neighborhoods on the perimeter of the city were treated by the police and the ways much of the inner city was dealt with. On an almost daily basis for their reports, the police drew on stereotypes concerning the deviant lifestyles of people living in so-called infected neighborhoods to justify their actions. Depictions of specific public spaces in the media exerted a strong influence on the ways in which the police raids were planned and the actual results of the raids. The explanations given by the police for the formation of gangs in areas on the perimeter of the city differed from the explanations they gave for the formation of gangs in the inner city. The gangs in peripheral neighborhoods allegedly were formed in no small part as a response by adolescents to the violent treatment they endured at the hands of their parents, who led lumpenproletariat lifestyles (slum lifestyles). In contrast, the police regarded the members of the gangs that gathered at clubs and hangouts in the inner city (for instance a coffee shop) as the unprincipled children of wealthy parents in high positions who led extravagant, even dissolute lives (hence their children's heedlessness).[48] The names used to designate these gangs in the police documents reflect this. For instance, one finds references to a "Gresham gang," which is the name of an expensive restaurant and coffee shop in Buda by the Chain Bridge (the gang later came to be referred to as the inner-city gang.).

Otherwise, the members of these gangs were regarded as the offspring of "class enemies." This ideological mapping of the spaces of the city strengthened the stereotype according to which Budapest could be divided into peripheral areas—namely, working-class neighborhoods and slums, which were inhabited by people laying siege to the emerging socialist metropolis, and the areas under siege, or the spaces inhabited, in general, by respectable citizens. The shimmering shop windows in Váci Street, which in the beginning of the 1960s began to be transformed into a shopping area, and the Anna Coffee Shop (an elegant coffee shop and restaurant on Váci Street) were kept under close observation by the police,[49] much as were the poorer neighborhoods (or slums), the busy urban spaces, and, later, the underpasses, which were regarded as fertile ground for sin and corruption, although this latter group of sites was watched for different reasons and on the basis of different stereotypes.

Beginning in the early 1960s, the images of the transportation nodes of the city were influenced by the contentions of the authorities, who claimed from time to time to have found groups resembling gangs hanging out either around the intersections or in the underpasses. One of the groups was the so-called Alvarez gang, the name given to a gang that frequented the area around

Moscow Square, one of the busiest transportation nodes in Buda, in the early 1960s.[50] As a kind of logical consequence of hierarchical depictions of the gangs, the various spaces of the city were also arranged into a hierarchy in the narratives. In the 1960s, the police, prosecutors, and journalists "discovered" more and more gangs, and they began to write so frequently about these gangs that eventually they, too, came to believe in them. The goal, for the police, was to be sure to find a gang in every poor neighborhood and in almost every park and crowded public space.

According to Phil Cohen's model of subcultures, the social meaning of youth subcultures both replaces and at the same time refashions the image of the industrial worker, which, furthermore, is combined with reflections on new consumer-culture habits.[51] In other words, the socialist regime nominally working for the proletariat should not be targeting the proletariat or the workers. Instead, notions such as hooliganism made it possible for the regime to target working-class people without invoking the proletariat.[52]

Expanding this interpretation to the question of uses of public spaces and mental mappings of emerging urban communities, the problem can be expressed differently. In the second half of the twentieth century, official descriptions of the conflicts and rituals between police and workers in the late nineteenth and early twentieth centuries, which arose because of customs and habits concerning the use of urban space, persisted, if in an altered form, in the narratives concerning conflicts between so-called hooligans and the police. The notion, in the official discourse, of a "strike zone" or the working-class district surrounded by barricades[53] was replaced by the city space "under the rule of hooligans," from which dangerous young people would launch attacks against respectable citizens. The stereotypes concerning the working-class street culture were replaced by the discourse on the ways hooligans used public spaces.

The discourse on slums and/or working-class neighborhoods, which shaped the image of the city in the minds of its denizens,[54] also subsisted in the press reports concerning hooligans and the plans in which the police outlined the measures they would take to address the threats presented by hooligans, whether real, perceived, or deliberately crafted. In Hungary, this shift in the discourse away from the notion of the dangers presented by people from working-class districts toward the idea of the dangers posed by hooligans was influenced in part by the fact that, under socialism, the ideologically valorized working-class could hardly be made the focus of police investigations. Hooligans, however—the image of whom was in no small part drawn on the images and rhetoric concerning the lumpenproletariat—served this function quite well.

Figure 5.3. House party, Budapest, 1967 (Fortepan / István Péterffy).

One of the functions of the discourse on hooliganism, from this perspective, was to legitimize the presence of the police in public and semipublic spaces and the measures they took to identify passersby. As a consequence of this, the social meaning of public spaces also changed, as did the ways semipublic spaces, for instance taverns and coffee shops, were used. One example of this was the gradual spread, beginning in the 1960s, of the habit of holding parties in private residences. In the police reports, these "house parties" figured as a consequence of the battle between the police and the hooligans, since the hooligans were allegedly fleeing public and semipublic spaces, which the police were keeping under close observation, and taking refuge in private spaces, which, because of these parties, were themselves becoming semipublic spaces.[55]

According to a police report describing the creation of the so-called Gresham gang, "[in the case of] young people who, because of the circumstances of their families, spend too much time in the streets, on the squares, and in clubs and hangouts and whose families themselves were ethically unsteady, the Communist Youth League was unable to exert any influence, and they remained followers of the group."[56] According to this reasoning, the city spaces themselves carved deviant figures out of these young people, because the official ideology was unable to exert any influence on them. Thus, the fight against hooliganism (i.e., youth subcultures) included not only the fight against the remnants of the lumpenproletariat but also an ideological fight against the capitalist West. Meanwhile, local administrative bodies and youth policies adopted by the government were subordinated to the emerging tourist industry and new patterns of socialist mass consumerism. Accordingly, police measures to control the youth were adapted also to the requirements of tourism and consumption.

## A SHOPPING CITY AND SOCIALIST CONSUMERISM

Although the alleged fight against capitalist values was a constant trope in the public discourses, in December 1969, while the investigation against the members of the Great Tree Gang was underway, the Communist Youth League published an issue of the international edition of *Magyar Ifjúság* (published in English for an international readership) depicting Hungary as a country of youth clubs: "There are 2,200 active youth clubs in Hungary. Half of the clubs took part in a competition conducted by the Hungarian Communist Youth League for the title of 'Excellent Youth Club.' About ten percent of the clubs for young people are held in romantic settings: in factories, Houses of Culture, and schools and universities. There is a growing trend of running a club in a cellar."[57] The clubs were presented as part of a narrative of movements without any political control, which was a prevalent motif of the official discourse of the entire socialist period and the 1960s in particular. This narrative formed part of the image of a so-called humane socialism, which was the form of socialism advocated by the regime in Hungary and the regimes in other Eastern Bloc countries after Stalin's death. The creation of relatively free spaces for youth cultures was accompanied by an increase in tourism from the West, which served economic goals and also gave the regime a greater degree of legitimacy internationally. Tourism and the clubbing scene frequented by young people represented the so-called human face of this new type of socialism, so both were emerging hand in hand in the 1960s. However, even while the international public was being told of the vibrant Hungarian clubbing scene, youth magazines and police journals for Hungarian readers were filled with reports on youth violence and, in particular, on the threats allegedly posed by youth gangs and hippies alongside the reports about the prosperous socialist state.

During this time, Hungarian films depicted Budapest as a colorful array of shop windows. In these films, Budapest represented a new kind of consumer socialism not only because of the influx of Western tourists in the 1960s but also because the state authorities took pains to make a conspicuous show of the regime's proconsumer attitude to legitimize their hold on power. The new

Figure 5.4. The Bercsényi youth club, Budapest, 1964 (Fortepan / Zoltán Szalay).

symbols of this decade—the sites of consumer lifestyle (e.g., the coffee bars [or *presszók*] and the new department stores) and the new housing estates—became the preferred locations for film shoots. Whereas in the films produced in the 1950s the images of the city had been rather homogeneous, feature films made in the 1960s represented Budapest as a spectacular, colorful, and varied shop window display.[58] All of the modern buildings, housing estates, and public institutions built at the time were featured in these films. New magazines and feature films sometimes portrayed the city as a European metropolis similar to Paris or Rome.[59]

The media also offered more varied representations of the city and sometimes even acknowledged social segregation. Illustrated magazines, such as the popular *Nők Lapja* (Women's magazine) and *Magyar Ifjúság*, often published reports about different city districts in Budapest, the problems faced by the people who lived in them, and the different modes of behavior of people living in the inner city or on the outskirts of the metropolis.[60] These representations contributed to the emerging definition of urban life and a reinterpretation of urban spaces. The image of Budapest changed in part because of an influx of migrant workers from small villages or agricultural towns. Few of these migrant workers were able to get an apartment in Budapest, however, due to residency restrictions that were put into place in the capital in 1962.[61]

Alongside the new housing estates, new hotels and modern department stores were the most important investments in urban development in Budapest in the 1960s. However, the construction of new hotels on the banks of the Danube was prioritized over the construction of residential apartment blocks because these hotels symbolized both the new age of consumerism under socialism and a greater openness to the West.[62] A photo reportage published in 1959 in the new popular newspaper *Esti Hírlap* characterized Budapest as "the city of nice department stores and shops."[63] Consumerism, tourism, and openness to the West were key concepts in the process of winning legitimacy for the Kádár regime and promoting de-Stalinization in Hungary after 1956.[64] For the young people who became the main characters in the story of the Great Tree Gang, in the late 1960s, the black market, Western tourists, and the new shops in Váci Street and on Rákóczi Avenue were already perfectly normal and familiar parts of life in the city.

The cleansing of the inner city and the campaign against the ruralization (the inundation of cities by migrants from rural areas) of Budapest were closely interrelated. Negative discourse about migrants from the countryside, in which they were depicted as a problem, spread widely. At the same time, slum sensationalism became a popular genre in the tabloid press (for example, in *Esti*

*Hírlap*), as public policy making transformed and appeared to lead to a rise in living standards in stark contrast to the beginnings of rapid industrialization in Hungary in the early 1950s. In the 1960s, a new type of popular reform journalism took an interest in the subject of the Budapest slums. The people who lived in the slums on the outskirts of the city came to represent Budapest's new urban villagers. As the problem of ruralization was closely connected to the question of legitimate and illegitimate forms of consumption, it became highly relevant in the context of the Kádár regime's efforts to build its refrigerator socialism, which offered the promise of a consumer lifestyle under a socialist system. In the era following the lifting of the Iron Curtain, the ideological battle between East and West relied heavily on the promotion of different lifestyles and different "consumer ethea," one example of which is Khrushchev and Richard Nixon's famous "kitchen debate" in 1959. The official discourses on consumerism made use of the idea of modernization to such a degree that modernization became synonymous with consumerist politics in both capitalist countries and the countries of the Eastern Bloc.[65]

The Iron Curtain became more permeable in both directions and not simply from the perspective of culture but also, in practice, with the consumption of popular culture.[66] The promotion of tourism from the West in Hungary in the 1960s served several important goals. It strengthened Hungary's image in the West and thereby established some legitimacy for the regime, which had implemented oppressive and even brutal reprisals after 1956. Furthermore, tourism also meant a significant influx of foreign currency. In addition, in the urban spaces created for tourists, patterns of consumption that resembled consumer lifestyles in the West were prevalent.

According to the Hungarian Central Statistical Office, whereas in 1957, 76,000 people had traveled to Hungary from abroad (before 1957, the number of tourists who had come to Hungary had been much lower), in 1968 this figure had jumped to almost 2.5 million.[67] Thus, in the area of the inner city where young people had taken their infamous stroll in the summer of 1969, it would have been quite possible on any given day to have passed more foreign tourists in the streets than locals since several of the main tourist attractions are found in this area (Gellért Hill, Erzsébet Bridge, Váci Street, St. Stephen's Basilica, and Liberty Square). This also may have been one of the reasons why the people who first reported the young people to the police mistook them for German tourists.[68]

As of 1960, with a restructuring of the work of the Budapest Tourist Industry Office and state investment in the construction of hotels, the Hungarian capital officially became a tourist attraction. In the wake of these decisions, the

Citadella at the top of Gellért Hill (which had undergone important renovations) was opened in 1961, and these renovations also included the opening of the Youth Park by the Castle Hill.[69] Without the Youth Park or the emerging tourism and consumer lifestyle in Hungary, the story of the Great Tree Gang could not have been constructed. By promoting tourism, the Kádár regime sought to strengthen its legitimacy internationally, even while it continued to hold more than twenty thousand people in prison for alleged political crimes as part of the reprisals that had been taken after 1956.[70] Thus, while on the one hand the state provided support for tourism as a service-based form of consumerism, on the other it continued to use oppressive measures against its own people to consolidate its hold on power. During a sitting of the Council of Ministers on December 10, 1956, a proposal was made concerning the necessity of increasing the number of available hotel rooms, even while strikes were being held in several factories as protests against the politics and policies of the Kádár government. Though the city was hardly prepared, from the perspective of its infrastructure, to welcome an influx of tourists, IBUSZ (Idegenforgalmi Beszerzési Utazási és Szállítási Rt. [Tourism Procurement Travel and Transport Ltd.]), the state-run tourist office, was expected to take measures to ensure that 60 to 70 percent of the tourists coming to Hungary "come from the capitalist countries in the interests of reaching the planned foreign currency income."[71]

Because of the compulsion to meet the goals established in these kinds of plans, beginning in 1959, the Budapest Tourist Industry Office worked hand in hand with the Budapest City Council in the adoption and implementation of numerous methods based on Western models to spur tourism and consumerism in the tourist industry. Novel depictions of the spaces of the city were intended to transform Budapest into a kind of consumer good, and not only for foreign tourists.

In 1960, 75 percent of the money that came into Hungary through the tourist industry went to Budapest. Given the popularity of the city among tourists, the government thought it important to increase revenues from tourism by making additions to the infrastructure within the city that would make it possible to welcome larger numbers of visitors from abroad. Over the course of the decade, the transformation of the city was shaped to a large extent by the goals and needs of the tourist industry. The construction of hotels along the banks of the Danube River,[72] the reconstruction of the so-called Danube Promenade (a pedestrian area between the Széchenyi Chain Bridge and the Erzsébet Bridge on the Pest side of the river that had been badly damaged during the siege of the city at the end of World War II), new emphasis on the many thermal baths in the city, the transformation of Gellért Hill and the surrounding area into a tourist

Figure 5.5. Tourist bus in Buda Castle, 1958 (Fortepan / Sándor Bauer).

attraction (including the reconstruction of the Youth Park), and the creation of the Hungarian Village near Szentendre (an open-air museum of ethnography) continue even today to shape how the city is experienced by tourists, and these proposals were all raised in the early 1960s and were implemented by the end of the decade.[73]

In order to maintain the image of the happy, shop window city, authorities believed it necessary to keep any event or trend that was deemed unsuitable or inappropriate under observation and at a distance. The Hippie Stroll was one such event. One could also mention the expulsion of beggars from the inner city (which was a common agenda item) because of the potential negative effects they might have on the tourist industry.[74]

In 1967, Budapest chief police commissioner György Sós (mentioned in earlier chapters) even got letters from the directors of the Tourist Industry Office and the Inner City Parish in which they complained about beggars loitering in ever greater numbers in the area around the hotels. At a sitting of the Executive Committee of the Budapest City Council, Sós himself made the following complaint: "Each and every one of these letters calls on us to take radical action concerning the beggar question. I would like to inform the Executive Committee that no authorities of any kind can take steps against beggars. In Hungary, begging is legal as long as the person begging is not leading a heedless lifestyle or engaging in any kind of rowdy behavior.... The new code of criminal offenses will make it possible for us to take measures against pretend beggars." According to Mrs. Ferenc Csehik, another member of the Executive Committee, "this is a major problem in the inner city. . . . But it doesn't make a pretty picture if ragged, filthy people cover the inner city." Sós regarded measures to ensure public safety as the most effective tools against the problem (allegedly) presented by beggars, but he raised the following question: "We hassle them with identity checks and if they are young or able to work, then we take them away, but what should we do with the elderly and the sick?"[75] The moocher young people, in the eyes of the authorities, who belonged to the Great Tree Gang and in many cases had come from various state institutions were in the category of people who could be removed from public spaces for presenting a danger to the public by avoiding work. By the end of the 1960s, the police were taking action against young people like them on a daily basis, in part because of the growth of tourism.

One gets a sense of the wide array of shops in the inner city of Budapest at the time not only from the depictions crafted by government bodies (and therefore a bit suspicious, since they may reflect pressure to satisfy the expectations of higher bodies of government as much as they did the actual situation) but also from the wide variety of businesses mentioned in the documents produced from petty crime trials. For instance, in the course of proceedings launched in 1969, a group of young people who allegedly sometimes gathered to form gangs was accused of having stolen windbreakers from the Corvin Department Store; black turtlenecks from the Lottó department store; sweaters, women's latex pants, electric razors, and pocket radios from the Fashion Halle; pants and terylene skirts from the Calvin Square department store; silk kerchiefs from the Verseny department store; crystal ashtrays from the Otthon ("At home") department store; and sweaters from the Luxus and the Extra department stores in 1968. They had used these things for a time and then sold them to a consignment shop, and thus the articles in question had come back into circulation as secondhand goods.[76] (For people living in the poor neighborhoods on the perimeter of the city, the sale of articles that constituted luxury consumer goods to consignment shops was a common way of bringing in a modest income.)[77]

The press at the time contained arguments against and in favor of the consumer lifestyle. In the 1960s, the press began ever more frequently to depict the accumulation of consumer articles and consumerism itself as perfectly acceptable goals, since the press also regularly ran advertisements.[78] At the same time, in a debate that took place in 1961 and 1962 in a monthly art periodical entitled

*Új Írás* (New writing), the consumer lifestyle and the "society of surfeit" were characterized as forms of the petty bourgeois ideal of life (the debate later became widely known as the refrigerator socialism debate):

> The craving to own personal goods continues to grow. . . . the question arises: the years of galley slave work to own a television, a refrigerator, a weekend house, a car, do they not foster a petty bourgeois mindset? . . . And when one has satisfied his yearnings, does not the fact that, because of his new television, he now shuts himself up inside his apartment day in and day out turn him into a deformed petty bourgeois and philistine, that in his car he isolates himself from pedestrians and in his weekend house from the human experiences of shared, communal life spent in the company of others?[79]

The other public debate concerning the consumer lifestyle was dubbed the "a kid or a car" debate. The name refers simply to the dilemma between two mutually exclusive (at least, according to the name) possibilities. One could choose either to have children or to live as a consumer with some disposable income. The implication was that young couples often preferred to set aside money to purchase consumer goods instead of starting families, which was why birth rates were dropping.[80]

In the debates about lifestyles that took place in the 1960s, the petty bourgeoisie represented the consumer lifestyle and the defense of the capitalist institution of private property. At the twenty-second congress of the Communist Party of the Soviet Union in 1961, as part of a twenty-year program, the manner in which a communist society would be built was announced. The same program was announced in Hungary in 1962 at the eighth congress of the Hungarian communist party as "the construction of socialist society." According to this program, a shift to publicly owned property was a precondition of abundance. This proclamation made it possible for the first time to have open debates about the accumulation of personal belongings. In the 1961 debate on refrigerator socialism, one of the most powerful criticisms of the consumer lifestyle was the contention that as a consequence of the production and proliferation of material goods, the petty bourgeois mentality would become a dominant force in the country.[81]

The city was transformed into a kind of consumer object. Even the print media and television programs that presented their audiences with images of the city that met the expectations of the regime became products of mass consumerism. The television had a significant role in representing everyday life, with ordinary people appearing daily on the screen talking about their experiences during the 1960s, also in accordance with the expectations of the regime, and this further bolstered efforts to legitimize post-1956 policies.[82] Hungarian television in the 1960s changed the way in which people perceived their pastimes. They watched television with little concern for what they were actually watching, and 70 percent of the people asked said they did so simply to amuse themselves.[83]

The city that people saw on television was presented mainly as a city of shop window displays. According to a report on television habits, "the entertainment is too much like the culture of Pest in its nature. It strives to meet the demands that the capital itself produces. The mentality and attitudes of audiences living elsewhere in the country do not influence the programming at all, not even negatively."[84] The norms that came to be regarded as acceptable and widespread in the city were more strongly influenced by the images people saw of the city on television than they were by people's everyday experiences of the city. At the same time, various elements came to be perceived as part of everyday life that the socialist regime was able to characterize as the elements of a consumer lifestyle. In other words, they harmonized with principles that were regarded as Western but, in an unusual way, were also considered socialist.

Consumer habits were used by young people as a rebellious gesture or a way of expressing nonconformist thinking, since ownership of forbidden Western items could in and of itself be characterized as an act of opposition to the regime.[85] Young people could also fashion rebellious identities by refusing to adopt prevalent consumer habits, since the consumer lifestyle was being propagated by the socialist state. As noted in chapter 3, by the time the stories about the gang began to disappear from the newspapers around 1975, young people who a decade earlier would have been dubbed hooligans had been given a new name, csövesek, which meant bums or vagrants. The expression also became a synonym for homeless young people. The homeless lifestyle of these hooligans can be understood as another attempt to act out symbolically the contradiction between traditional working-class puritanism and the emerging ideologies of hedonistic consumerism. Hedonism was embodied by the *digó* (Italian) style connected with the new disco culture, which was much more palatable to the state. The police campaigns against the csövesek were based primarily on a new moral craze about drug abuse, which mostly meant sniffing glue.[86] Most of the csövesek were depicted as representatives of old-style working-class and/or proletarian culture: "They all come from the working class and from working-class districts. They come from traditional families which have broken up because of the central problems of our society: the housing shortage, alcoholism, emigration, and divorce. They are being brought up by single mothers or aunts or in state institutions. The older ones

Figure 5.6. Concert held by the rock band Beatrice, one of the symbols of csöves (vagrant) culture, 1978 (Fortepan / Tamás Urbán).

have already been in juvenile prisons or some of the country's reformatory schools."[87] The puritanism embraced by the *csöves* subculture was regarded as an attack on the Hungarian state of the 1970s and 1980s, the propaganda of which was intended to spur consumerism. The disco culture that emerged at the end of the 1970s, which embraced consumerism, received strong support from the state and the Communist Youth League because it was seen as an antidote to the puritanical punk and csöves subcultures. The socialist DJs who organized disco clubs in the houses of culture and youth benefited from this identity politics. Some of them were even allowed to manage their clubs as capitalist entrepreneurs.[88]

After the Youth Park had been closed because of an accident in 1981, the Starlight Disco Club (Csillagfény Diszkó) became one of the most supported places of amusement in the 1980s. Every Saturday night, some three to four thousand youngsters met at the club, which was run by the Communist Youth League. When asked to compare the Starlight Disco Club to its Western counterparts, one director of the club highlighted its purported educational mission: "The big foreign discos employ lots of go-go girls, and sexuality is part of the scene there. We also have live shows and dance. But we only let youngsters on stage, and the dancers are of the same age group as the spectators. Our dancers are young girls who have learned rhythmic gymnastics, and they are not only attractive, you can also see how much they have worked for their beauty, their figures, and their harmonic motions. Our programs also include elements of sexuality, because this is generally accepted nowadays, but we do it with good taste."[89] It was necessary to insist on the educational value of the discos to be able to draw a distinction between an acceptable socialist mode of consumerism and patterns of consumerism in the vilified West. Consumerism was not only tolerated but supported as long as it had alleged educational or moral functions. Although it had become legal to purchase, use, and consume Western goods, this was not officially encouraged. This is why many nationalistic young people used jeans and Western products as symbols of their rebellion against the socialist regime. A show of contempt for the officially propagated products became equivalent to rejecting the socialist petty bourgeoisie.

## CONCLUSION

One of the recurring strategies used in attempts by authorities to create a sense of moral panic is substitution: if it is not possible, for institutional reasons, to launch a campaign against a given or perceived threat (for example, the working class), then a campaign should be launched against another group, real or created (in this case, hooligans). The fight against alleged gangs in Hungary was really a pretext for numerous other campaigns by the police. It would have been unpersuasive at best for the authorities to have contended, in the 1960s, that they were launching investigations and campaigns against counterrevolutionary forces, but at the same time, given the ideology and purported goals of the socialist state, any campaign against poverty or hedonistic lifestyles would have been taboo. So instead, the authorities brought these socially unsavory subjects (allegedly deviant sexual habits, living in squalor, etc.) under the umbrella of their campaigns against hooliganism, which in the 1960s meant campaigns against gangs and in the 1970s against so-called csövesek, or derelicts and vagrants. In an era of urban planning, any narrative implying the impenetrability and inscrutability of the city as a place of unforeseeable dangers could hardly have figured as part of the discourse on urban spaces.

With the creation of the stories about gangs, it became possible for the authorities to present to the public a chaotic, dangerous side of the city that served as a foil to the new consumer-friendly inner city visited by tourists. In other words, the narrative construction of hooligan hangouts and haunts (formerly depicted as working-class areas) transformed the image of urban spaces and also harmonized better with the public's perceptions about the city, which differed from the official image of the prospering utopia of a socialist metropolis, and especially from its image of the inner city. The narratives concerning parts of the city under the reign of hooligans confirmed prevalent stereotypes that earlier had been used as justifications for keeping the residents of working-class neighborhoods under close observation. Furthermore, they served to reinforce the self-perceptions of residents of more affluent neighborhoods, helped denizens of the city from different social backgrounds feel at home in similarly different spaces of the city, and distinguished the areas seen as hangouts from parts of the city envisioned as tourist areas.

While the police regularly used force (which was not surprising, given their goals and tasks), they also had to offer justifications for this force if they wanted the government to provide more resources, both human (for instance, additional staff) and material (for instance, motorized vehicles). Thus, in their reports, the police presented the social spaces of the city as an opposition between chaos and order, a place where law-abiding citizens came into conflict with hooligans. The nightstick, in these narratives, was one of the most important tools in the restoration and maintenance of public order. According to a 1967 memorandum on the practice of using nightsticks and the observed consequences of their use, which was issued to the effective force in charge of maintaining public order, the police had to provide a justification for how and why they used nightsticks in the Youth Park, the area around the People's Stadium, and in front of the American embassy. According to the logic of a report that offered an analysis of protocol breaches, a policeman who made unjustified use of the nightstick "seriously damages the politics of our party," so the use of the nightstick had to be regulated in detail. The report contained the contention that the act would seem more lawful if, when using a nightstick, the policeman would say "in the name of the law" or would warn the suspect that he was about to use a nightstick on him or her.[90]

As another way of trying to legitimize force, efforts were also made to change the image of the police in the public mind. The pictures that were used on the title pages of the newspaper *Magyar Rendőr* (Hungarian policeman) offer good examples of these attempts. These images included a picture of police doing an identity check at night, which obviously would have been seen as an intimidating representation of authority, but later issues of the newspaper had on their cover pages a picture of two policemen in a snowy park at night, a uniformed man on the street ensuring the safety of people celebrating New Year's, and a bicycle patrol guarding the peace at a socialist housing project.[91] In another attempt to improve the image of the police, in 1959 the police who kept theaters and cinemas under observation were no longer allowed to carry arms because "the fact that the uniformed people on duty wear waist belts and are armed has a displeasing effect and creates a stern and unfriendly mood, thus it does not mirror the intention to deepen their relationship with the workers."[92]

Egon Bittner has characterized the modern police as a mechanism that, from its origins, has served to reinforce social hierarchies.[93] The police of the Kádár era functioned, furthermore, as a tool with which the regime sought to achieve its ideological agenda. This is one of the reasons why regular efforts were made to assess the police officers' and deputy officers' knowledge of socialist political ideology and their education in general. In spite of the fact that in 1958, 82 percent of the police officers and 70 percent of the deputy officers subscribed to *Népszabadság*, which was one sign of their loyalty to the regime, there were some among them who referred to the Soviet Union as Russia and who considered Asia and Africa independent great powers. As far as political questions were concerned, however, the police officers were only knowledgeable about issues on which they had been regularly informed through word-of-mouth propaganda.[94]

The creation of youth subcultures and the emergence of new social identities were both related to the goals of the socialist regime. The depiction of these folk devils of socialism played a significant role in the assertion of alleged differences between Eastern and (stereotypes of) Western consumer culture. Proper socialist modes of behavior and consumerism were addressed mostly in an indirect way. The expansion of social institutions dealing with adolescents and the commercial youth market helped establish the "teenager" as a social construct. In order to represent society as classless, the West and the East needed to find new folk devils among one of the social groups of this "classless" world, and the disaffected members of the younger generation were seen as the perfect candidates. The discourse concerning teenagers served to outline ideological norms and highlight the differences between socialist and Western modes of behavior. Thus, the construction of a new class made up of the teenagers helped the state represent the Hungarian version of consumer society. This kind of controlled consumer society was popularized in the official discourse as "goulash communism" or refrigerator socialism. In the West, it was perceived as a special type of socialism, or the "happiest barrack" in the Eastern Block.

Thus, the creation of youth identities cannot be separated from strands of discourse that dealt with members of the younger generations as the new folk devils and the corresponding habits of consumerism. As the youth problem was closely connected to the question of distinguishing legitimate and illegitimate forms of consumerism, it became highly relevant in the context of the Kádár regime's effort to build its refrigerator socialism and extend the promise of a satisfactory consumer lifestyle in a socialist system. The consumption of Western popular culture, as opposed to its refrigerator-socialist counterpart, also became a mode of affirming an anticommunist national identity. As the Kádár regime was permeated by a deep uneasiness about what it saw as nationalist sentiment, which had been at least one of the factors that led to the 1956 uprising; the use of consumer habits as a way of expressing these kinds of sentiments was more of a countercurrent than part of an official discourse on (youth) consumerism.

The rise in the number of tourists coming to Hungary from the West, the transformation of Budapest into a city of shop window displays, the various debates concerning the consumer lifestyle and critiques of the consumer lifestyle, and the media, which presented these debates to the public, all contributed to a general shift in people's perceptions of the world around them. This in turn changed the prevailing image of the goals of the socialist state and citizens' perceptions of Budapest, and whereas the first half of the 1960s had seemed a time of oppression, the second half had come to be seen, gradually, as an era of socialist consumerism.

Alongside the police and the organs of the state responsible for youth policy, the socialist tabloid press also played a considerable role in shaping the public discourse on the younger generations. After 1956, the tabloid press began to reach an ever-wider readership, and it played an important role in creating the story of the Great Tree Gang. In the next chapter, I examine the ways in which the tabloid press became increasingly influential in shaping public perceptions in socialist Hungary and the functions it played as one of the tools of the regime.

## NOTES

1. Tolnai, *A Mohikán-galeri*, 25.
2. See Fürst, *Stalin's Last Generation*, 193.
3. Katz, "What Makes Crime 'News'?," 48.
4. *Magyar Rendőr*, January 11, 1969, 15.
5. On the sources and functions of the creation of the communist police, see Shelley, *Policing Soviet Society*, 3–15.
6. Lüdtke, *"Gemeinwohl"*; Lüdtke, *Police and State in Prussia, 1815–1850*; Jessen, *Polizei im Industrierevier*; Lindenberger, *Straßenpolitik*; Lindenberger, *Volkspolizei*; Gyáni, *Az utca és a szalon*, 74–85, 96–109.
7. Cf. Bauman, *Liquid Modernity*, 94.
8. For more on these consumerist politics, see Péteri, "Nylon Curtain"; Bren, *Communism Unwrapped*.

9. Müller, *Politikai rendőrség a Rákosi-korszakban.*

10. MNL OL, f. XIX-B-14, Országos Rendőr Főkapitányság (ORFK) [National Police Headquarters], b. 128, Report on the Ministry of Interior, August 26, 1969, 301.

11. MNL OL, f. XIX-B-14, ORFK, b. 464. The gradual introduction of the system of district commissioners began in 1953.

12. BFL, f. XXIV-1-66-d/1, BRFK, 111–002/1974, the situation in the capital from the perspective of public order and public safety, containing a summary of the work of the district commissioners and their dispatch into the city in 1972.

13. On the police and the monitoring of the private lives of members of the police force under socialism, see Pető, *Nőhistóriák*, 141–61. In 1950, the Budapest police wrote a report regarding "marriage fever" among the policemen and ways in which it potentially could be brought under control (MNL OL, f. XIX-B-14-3, ORFK, b. 446, 1950).

14. Cohn, *High Title of a Communist.*

15. See Glaeser, *Political Epistemics*, 320.

16. MNL OL, f. XIX-B-14-3, ORFK, b. 446, 1950,, report on the work of volunteer policemen.

17. BFL, BRFK, f. 56/10 111-026/4-1968.

18. MNL OL, f. XIX-B-14, ORFK, b. 499, 1956.

19. Ibid., 1962, 85/182.

20. Ibid., 50-840-1959, 10.

21. BFL, f. XXIV-1-24-d, BRFK, 43/1947, vice squad.

22. MNL OL, f. XIX-B-14, b. ORFK, 446, no. 3. 1950.

23. Ibid., no. 13. 1951.

24. BFL, f. XXIV-1-71-d, BFRK, 091–12/1958, prostitution in Budapest, September 15, 1958, 9.

25. Majtényi and Majtényi, *Contemporary History of Exclusion*, 31–62.

26. Beginning in 1962, the National Police Headquarters methodically collected and studied the criminal acts that were considered "characteristic of Gypsy crime and also asked the county police headquarters to submit reports on the subject (MNL OL, f. XIX-B-14, ORFK, b. 583–84). On the use of agents in Roma communities, see MNL OL, f. XIX-B-14, ORFK, b. 122, 1959.

27. For instance, an indication that Roma would have been well represented in state care institutions is that 90 percent of children in state care had parents who had "physical occupations" (almost half of them were unskilled laborers) (Hanák, *Társadalom és gyermekvédelem*, 54–55, 85–88).

28. Quoted by Dupcsik, *A magyarországi cigányok/romák*, 143.

29. Majtényi and Majtényi, *Contemporary History of Exclusion*, 94.

30. Szendrei, *Romák a rendészeti*, 93.

31. Tauber and Ferencz, "A fiatalkorú cigány," 101.

32. https://adt.arcanum.com/hu/ (June 1, 2021) Based on the analysis of how often the press mentioned the term *Roma crime*.

33. For instance, the article "Rendőrkézen a galeri" [A youth gang captured by the police] mentions a boy nicknamed "Cigány" [Gypsy] among the leaders of a youth gang on the outskirts of Budapest (*Népszava*, December 4, 1962, 1). The novel by Kálmán Tolnai about a fictious youth gang includes a story about a boy nicknamed "Gypsy" who identifies himself as a Roma, not a Gypsy: "I would rather be a Roma than a Gypsy!" (Inkább roma legyek, mint cigány!), he says to a girl who asks him about his ethnic identity (the remark is rich with irony, since it implies discrimination within a group that is discriminated against) (Tolnai, *A Mohikán-galeri*, 13).

34. BFL, f. XXIV-1-13, BRFK, d, 005/1952.

35. MNL OL, f. XIX-B-1-Z, BM Kollégium [Panel of the Ministry of Interior], b. 39, June 11, 1970, report on the circumstances concerning some violent criminal acts of a rowdy nature. In 1969, in the course of three nationwide and 2,259 local police campaigns to ensure public safety, 8,594 people were detained. In 3,710 of these cases, the police were "taking action against vagabonding children and adolescents."

36. On the reasons for the increase in the number of campaigns to protect public security and the changes that were made to the police budget, see MNL OL, f. XIX-B-1-Z, BM Kollégium [Panel of the Ministry of Interior], b. 39, June 11, 1970, report on the circumstances concerning some violent criminal acts of a rowdy nature; MNL OL, f. f. XIX-B-14, ORFK, b. 164 50–362-1970, proposals and budget in detail.

37. Benda, "Budapest társadalma."

38. BFL, f. XXV-60-f, Fővárosi Főügyészség [Budapest Municipal Public Prosecutor's Office], TÜK igazgatási iratok, 0017/61, 480–81.

39. Ibid., 483–84.

40. Ibid., 483–84.

41. BFL, f. XX-60-f, Fővárosi Főügyészség [Budapest Municipal Public Prosecutor's Office], TÜK igazgatási iratok, 0017/61, 410.

42. Szamos, *Barakkváros*, 17–23.

43. The dilapidated buildings next to the Városmajor Park in Buda; a neighborhood known as Juhász-falu (which literally means "shepherd village") in Óbuda next to Bécsi Avenue; areas in Angyalföld, including Tripolisz; and so on (BFL, f. XXV-60-f, Fővárosi Főügyészség [Budapest Municipal Public Prosecutor's Office], TÜK igazgatási iratok, 0017/61, 514–20).

44. BFL, f. XXV-60-f, Fővárosi Főügyészség [Budapest Municipal Public Prosecutor's Office], TÜK igazgatási iratok, 0017/61, 400, to Budapest public prosecutor Lieutenant Colonel Dr. Sándor Tihanyi, February 28, 1961.

45. For instance, the letter by Dr. György Gönczi, prosecutor and head of department, to the chairman of the Pest Central District Court, in which Gönczi asks the court to treat several cases involving individuals as one case (BFL, f. XXV-60-f, Fővárosi Főügyészség [Budapest Municipal Public Prosecutor's Office], TÜK igazgatási iratok, 0017/61, March 3, 1961, 403).

46. BFL, f. XXV-60-f, Fővárosi Főügyészség [Budapest Municipal Public Prosecutor's Office], TÜK igazgatási iratok, 0006/61, 228.

47. Ibid., 0017/61, 419.

48. PSZL, f. 289/8, ő.e. 282, 2–4, Richárd Nagy: memorandum on the Budapest campaign to eliminate hooliganism, November 30, 1959, and February 25, 1961; BFL, f. XXV-60-f, Fővárosi Főügyészség [Budapest Municipal Public Prosecutor's Office], TÜK igazgatási iratok, 0017/61, 396, reminder, Budapest Public Prosecutor's Office.

49. As an example of this, one could mention the area over which agent "Répási" was supposed to keep watch between 1959 and 1967 (ÁSZTL, M-16170, "Répási" [Répási]).

50. BFL, f. XXV-60-f, Fővárosi Főügyészség [Budapest Municipal Public Prosecutor's Office], TÜK igazgatási iratok, 0017/61, 457, 525.

51. P. Cohen, *Subcultural Conflict and Working Class Community.*

52. According to LaPierre, the hooligan of Khrushchev's era was the "offspring of the ugly underside of everyday life of the supposed workers' utopia" (LaPierre, *Hooligans in Khrushchev's Russia*, 8).

53. On the meanings of this from the perspective of the use of space, see Gyáni, *Az utca és a szalon*, 96–106.

54. On this term, see Lynch, *Image of the City.*

55. BFL, f. XXV-60-f, Fővárosi Főügyészség [Budapest Municipal Public Prosecutor's Office], TÜK igazgatási iratok, 0017/61, 396.

56. Ibid., 438.

57. *Magyar Ifjúság*, December, 1969, international edition, 16.

58. B. Varga, "Várostérkép," 502–4.

59. Ibid., 515.

60. See, for example, "Angyalföld az emberek földje" [Angyalföld, the Land of the People], *Nők Lapja*, January 6, 1962; "A kör bezárul" [The circle closes], *Nők Lapja*, January 6, 1962; "A mi Budapestünk" [Our Budapest], *Nők Lapja*, January 20, 1962; "A Rákóczi útra kiküldött tudósítóink jelentik" [Our correspondents report from Rákóczi Avenue], *Nők Lapja*, February 17, 1962.

61. Benda, "Budapest társadalma."

62. In early 1960, the government decided to proceed with a project to build new hotels and new department stores on the banks of the Danube, despite the fact that only one new housing estate was in the planning and "testing" phase in Budapest at that time (BFL, f. XXIII-102-a, Budapest Főváros Tanácsa

Végrehajtó Bizottsága üléseinek jegyzőkönyvei [Minutes of the meetings of the Budapest City Council's Executive Committee], April 6, 1960, Jelentés a Budapesti szállodák és áruházak építése, valamint rekonstrukciója tárgyában [Report on the construction and reconstruction of hotels and department stores in Budapest],).

63. "Budapest, a szép üzletek városa" [Budapest, the city of nice department stores], *Esti Hírlap*, November 28, 1959, 1.

64. See Rainer and Sereda, *Bevezetés a kádárizmusba*, 95–184; Apor, *Fabricating Authenticity in Soviet Hungary*, 168.

65. On how modernization and lifestyle became a product, see Reid, "Khrushchev Kitchen."

66. See Péteri, "Nylon Curtain."

67. Including people who were merely traveling in transit, the numbers were 213,000 in 1957 and 4,307,000 in 1968 (Révész, "Számtükör")

68. ÁSZTL, 3.1.9, file V-158094/1, Sz. Gyula és társai [Gyula Sz. and his associates], minutes of the hearing of witness Péter Bognár, 37.

69. The decisions concerning the construction of hotels and the restructuring of the tourist industry were made in 1959–60. (BFL, f. XXIII-102-a, Budapest Főváros Tanácsa Végrehajtó Bizottsága üléseinek jegyzőkönyvei [Minutes of the meetings of the Budapest City Council's Executive Committee], sittings held on October 28, 1959, and April 6, 1960; BFL, f. XXIII-101-a, Budapest City Council, September 29, 1961; BFL, f. XXIII-102-a, Budapest Főváros Tanácsa Végrehajtó Bizottsága üléseinek jegyzőkönyvei [Minutes of the meetings of the Budapest City Council's Executive Committee], April 19, 1961).

70. Kende, "Mi történt a magyar társadalommal 1956 után?," 9.

71. Rehák, "Szállodaiparunk és idegenforgalmunk fejlesztése tárgyában soron kívül teendő intézkedések," 336.

72. BFL, f. XXIII-102-a, Budapest Főváros Tanácsa Végrehajtó Bizottsága üléseinek jegyzőkönyvei [Minutes of the meetings of the Budapest City Council's Executive Committee], April 6, 1960, the construction and reconstruction of the Budapest hotels and department stores, summary.

73. Ibid., the work of the Budapest Tourist Industry Office and the development of the tourist industry in Budapest, April 6, 1960, 7.

74. "They beg and they loiter. They ruin the cityscape, and they have a particularly bad effect on the tourist industry, since for the most part, they beg in the areas of the inner city" (ibid., debate on the report on the provision of medical care for the elderly, with particular focus on social political implications, November 2, 1960, 104).

75. Ibid., December 20, 1967, 104–5.

76. BFL, f. XXV-44-b, PKKB, 21054/1970, 616, Endre d. E. and his associates, sentence number 22. B. 544/1969/96.

77. In 1970, for instance, clothes that had been made for Tito's wife in the fashion salon owned by Klára Rotschild were stolen from a car parked in front of the Astoria Hotel and sold by a couple who worked in the construction industry and lived in a poor district of Óbuda that had been scheduled for demolition (ibid., 394, József d. B. and his associate, 964/1971).

78. See, for instance, *Esti Hírlap*, September 5, 1959, 3.

79. Editorial Board, "Kultúra és életforma" [Culture and lifestyle], *Új írás*, no. 8. (1961): 736–37.

80. Fekete, *Éljünk magunknak?*

81. For a summary of the debates, see Pótó, "A kommunizmus ígérete."

82. More on the role of television during normalization in Czechoslovakia, see Bren, *Greengrocer and His TV.*

83. MNL OL, f. M-KS-288, Central Committee of the Hungarian Socialist Workers' Party, cs. 36, 1969, ő.e 13, Cultural Division, report on the habits of television viewers, September 29, 1969.

84. Ibid., 9.

85. Mazurek and Hilton, "Consumerism, Solidarity and Communism," 316.

86. For example, one could mention a case in Győr from 1980–81: ÁSZTL, O-17638, "Csövesek" [Vagrants]. On the moral panic over drugs and the rhetoric used in narratives of this moral panic, see, for example, Ellwood, *Rhetoric in the War on Drugs.*

87. János Kőbányai, "Bőrnadrád és biztosítótű" [Buckskins and safety-pin], *Mozgó Világ*, 1979, 4, 64–76.

88. In 1982, some of these DJs would make as much as HUF 10,000 in a single night. This was the average monthly salary (ÁSZTL, M-41158, "Dejkó," [Dejkó], 67–68).

89. Riskó, *Diszkó A.B.C.D.*, 132.

90. MNL OL, f. XIX-B-14, ORFK, b. 456, 50-137-1968.

91. The 1965 title pages of *Magyar Rendőr.*

92. BFL, f. XXIV-1, b. 43-d/19, BRFK, 011/20-1959.

93. Bittner, *Function of the Police in Modern Society*, 39.

94. Tarján, "A Budapesti Rendőr-főkapitányság 'mindennapjai' 1957–58-ban," 48–49.

SIX

# THE SOCIALIST TABLOID PRESS

THE TRADITION OF INVESTIGATIVE JOURNALISM in Hungary survived in the police news in a very limited way in the 1960s and 1970s, and journalists cast themselves as willing servants of justice and fair play as they essentially did little more than transcribe the police reports into "investigative articles." The Sovietized press was the key organ with which the state represented itself (including the police) to the citizens, and it had another important function: namely, to offer a forum for what were represented as "voices from below," though these voices were in fact strictly filtered. As Natalia Roudakova has observed in connection with Soviet journalists, they were entrusted with the governmental task of "monitoring the very governing bureaucracies of which the press was part,"[1] which could mean that "investigative journalism" was sometimes based merely on denunciations, police actions, or transcribed police reports. After 1956, the press became more market oriented, meaning that a socialist tabloid press was created, and new magazines and newspapers were founded or old ones were transformed into more popular formats which included a lot of pictures. These new or transformed magazines and newspapers sold well, and they targeted different audiences, including the youth, women, and also "ordinary people." The new tabloid press included a lot of articles based on crime stories and police reports. Accordingly, in the 1960s in Hungary, more and more crime stories were published focusing on young people. These stories had the function of fashioning depictions of the younger generation that harmonized with and reinforced characterizations of the youth in the official rhetoric. The diversification of the press in the 1960s helped spread notions of youth cultures as potential threats to the public order.

Figure 6.1. Newspaper vendor on the outskirts of Budapest, 1962 (Fortepan / Budapest City Archives / Photographs of the Department of Urban Planning and Architecture).

In this chapter, I examine how the press and, more narrowly, the socialist tabloid press functioned and operated. I situate this discussion within a larger theoretical framework according to which "reality" and the spaces in which "reality" is perceived and experienced are constructed by society—a process in which the press plays a crucial role.[2] In this regard, methods that become part of everyday routine in the production of printed matter were decisive.[3]

Accordingly, I explore how reports published in the press became news, how the socialist tabloid press evolved in Hungary after 1956, and how the press created news stories out of the criminal cases involving young people. I argue that the socialist tabloid press had the function of legitimizing political campaigns against the younger generations in close cooperation with the police,[4] which sought to politicize the youth revolt. Accordingly, the symbolic link in the propaganda between the 1956 uprising and deviant people who were officially responsible for the revolution helped legitimize the measures taken by the police and also the official narrative of a counterrevolution. The regime after 1956 allowed a tabloid press to emerge, the popularity of which depended partially on crime reporting and with which the police were instrumental in placing crime stories.

## THE DEVELOPMENT OF SOCIALIST TABLOID PRESS AFTER 1956

Although the propagandistic newspapers still circulated widely and even people who were against Soviet rule could read the newspapers against the grain for information, the press mostly included state propaganda, and the tabloid papers, which earlier had enjoyed popularity, were shut down in the first decade after the war. After 1956, one method adopted by the Kádár regime in its efforts to consolidate power was to support the establishment of printed materials that were more suited to readers' tastes and expectations. Propaganda was neatly bundled together with illustrations, criminal reports, and an increasing number of reports on consumerism. As a result of these efforts, people began to purchase the papers not simply because they were expected to or had to, but also because they took some interest in at least some of what the papers covered.

Before 1956, the press of the socialist era was not very market-oriented, because, quite simply, it was primarily a tool for party propaganda. Nevertheless, from time to time the various organs of the press tried to make at least some of the publications less "deficit prone," though they were not terribly successful. One of these attempts involved the sensational reporting, in the early 1950s, on the (alleged) successes of workers in reaching the goals set in the various plans (though the press was obliged by the regime to produce these sensational reports).[5]

After the 1956 revolution, the regime realized that it needed new tools that could also be used in the de-Stalinization campaigns in the East-Central European countries. On September 7, 1957, the secretariat of the Central Committee of the Hungarian Socialist Workers' Party held a meeting to discuss potential changes to the management of the press and the responsibilities of editors. According to the minutes of the meeting, János Kádár himself insisted on the importance not of controlling the press but rather of making it more consumer-friendly and more appealing to the public.[6] As a consequence of this, after 1956, newspaper articles were less rigorously checked before being sent to the press. Because censorship became less severe and less consistent and was also often exercised only after issues had gone to press, some newspapers were able to write about questions that were regarded as "immaterial" by the regime in a manner that suited the tastes of the larger readership, especially papers that bore new names and were printed in new formats. Thus, for instance, in the winter of 1956, it again became permissible to print reports on criminal cases in the newspapers because these reports made the papers considerably more popular. Thus, the first articles were published precisely thanks to close cooperation between the police and the press, and while the press may not have remained a consistently direct mouthpiece of the regime, it nonetheless continued to function as an important implement in the legitimization of the exercise of power by the authorities.

Before 1956, articles that resembled police news or gossip could only be published as "short miscellaneous news" in the newspapers' feuilletons. This was why, in the press of the early 1950s, "notes" recording the phenomena of urban life began to resemble articles in the tabloid press, with their typical heroes and venues: the overdressed or underdressed lady and the ungallant jampec or teddy boy at the pool, on the river shore, on a dirty, crowded bus, or in a noisy bar.[7]

Between December 1956 and February 1957, new papers were launched, and old publications were relaunched with new titles and in new formats.[8] All of these publications, which included more illustrations and articles that, it was hoped, would better suit readers' interests than the articles published in newspapers before 1956, needed both official subscribers and broad appeal among everyday people.[9] They were made more visually arresting, given new formats, had fewer articles on politics, included more illustrations, and were sold for less. The new periodicals often sold out within a few days, even when, at first, they were only sold on the streets, a fact that offers clear proof of their popularity. Readers could not subscribe to *Magyar Ifjúság* until 1958 because every copy was immediately sold on the street. The print run of *Magyar Ifjúság* was 180,000 in 1958, 225,000 in 1961, and 246,000 in 1964.[10] In 1964, 55 percent of the copies were sold to subscribers, and between 65 and 70 percent were sold in parts of the country outside of Budapest, mainly in larger towns. The paper made a steady profit, and its profit margins grew continuously.[11]

The appearance of a newspaper, including the generous use of illustrations, became an increasingly important tool in attracting a readership. In the socialist tabloid press, when the publications were being typeset, illustrations of women in bikinis or revealing garb were given priority,[12] but it didn't hurt to link the pictures to some kind of ideological message. For instance, articles about socialist construction camps, officially designed to educate members of the younger generations in the new spirit of socialism, were regularly illustrated with photos of young girls in bikinis picking fruit. Perhaps this is why the news about a trip taken by János Kádár and Jenő Fock to East Germany was placed in the upper right-hand corner, the least noticeable part of the cover. According to the headline in the middle (the most eye-catching part of the cover), Maria Eugenia Pretel, a sixteen-year-old Colombian film star who bore a strong resemblance to the famous Italian actress Claudia Cardinale, had gotten an

Figure 6.2. Cover of *Magyar Ifjúság* [Hungarian youth], January 30, 1970.

important role in a film. The headline included an illustration of Pretel in tight shorts and a bikini top and the additional remark of "who is said to be talented too." To the right of the photo of the young film star was a picture of the newly opened television tower in East Berlin rising from the bottom to the top of the cover and, above it, the mention of Kádár's trip.[13]

The press also widely propagated the "Young people for socialism" movement in the beginning of the 1960s, though without much success. After the failure of this movement in 1964, the Communist Youth League launched its club movement, and *Magyar Ifjúság* was given the task of propagating the clubs, mainly through popular music. The impact of Western papers on the Hungarian press was palpable in this period: influenced by the programs broadcast by Radio Free Europe, the Hungarian Broadcasting Company restructured its broadcasts in the mid-1960s and launched new programs. Nevertheless, a 1968 report written by the Department of Agitation and Propaganda of the Hungarian Socialist Workers' Party, analyzing the programs of the Hungarian Broadcasting Company, stated that although the radio program entitled "Dance Music Cocktail" was a huge hit, they were still unsatisfied: "Our hopes for improvements to the broadcasting relations have not yet been fulfilled, although this issue is gaining more and more significance in relation to Radio Free Europe, and it appears to be getting worse."[14]

The interest shown by young people and the clubs organized by the Communist Youth League created opportunities, beginning in the mid-1960s, for the publication of an increasing number of illustrated news articles about the lives of rock and film stars, following the Western model. As articles about stars became more frequent, an ideologically critical discourse on "star cults" became a vital element in the power struggles surrounding the newspapers. In the reports on the youth magazines, Communist Youth League officials praised the papers for their improvement in cost-effectiveness but also provided a detailed criticism of the film and rock star cult.[15] News regarding Western stars became a regular topic in the socialist popular press in the 1960s, not only in Hungary, but also in other socialist countries—for instance, Yugoslavia.[16]

Illustrated reports on youth cultures played an essential role in the development of news photography all over the world.[17] One can observe a similar phenomenon in Hungarian illustrated papers in the 1960s, in which pictures of young people were an increasingly common and striking feature of the illustrated periodicals that were being published in an increasing number of copies. One of the reasons for this was perhaps simply that hooligans and the alleged threat they posed were common topics of conversation on the street (as it were). It was, furthermore, quite easy to fashion visual images of hooligans as threats

Figure 6.3. Actress Ildikó Piros and István Kotroczó, photojournalist for the magazine *Magyar Ifjúság*, 1970 (Fortepan / Tamás Urbán).

thanks to the eye-catching and distinctive clothing popular in youth culture, which the press tended to emphasize.

The columns Tallózó (Browser) and later Panorama of *Magyar Ifjúság* had the most modern look of the time. Individual photos were, in general, linked to a short headline or news item: for example, an accident that had befallen a star, a meeting between a fetching American stewardess and a koala, or a training program for secretaries of the Communist Youth League in Dobogókő.[18] The pictures used as illustrations in Western newspapers at the time were hardly ever used in Hungarian newspapers in the first half of the 1950s, and when they were, they were borrowed only for the sake of evidence that socialist society was more developed. This is why one of the favorite topics in the Hungarian press in the first half of the 1950s was discussion of the morally harmful nature of American comics.[19] By the end of the 1960s, the cost of including photographs in print material had dropped, and in the fight for readers, Hungarian periodicals began to use images from the Western tabloid press in the Colorful Stories and Panorama sections or to accompany (primarily ideologically neutral) news about some passing curiosity.[20]

In addition to pictures of celebrities and politicians, images of urban life with ordinary people (a child with a woman or alone, couples against the sentimental backdrop of the city), photos of urban traffic (accidents, traffic policemen,[21] traffic jams), and pictures taken during police raids[22] became increasingly common in newspapers. As one of the essential tools used to create what Roland Barthes refers to as the reality effect,[23] the photos mainly represented the urban environment in which the papers were sold. These newspapers used the images to help readers identify with the paper, and they transformed and reshaped perceptions of spaces in the city that were considered important. Images of hooligans regularly popped up alongside (and in clear juxtaposition with) idyllic pictures of urban life and the vibrant dynamism of the burgeoning city. Thus, they were cast as deviant figures who subverted social norms and disrupted the harmony of everyday life.

## WRITING FOR THE PARTY AND THE READERSHIP: THE RELATIONSHIP OF THE POLICE AND THE PRESS

The newspapers, which were increasingly flooded with reports on criminal cases, were sold using tools typical in the marketing of organs of the tabloid press. The impact of *Esti Hírlap,* which reported on police raids and cases of rape and murder (and, later, political trials), on *Népszabadság,* which was the most important newspaper of the communist party in Hungary and was definitely considered part of the respectable press, was already palpable in the January 1957 issues. Although initially typeset separately, reports on courtroom cases and criminal news regularly appeared on pages 8–10 of *Népszabadság.*[24]

Reports on courtroom cases were usually placed in the most striking part of the page, and they often contained passages printed in bold font for emphasis.[25] Sensationalist articles, reports on international celebrities,[26] and articles on crimes became the drawing card of the newspapers that were revived after 1956 and helped them sell issues in large numbers. Reports on crime and crimes, however, were not useful simply as a way of selling papers and appealing to readers' interests. They also helped the police persuade the reading public that the police campaigns (for instance, campaigns against hooligans) were justified and that the police closely cooperated with the press. In the early 1960s, the police regularly invited the crime scene and court reporters of the daily and weekly papers and the radio and television to press conferences. In late 1963, police major Dr. Endre Bodor expressed his approval of the situation with the following observation:

> The press conferences are regularly attended by the central division heads of the Budapest Police Headquarters and their deputies, who regularly speak their minds, and indeed the police chief deputies of the Budapest Police Headquarters also regularly take part in these discussions. This year, for example, more than 260 police-related articles were published in the newspapers. This number does not include announcements concerning traffic accidents (estimated at several hundred cases), nor does it include the news provided daily by the Hungarian Telegraphic Office (Magyar Távirati Iroda—MTI) about unexpected incidents in the capital (such as fires, explosions, major work accidents, cases of assault and battery, stabbings, deaths by gas, food poisoning, and accidents on the grounds of the Hungarian Railways). . . . Staff members of the press have a permanent pass to enter the building of the headquarters.[27]

Nonetheless, the authorities still wanted the papers to include more police news. Having assessed the views of the population of Budapest, the Budapest Police Headquarters found that "the residents are not satisfied with the information provided by the press, radio, and television about public order and safety, although they recognize that there has been considerable improvement in this field recently. They expect regular and more detailed information, which serves the purpose of preventing crime and, furthermore, the rapid discovery and investigation of a criminal act will enhance the prestige of the police and people's faith in the police force."[28] The institutional framework of cooperation between the press and the police was established just before the autumn of 1956; however, it began to exert a decisive influence in how news was based, for the most part, on police reports only after the revolution. According to a ministry directive, the Press Office of the Ministry of Interior had to "pay special attention" to regularly providing information about "the protection of social property, the harmful effects of alcoholism, the dangers of prostitution, the issue of crime among juvenile and underage children, and recidivism." On August 22, 1956, the Budapest police chief set up his own press service, one of the functions of which "was to collect materials coming in from the police forces in the capital for public release and to process some cases highlighted in the daily reports and hand them over to the press." Before the articles were printed, they had to be shown to the Press Office of the Ministry of Interior, a practice that was not affected by the shift in the general management and oversight of the press after 1956; this was, in other words, the introduction of the principle of responsibility of the editor in chief,[29] meaning that the articles did not have to be authorized in advance because the editor in chief took responsibility for their content.[30] From the point of view of the journalists, the press office was a kind of preliminary censorship office, and of course sometimes the journalists and the officials were on friendly terms, and in some cases, even the officials were involved in the production of the articles. As Éva Bedecs, a journalist for *Magyar Ifjúság* who reported on police affairs, recalled,

> They [the Press Office of the Ministry of Interior] were actually quite nice, because if I wanted to go, for example, to a prison, they arranged it for me. There was someone waiting for me and showing me around. But they wanted to see the article. If they didn't like it, they grimaced. They tried to hamper me. So it was worth being on good terms with the police—that is, with Csáki[31] and his fellows—so that they would be nice to me. But sometimes they did stop me. And then they didn't argue with me but immediately called the editor-in-chief and said, "This Bedecs, we can't have her stuff." . . . Later, the situation improved a bit, because Csáki retired and the man who filled his position was a good friend of mine; he still is. And he never gave me any materials that were not public; when I asked for his help, he helped. He found, organized, and prepared the materials for me.[32]

One sees the impact of the Ministry of Interior's 1956 directive on the choice of topics in cases of later crime articles as well. In addition to reports on murder cases, the December 24 issue of *Esti Hírlap* featured reports on "public safety operations" (namely, police raids) primarily concerning prostitutes and alcoholics. As a result, the following dialogue took place at one of the first press conferences after the revolution on December 31, 1956 (to which correspondents from "reliable, left-wing" Western, predominantly communist newspapers were invited). The questions raised and interpretations offered by these friendly newspapers were often based on the explanations of the 1956 revolution given in the state propaganda:

> UNITA [l'Unità, the official newspaper of the Italian Communist Party]: I would like to hear a few words about the revival of prostitution.
> REPLY: Prostitution still exists in Budapest.
> UNITA: Under a popular democratic system, to his knowledge, prostitution ceases to exist. So apparently this theory was not true.
> REPLY: In countries with popular democratic systems, the institution of prostitution ceases to exist, but of course this does not mean that there are no prostitutes at all.

UNITA: Explains that the question was raised because it is a well-known fact that the counterrevolution always relies on and is supported by these elements.

REPLY: There may be several factors that determine the extent of prostitution in a country. It is closely related to social conditions and unemployment. The police deal with these issues and prosecute prostitutes to the full extent.[33]

In late 1956 and early 1957, the police force was portrayed by the press as fighting primarily against prostitutes, tramps, and murderers. One of the functions of this portrayal was to cast the people who had been arrested after 1956 for political reasons as little more or little other than "deviant members of society"[34] and also to reinforce the legitimacy of the police. Making social divisions visible (by frequently featuring articles on the homeless, prostitutes, and nonpolitical criminals) could also strengthen the functions of the police. Furthermore, as was indeed often the case in the West, journalists needed the police more than the police needed the press, since the police provided journalists with the information necessary to write articles that would appeal to readers and keep up sales.[35]

The police news in the newspapers was often based on documents of ongoing criminal cases, but there are very few written records left on which to draw, given the informal nature of the relationships at work. A good example of this is Endre Fejes's *Jó estét nyár, jó estét szerelem* (Good evening, summer, good evening, love), which originally was probably intended to be a film script and was first published in the periodical *Tükör* (Mirror) and later as a novel. *Tükör* frequently featured writings that focused on crime. At the request of the Propaganda Department of the Ministry of Interior, József Smetana, police lieutenant and head of the Police Department Division for the Protection of Children and Minors, requested the documents of the trial that was underway against György Sz. in September 1967, which he passed on to writer Szilárd Rubin. Smetana had earlier discussed the case in *Rendőri Szemle* (Police review). In early 1968, Rubin decided not to continue work on the screenplay, and he sent the documents back to the police. A few weeks later, Smetana was informed that Endre Fejes would write the script, and he was ordered to hand the materials over to Fejes. A few months later, when Smetana asked for the materials back, director Frigyes Mamcserov[36] called him and (according to Smetana's report) said that Fejes had terminated his contract with the film studio and was not willing to write a screenplay based on the crime. Not long after this, Fejes's narrative based on the case was published in serial form in *Tükör*. In 1969, it was also published by Magvető publishing house as a novel, and in 1972, it was released as a film. In 1977, it was turned into highly successful musical with music written by Gábor Presser, leader of the progressive rock band LGT.[37]

In February 1970, György Rudas, the police major general, proposed that following the model of the West German illustrated paper *Stern*, one of the Hungarian newspapers should also feature news of warrants for arrest. He also suggested that the news featured in the Investigate with Us section of the police television show *Blue Light* not be published in the periodical *Tükör*. Rather, he thought that the Ministry of Interior should publish its own illustrated periodical, which would be issued in connection with *Blue Light*. He argued that "a paper like this concerning domestic affairs would have a large readership and would probably also make it possible for the other newspapers to publish without deficits."[38]

Smetana did not let his bosses make him a scapegoat in the scandal concerning authorship of the work. In his report he insisted,

> I contacted Endre Fejes and his wife personally and contested the way he was handling the matter. I told him that he had not been given permission by the Ministry of Interior and that his conduct violated copyright, because I had first published on the case in *Rendőri Szemle*. I had requested permission from comrade Lieutenant Colonel Csáki to make contact. In the end, Fejes sent a letter to the party center asking them to resolve the dispute between him and the director, Mamcserov, and he also mentioned me. I was then ordered to go to the administrative department of the party center and I was asked questions concerning antecedents to the case.

In light of later developments in the case, it seems that the party center took Fejes's side, as it refused to accept Smetana as the original author.[39] This row of sorts indicates just how popular the stories that first appeared as police news items were. Writers could use them to write about social problems, since the publication of these kinds of stories had been permitted beforehand.

Although the press was controlled by the state (and party) bureaucracy, the state needed the press not only as a bureaucratic propaganda organization but also as an institution that buttressed its legitimacy. And the police needed the tabloid press to present itself as an important institution that deserved preferential treatment by the party bureaucrats when it came to the distribution of state resources. The police reports that appeared as transcriptions in the press, most of which were compiled by the Press Office of the Ministry of Interior,[40] were edited to suggest that chaos was on the verge of erupting and that law and order were in danger. Thus, the police transcripts nurtured both fear and a craving among the wider public for the restoration of order, which of course meant the socialist regime's vision of order.

The articles and headlines on crime in the respectable newspapers and the tabloid press were not useful only for the police. The press was able to cast itself as a vital social institution, one that differed from the press before 1956 because it addressed awkward and unpalatable issues and abuses in socialist society and dealt not only with the official plans proclaimed by the regime but also with smaller matters and the everyday concerns of the people. The papers that published news on crime met the expectations of the Ministry of Interior and also attracted ever larger readerships. From the perspective of financing, it was important for the newspapers to present themselves as organs of the press that in no way clung to the schematic writing of the early 1950s. Journalists themselves may well have seen this as an act undertaken in the interests of furthering social change and a kind of reform journalism, as indeed Éva Bedecs characterized it decades later:

> To tell the truth, the things I poked around in were the things that did not exist. That did not exist in practice. That's why the Hungarian Communist Youth League hated me. Because in the major papers you couldn't read about such things. *Népszabadság*, for instance, never wrote about little whores. Or big whores, for that matter. Nor about the old men who rented out the rooms. Because these things did not exist. But I loved to write about this. I had a feeling—and this is the naivety of the journalist, the inexperienced journalist—I was really hoping that if I wrote about these things, I could bring about change.[41]

Several procedures became part of regular routine in the process of producing tabloid press publications and respectable papers.[42] The staff of the Press Office under the Information Department of the Ministry of Interior had the twofold task of giving materials to the press and checking articles before they were published. It was therefore not by chance that the texts of police reports were often the same as the texts of articles. Even the police agents themselves sometimes used the press texts to write their reports.[43] For instance, the text of a report entitled "Information about the Hippie Phenomenon and the Measures Introduced by Police" that was forwarded to the Budapest committees of the party and the Hungarian Communist Youth League resembles and at times is entirely identical to the text of an article published some six weeks later.[44] Bedecs's article in *Magyar Ifjúság* on the trial of the Great Tree Gang was based on the indictment, and in some sections, she only slightly rephrased what had been said at the hearings.[45]

## YOUTH PROBLEMS AND HOOLIGANS IN THE PRESS

After 1956 the papers published a growing number of articles about young people, and especially hooligans and gangs. However, the extreme, exaggerated portrayals of young people were criticized even by institutions commissioned to speak out against hooligans, such as the Communist Youth League, and by leaders of the public prosecutor's department: "Discussion of the hooligan issue has become quite fashionable in the press, on the radio, and among the general public recently. One of the advantages of this fashion is that they strive to draw attention to the problem. The disadvantage, for the most part, is that they exaggerate it, sensationalize it, and spice it up using journalistic imagination . . . There should not be more propaganda devoted to hooliganism, whether positive or negative, than the necessary dimensions of the given case demands, neither in the press, nor on the radio, nor anywhere else."[46] When writing articles about young people, the editorial boards of the newspapers and magazines cooperated closely not only with the police but also with the institutions that maintained their offices, such as the Communist Youth League. Accordingly, the words *youth gang* (galeri) and *hooligan* (huligán) were mentioned in the press most often during the police campaigns against the youth gangs in 1961, 1969, and 1970 (the analysis is based on six dailies and three national magazines, including two youth magazines). The words *hooligan* and *hooliganism* started to be used with more frequency after 1957, especially in connection with the people who participated in the 1956 revolution (to represent them as deviants). Meanwhile, 1958 was the year in which the word *jampec* was used the most often in the press, but it almost disappeared in the 1960s. The year in which the most references to alleged hooligans were made in the press was 1961, which was the starting year of the police campaign against the youth gangs. Between 1962 and 1965, the topic was mentioned very frequently (more than 150 times in a year), but by 1965, there was a slight decline in its use. Between 1966 and 1968, hooligans as a topic or trope started to be important again, and it was mentioned with increasing frequency in 1969 and especially in 1970, during the judicial proceedings against the Great Tree Gang. The word *galeri* was used with almost the same dynamics: the years in which it was used the most frequently were 1961 and 1970, and after 1970, its use in the press included in the sample declined quickly and consistently. Thus, the press reports on juvenile delinquency followed the dynamics of the measures taken by the police against young people.[47]

Youth problems were represented in the press in part as problems facing and caused by the new "teenage" generation and originating in the age of adolescence. A new series of press debates was started to discuss the youth as a problem in *Magyar Ifjúság*, including many articles regarding the generational conflicts in 1961.[48] The conflicts represented in this debate covered mostly the question of the independence of young people from their parents and the dangers allegedly faced by young people who did not have proper moral role models to learn from. The parents in the articles published in the series were presented as embodiments of socialist morals who would never let their children mix with hooligans (or be part of youth subcultures), who undermined and threatened the morals of the people's democracy.

One of the issues that came up repeatedly in the rhetoric concerning alleged youth problems concerned proper or productive ways of spending time. According to the article published in the tabloid press, the fight in this case was between the socialist and capitalist modes of behavior. In other words, it was also a fight against "idleness," which was depicted as the nest of hooliganism.[49] According to the youth magazines, young people who participated in the programs organized by the Communist Youth League spent their free time usefully. Thus, alongside the ideological functions the youth league had, it was also entrusted or charged with the task of organizing proper leisure time activities for young people, including popular programs, like concerts in houses of culture.[50]

While at the end of the 1950s the expression *youth problem* (*ifjúsági probléma*) was mentioned only once or twice in a year in *Népszabadság* and *Magyar Ifjúság*, the expression gained widespread use in the 1960s, and it was mentioned more than ten times a year from the second half of the 1960s onward.[51] Articles on young people in the press started to mean, simply, articles on youth problems, and the depictions of members of the younger generation were influenced by the Communist Youth League and by the police.

Many of the newspaper articles that served up salacious stories about popular subjects and the misdeeds of adolescents were based on the interviews done by the police in the course of raids or on the minutes of hearings and the records of interrogations. When looking back on their careers, journalists often tended characterize their personal relationships with members of the police force as a kind of solidarity and community experience, especially when writing articles on the youth problems: "And then we held raids together, from dusk till dawn. Then we drank one or two shots of rum in Bonbon, and then we told cop jokes. . . . They would let me know if there was going to be a raid, and then they asked if I was coming. And I happily went."[52] The number of scandals reported in the press grew continually as the number of papers and other sources of news grew; meanwhile, the youth was represented as a growing problem that threatened every strata of society. However, the scandals could never touch on political questions that were regarded as taboo by the authorities—for instance, the 1956 revolution or the reputations of leading politicians—but they could involve questions concerning everyday aspects of the relationship between the regime and society.

Thus, one could analyze the tabloid press as an institutional arena in which social problems were discussed that were never raised in the respectable press. The narratives through which these social problems were crafted served mainly to reinforce the legitimacy of the institutions of power, but as cases involving allegations of slander reveal, they had numerous other functions. An analysis of these cases provides a subtler understanding of the ways in which the fashioning of cases of media scandals became a matter of routine.

It is difficult to decide in retrospect whether a given newspaper article stirred up a scandal at the time it was printed or not. If an individual mentioned in the article brought charges of slander against the author, this clearly indicates that the article was met with at least some indignation, since the accuser clearly felt he or she had been offended. Charges of slander were brought against not only authors who published articles in the socialist tabloid press but also authors (and in no small numbers) who worked for *Népszabadság,* which regarded itself as a serious, respectable newspaper. In the various documents concerning accusations of slander and requests for corrections that have survived in the materials of the Pest Central District Court (which had jurisdiction in cases involving the newspapers published in Budapest), László Szabó, the host of the television show *Blue Light,* which was launched in December 1965, appears most often among the accused. This is not surprising, since the articles by Szabó, which were published in *Népszabadság,* bore strong affinities with the stories of scandals published in the tabloid press and regularly drew the attention of the reading public to matters that otherwise probably would have remained little more than local gossip. Some of these articles, indeed, resembled narratives involving criminal acts. Thus, at times, they blurred the border between the tabloid press and the respectable press.

The similarities between detective stories and the narratives produced by the police and used in the media did not escape the notice of scholars at the Institute for Literary Studies of the Hungarian Academy of Sciences. Drawing on the notion that at the time was considered unquestionable—namely, that discussions of violence in the media would lead to acts of violence—at the suggestion of the Cultural Division of the communist party, the scholars made the following proposal concerning television programming: "the number of crime stories, which have dubious value and unpredictable effects (one might think of sadism), should slowly be reduced with the addition of programs like 'Blue

Figure 6.4. Cartoon of the *Blue Light* police television show: "Convict: And how much will I get if the show is repeated?" (*Ludas Matyi*, November 2, 1967).

Light.' Here too there is excitement, but it is presented in a manner that serves unmistakable ethical goals."[53]

Behavioralist analyses that linked the portrayal of violence with the actual commission of acts of violence became an increasingly conspicuous element of the discourses on violence. According to this approach, young people committed acts of violence because they had been exposed to violence in the media, not simply because they were imitating their parents' generation. For instance, a police colonel wrote the following in connection with problems involving young people in Vas County who were having difficulty adjusting to social norms: "influenced by the television film *A Tenkes kapitánya* (Captain Tenkes), which was made with an admirable goal and which, indeed, has a good influence on the upbringing of young people, the youngsters in one of the agricultural cooperatives stole the cooperative's horses, because they wanted to play the part of Captain Tenkes in their games."[54] (Captain Tenkes, or *A Tenkes kapitánya*, was a thirteen-part, black-and-white television film made in 1963 and put on air in 1964. It is set in the early eighteenth century, when Hungarian prince Ferenc II Rákóczi was fighting for independence from the Habsburgs. Not surprisingly, it contains many scenes in which Hungarians fight on horseback against the Habsburg forces.)

The fact-finding newspaper reporters were not the only people who wanted to play the role of detective, even if (or perhaps especially if) this meant causing scandals. All of the slander cases brought against László Szabó, who in addition to being the host of *Blue Light* was perhaps the most widely known reporter of police news working for *Népszabadság* at the time, involved articles in which Szabó depicted a local, isolated affair as a great scandal and then began the investigation of the affair with the question "So who was the perpetrator?" Sometimes, the direction of the investigation flipped, and Szabó began to portray the character in the drama who had been depicted positively as the victim (and whom Szabó had already known for a long time) as someone whose actual motives were shrouded in mystery.[55] By the end of the article, the perpetrator had always been caught, of course, but if one reads all of the documents of the proceedings that were launched against Szabó, it becomes clear that he knew the perpetrators when he began writing the articles, since the articles themselves were originally narrative summaries of the investigation materials.[56]

Journalists manufactured (as it were) fact-finding articles on the basis of the investigation materials that they were given by the police almost as a matter of routine. This freed them from any fear of accusations of slander, and indeed they were given further encouragement by the B. I. 249 / 1961 decree of the Supreme Court, according to which, "the organs responsible for pursuing criminals expose and reveal; the identities and the crimes committed by the perpetrators are put on the pillory in front of the public by the press, on the basis of and in harmony with the facts discovered."[57] In their articles, journalists narrated the events as if they themselves had done the investigative work, thus adopting a further stylistic feature of the crime story, although frequently they were in fact using materials from an investigation that had come to an end.[58]

When selecting the various characters who would figure in a given article, journalists had to find a victim with whom readers would be able to identify and a perpetrator or perpetrators whom the reader could blame for the fact that we do not live in the best of all possible worlds. The kulak, the deviant, the saboteur, and the counterrevolutionary were no longer plausible villains, so the police and journalists had to come up with new, more believable malefactors who could be cast as threats to safety and order. The hooligan and the gang member were ideally suited to this role, since they enabled the police to give political meaning to tensions and conflicts between different generations and also between different spaces of the city.

In descriptions of events that cause panic, one often finds references to natural disasters as metaphors for the deeds of the groups that have struck fear into

Figure 6.5. On the shore of Lake Balaton, Balatonföldvár, 1964 (Fortepan / Zoltán Szalay).

the hearts of the larger public. For instance, in the sensational descriptions of clashes between the mods and rockers in England, the seashore was used as the backdrop. It functioned as an idealized site where hardworking members of decent families would come to rest and relax, but alas, in the standard the narrative about these two youth subcultures that were a constant threat to the public, the mods and the rockers would arrive on the scene and ruin everything.[59]

The people who crafted stories of Budapest bulletins also liked to choose settings for their stories that represented ideal sites for good denizens of the city to spend their free time: for example, public swimming pools and parks. According to the police, the Gresham gang liked to hang out at the Palatinus swimming pool complex on Margaret Island, and this innocuous habit was depicted as a growing problem in the press.[60] In a propagandistic pulp novel by László L. Lőrincz about the Great Tree Gang, the gang leader uses West German girls in bathing suits to entice the protagonist to join the gang at the swimming pool complex in Csillaghegy (a neighborhood in north Buda).[61] The so-called hippie meetings that were organized along the shores of Lake Balaton became infamous (primarily because of reports in the press), though according to some sources there were more plainclothes policemen at these events than there were long-haired adolescents.[62]

Figure 6.6. Hitchhikers on the border of Budapest, 1966 (Fortepan / *Magyar Rendőr*).

The police narrative that was crafted concerning hooligans and gangs at the swimming pools and on the shores of the Danube and Lake Balaton reached its culmination in the fashioning of a "hooligan meeting in Balatonföldvár."[63] In order to prevent this meeting, the police began to stop people on the roads between Budapest and Lake Balaton and at the two train stations in Budapest (Déli and Kelenföldi) from which southbound trains departed to check their papers and ensure that "the hooligans [are] unable to leave Budapest." They took in several people who had been trying to hitchhike at the border of Budapest, and people who were traveling by train without having bought tickets were forced to get off. The police even detained numerous adolescents who were "garbed in clothing that offended good taste." Nonetheless, it was determined that, "in spite of the police measures that were taken, the goal of the gathering was not identified, nor were the people who may have organized it. The people who were going to the gathering themselves were not clear on this."[64]

The authors of the reports on the hooligan gathering on the shores of Lake Balaton and the police who participated in the measures to ensure that this gathering not take place were able to portray themselves as indispensable protectors of the peace in an area that functioned, in the narrative of the socialist state, as a site where law-abiding families came to rest and recover from the hard work they had done all year, a site that—were it not for the assiduous efforts of the police force—would have been ruined by adolescent deviants.

Alongside swimming pool complexes, public parks were another site where hardworking citizens might escape the city and fulfill their craving to be in nature—and one that was marred, in the narratives crafted by the authorities, by hooligans. According to one of the most effective descriptions offered by *Blue Light* of the Great Tree Gang, the members of the gang had gone to Margaret Island the day before their infamous stroll to trample flowers, do a round dance, and disturb the public with their hollering.[65] In Lőrincz's novel, the narrative often alternates between descriptions of the beauties of nature on the one hand and the escapades of the gallivanting hooligans, who were utterly indifferent to its charms, on the other.[66] The police reports that influenced the newspaper articles also often linked the gangs to specific parks or specific areas in the city parks.[67] According to these reports, the presence of the hooligans transformed the parks from pleasant places where law-abiding citizens could rest or play into dangerous sites where one could never quite feel safe.

When the parks figured in the press as public urban spaces or in pulp literature as luscious natural landscapes, they served to create the impression of an idyllic scene ruined by the hooligans, but they also had a more implied metaphorical function. The descriptions of the landscapes, the leaves on the boughs of the trees, and the abundant flora evoked at least the impression of the wilderness—that is, of something foreign to the city. This may explain why the illustrator of Kálmán Tolnai's book on a fictional youth gang partially based on the press's depiction of the Great Tree Gang was fond of using images of lush vegetation in the drawings alongside the paragraphs narrating the ever more appalling deeds of the gang members. The novel was part of a genre of works composed under the socialist state with the purpose, similar to investigative journalism, of educating readers. Tolnai was the director of the Pálhalmai Law Enforcement Institute, where many young convicts were incarcerated. He later wrote several detective novels, and he sometimes incorporated episodes and elements from the lives of the people imprisoned in the institute into the plots of his narratives. Most of the characters in his stories end up in similar penitentiaries, where, thanks to assiduous adherence by their caregivers to the ideas of Anton Makarenko, the Soviet pedagogue, they are finally given a proper upbringing that, for most of them, helps them mend their ways. Tolnai regularly held big dinner parties in his house on the Danube waterfront in the village of Kulcs for party apparatchik. He also went hunting, and he wrote detective novels and cookbooks for fun.[68]

Sometimes, the intertwining branches and vines in the illustrations in Tolnai's book are combined with images of women spreading their legs, which both catch the reader's attention and express visually the notion that the gangs engaged in orgies. Thus, the depictions of nature in the illustrations arguably reinforce the characterization of the gang members as people with robust sex drives and aberrant sex lives.[69] As a kind of essential component of their narratives, almost all of the police and press reports on gangs emphasized the intensity and violence of the sexual appetites and sex lives of their members. The park functioned in these narratives as a metaphor for a dangerous, wild place, in particular because it was a place where gang members might take advantage of the isolated setting and commit violent sexual acts.

In most cases, parties in private residences that became orgies, stories of rape and multiple and frequent sexual partners, and the provocative dress and conduct of girls who belonged to gangs were prominent elements of the narratives in the police documents and, eventually, the articles in the press concerning individual gangs.[70] The function of the bulletins that characterized the sex lives of young people as deviant was to legitimize the control maintained over young people by the police and the violent measures taken against them.

Along with the parks and the swimming pool complexes that were allegedly frequented by the gangs, the crowded pedestrian underpasses also came to be seen as urban spaces that had to be kept under close watch by the police because of the danger posed by hooligans. The notion of the underpass as a place seething with sin and licentiousness became a cliché in the descriptions in the press of hooligans and even a not infrequently used motif in the speeches made by party leaders. In one of his speeches, Kádár himself made the following contention: "No one can deny his responsibility—because we are all responsible for them . . ., that in the steamy underpasses we bring them to the windswept surface . . ., to where the country is being built, where the tasks of building the country are waiting for them too."[71] The underpasses, which were symbols of modernization when they were opened, turned into metaphors for sinful life in the modern city within only a few years.[72]

The youth problems reported in the press were not restricted to youth gangs, violence, or allegedly deviant behavior, but these topics were mostly all represented when an article was dealing youth problems. In the 1960s, articles on youth problems began to become more common, much as the number of scholarly research projects on the issues faced by members of the younger generations also increased. On February 16, 1970, a verdict was reached in the case of the Great Tree Gang.[73] The press immediately reported on it. The major newspapers, including *Népszabadság*, *Magyar Nemzet* (Hungarian nation), and

*Népszava* (People's voice), reported on the case when it began and when the verdict was reached, but the most detailed report was published on February 20 in *Magyar Ifjúság*.[74] At the same time, a position statement on youth policy was reached at the sitting of the Central Committee of the Hungarian Socialist Workers' Party on February 18 and 19 (the committee had endorsed the scientific study of the younger generation and its habits and lifestyles).[75]

The regime also needed widespread coverage in the press of the trial against the Great Tree Gang precisely at a moment when a party resolution was being reached with regards to youth policy to ensure that the following message was made emphatically clear: the question of youth policy had not yet been solved. In part as a consequence of the resolution adopted by the party, work began on a midterm program involving research on the problems faced by the younger generation. This happened at almost the same time as when Big Kennedy and Lord Blondie began to serve their prison sentences.[76] In 1971, a youth policy research division was created in the Social Sciences Institute of the Central Committee of the Hungarian Socialist Workers' Party. In 1970, the problems faced and (allegedly) caused by members of the younger generations were major issues both in the press and in the party meetings. More narrowly, focus was placed first and foremost on the problems faced by young people who were training to be skilled workers and were expected to play an important role replacing members of the older generations who were leaving the work force, in other words, young people like the members of the Great Tree Gang.[77] The fact that these two things took place at essentially the same time was no coincidence. Numerous newspaper articles were printed on the case involving the Great Tree Gang in part because these articles were useful to the tabloid press, which was always seeking salacious stories with which to draw in readers.

## CONCLUSION

During the socialist era in Hungary, the tabloid press created a kind of foil against which the representatives of the respectable press could clearly define their roles, mainly by distancing their coverage from the types of stories the tabloids published (for instance, the discourse of star culture in the 1960s). The various strategies adopted to make the organs of the tabloid press more marketable (numerous illustrations, narratives that transformed everyday people into stars, stories that turned gossip into scandal, etc.) unquestionably infringed on the interests of the respectable press in a number of ways, but mainly and quite simply because readers tended to prefer *Esti Hírlap* and *Magyar Ifjúság* to *Népszabadság*, which was the main paper of the communist party and was in a way representative of the respectable press. The respectable press responded to this consumer preference in two ways: discourse that emphasized the importance of the role of the press as entertainment grew stronger (for instance the assessments of sensationalist articles) and more articles published that presented local matters based on idle gossip as national scandals, following the crime story narrative style of much of the tabloid press.

The crime story narrative was useful in at least two ways. It entertained readers, so it was popular and made the newspapers more popular (presumably, as we have no sources regarding the reception of these stories). It also made it possible to present the news as a kind of socialist fable, since "in the detective story, one is always dealing with the emotion-filled violation of the moral borders within the community."[78] And the stories regarding youth gangs fit the crime story narrative very well. The crime story narrative could be used for propaganda purposes to influence the readership. Journalists passed on morals by satisfying the public's cravings, but they also strove to meet the needs of the party and thus were far more effective. In the late 1960s, the youth question was raised ever more frequently in the official forums of the party as a problem and threat and could be politicized in a popular narrative form that served propaganda purposes.

The tabloid press, however, was not simply one of the fountains of the discourse on the younger generations but also, as a consumer article, part of the consumer ethos that the socialist state created in the 1960s, and it played a decisive role in shaping perceptions of urban spaces in which the actors in our story, the story of the Great Tree Gang, moved. Their story, however, can nonetheless also be understood as a consumer product of its own, a product that itself spurred consumption of the officially supported tabloid media. It had all the necessary frills: violence, contrasting ideological views, sex, and a modified version of the Western discourse on generational conflicts. The Great Tree Gang's story made the press itself more appealing as a consumer product, since it was interesting to many readers, and it was useful to the authorities because it could be used to pass on moral lessons.

Clearly, however, the acts and attitudes of the young people who gathered around the Great Tree were not shaped entirely by state institutions, the police, the press, and changes to urban spaces and consumer patterns. Obviously, they also reflected personal decisions made by the individuals themselves. It would be difficult to know much about the motivations that lay behind these decisions on the basis of the kinds of sources that are usually available to the historian (newspaper articles, police documents, minutes from council meetings, etc.), but in this case, as it so happens, one of the teenagers who hung out with the others by the Great Tree and happened to be one of the more influential members of the group kept a kind of notebook that resembles a diary that has survived. This notebook also offers an example of the ways in which a young person internalized aspects of his portrayal in the press. In the next chapter, I will use this source as the primary basis for a discussion of what the boy might have been thinking and how he understood himself in the days immediately leading up to the infamous stroll, which for many of the members of the group forever changed their lives.

## NOTES

1. Roudakova, *Losing Pravda*, 33.
2. Particularly notable in the vast array of secondary literature on the subject is Berger and Luckmann, *Social Construction of Reality*; Fishman, *Manufacturing the News*.
3. On the process and function of the emergence of routines in the press, see Tuchman, *Making News*.
4. On cooperation between the penny press and the police, see Springhall, *Youth, Popular Culture and Moral Panics*, 148.
5. See the presentation of the Soviet Stakhanovisms during the 1960s in the Soviet Union: Wolfe, *Governing Soviet Journalism*, 75.
6. Feitl et al., *A Magyar Szocialista Munkáspárt Központi Bizottsága Titkárságának jegyzőkönyvei*, 149–56.
7. For instance, the column entitled "Budapest notes" in the 1952–53 issues of *Esti Budapest* (Evening Budapest; it was the predecessor to *Esti Hírlap*).
8. These periodicals included *Érdekes Újság* (Interesting news), *Esti Hírlap* (Evening herald), *Magyar Ifjúság* (Hungarian youth), a new format of the *Nők Lapja* (Women's magazine), and later *Ifjúsági Magazin* (Youth magazine) from 1965.
9. On the reorganization of the press after 1956, see Cseh, *Zárt, bizalmas, számozott*, 217–27.
10. With less than 2–3 percent of the issues left unpurchased.
11. In the first half of the 1960s, it had an annual profit of HUF 2 million (MNL OL, f. M-KS-288, ő.e. 41/52, memorandum on the economic and distribution problems faced by *Magyar Ifjúság*, December 15, 1965, 12–18). In 1958, half of the issues were sold in Budapest (PSZL, f. 289, A Kommunista Ifjúsági Szövetség iratai [Documents of the Communist Youth League], cs. 8, ő.e. 82, 1958, informational report on *Magyar Ifjúság*).
12. For instance, even in 1957, issues of *Esti Hírlap*, such as the April 30 issue.
13. *Magyar Ifjúság*, January 30, 1970, 1.

14. MNL OL, f. M-KS-288, ő.e. 36/1968/13, 14.

15. MNL OL, f. M-KS-288, ő.e. 41/52, 15, memorandum on the economic and distribution problems faced by *Magyar Ifjúság*, December 15, 1965; MNL OL, f. M-KS-288, ő.e. 22/1968/3, the position of the Agit. Prop. Division of the Central Committee of the Hungarian Socialist Workers' Party on the work and further tasks of *Ifjúsági Magazin*, August 27, 1968, 141–44.

16. Patterson, *Bought and Sold*, 174.

17. Harrison, *Young Meteors*, 34–37.

18. The stories mentioned here as examples are all taken from the same issue: *Magyar Ifjúság*, January 30, 1970, Panorama column.

19. For instance, *Esti Budapest*, August 12, 1952, 6; *Szabad Ifjúság*, March 19, 1952, 4; *Szabad Ifjúság*, May 11, 1952, 8; Vigyázat méreg (amerikai kultúráról fényképekkel illusztrálva) [Caution, poison (on American culture, with photographs as illustrations)], *Szabad Ifjúság*, May 6, 1952, 4; Amerikai nevelés [American upbringing], *Szabad Ifjúság*, May 11, 1954, 5; Ifjúsági irodalom—Amerikában [Youth literature—In America].

20. For instance, *Magyar Ifjúság*, Panorama column, but *Nők Lapja* also regularly used photographs taken from the tabloid press in the West.

21. Photographs of police raids were particular popular in the early 1957 issues of *Esti Hírlap*. For instance, *Esti Hírlap*, February 14, 1957, 3; March 3, 1957, 3; March 8, 1957, 3.

22. According to journalist Éva Bedecs, one of the photographers who worked for *Magyar Ifjúság* also regularly came on the police raids. Interview with Éva Bedecs.

23. See Barthes, *Camera Lucida*.

24. Examples from the *Népszabadság*, January 10, 1957, issue include the titles "They Beat Their Friend to Death," "Shot in the Stomach Because of a Dog," and "Thieves Can Be Robbed Too."

25. *Népszabadság*, February 7, 1957, 8.

26. For example, *Esti Hírlap*, December 31, 1956, 5.

27. Bodor, "Hozzászólás."

28. BFL, f. XXIV-1-f-59-d/11, BRFK, line number 111-49/1-1965, report on the opinion of the population of the capital city on the work of the Budapest Police Headquarters, September 28, 1965.

29. BFL, f. XXIV-1-f-2-d/10, BRFK, line number 1956, 222-18/7-1956, directive number 7 of the Budapest chief of police, August 22, 1956.

30. There were even cases when editor in chiefs were dismissed because of some publications, for example László Vörös, the editor in chief of the journal *Tiszatáj* (Gyuris, *A Tiszatáj fél évszázada 1947–1997*, 140–42). For more on how this self-censorship functioned, see Takács, "*Sajtóirányítás és újságírói öncenzúra az 1980-as években.*"

31. Police lieutenant colonel and then colonel Sándor Csáki, head of the Press Division of the Ministry of Interior.

32. Interview with Éva Bedecs, February 4, 2005. From 1965 until 1972, Bedecs wrote articles on police work and court affairs for *Magyar Ifjúság*.

33. BFL, f. XXIV-1-f-49-d/7, BRFK, line number 220-68/2-1957, respondent: Colonel György Sós, head of the Budapest Police Headquarters.

34. The people who fought in the streets in 1956, for instance, were often characterized as vagrants or prostitutes in the articles in the press. At *Magyar Rendőr*, A. P., a retired police lieutenant played this role. See, for instance, A. P., "Igaz történet a prostituált 'szabadságharcáról'" [A true story about the prostituted "freedom fight"], *Magyar Rendőr*, August 10, 1957, 2; A. P., "A zárdától a Corvin-közig" [From the convent to Corvin commons], *Magyar Rendőr*, August 24, 1957, 2.

35. Chibnall comes to a similar conclusion concerning the British press in *Law and Order News*.

36. He also directed the popular films *Mici néni két élete* [The life of old lady Mici, 1962] and *Alfa Rómeo és Júlia* [Alfa Romeo and Júlia, 1968].

37. MNL OL, f. XIX-B-14, ORFK, 76-d, 825–1970, the narrative summary of the case of Ildikó S.

38. Ibid., report 391-1970. February 16, 1970.

39. Ibid., the narrative summary of the case of Ildikó S. Report submitted by József Smetana, April 28, 1970.

40. BFL, f. XXIV-1, BRFK, 48-d/9, line number 14/1-1957, Ministry of Interior, the tasks of the Informational Division. The staff of the press office frequently were able to take part in any phase of a police procedure. The Budapest chief of police held the leaders of the individual organs specified in the daily report personally responsible for the precision and speed of the work of informing the press in December 1957, as he did not consider the briefing to have been adequate (BFL, f. XXIV-1, BRFK, 43-d/29, line number 011/52-1958).

41. Interview with Éva Bedecs. February 4, 2005.

42. Tuchman, "Making News."

43. T. Takács, "Az ügynökhálózat társadalomtörténeti kutatása," 123–24.

44. BFL, f. XXIV-1, BRFK, 207-d, 5015/2001, 1968. KSZ 5/107/68; Judit Kovács, "Magyar hippik" [Hungarian hippies], *Magyar Nemzet* June 11, 1968, 5; István Ivanics, "Hippik a körúton" [Hippies on the boulevard], *Magyar Ifjúság*, June 21, 1968, 3. On June 27, 1968, a series of articles entitled "A beat-hippie jelenségről" [On the beat-hippie phenomenon] was launched in *Magyar Rendőr*, which made use of the report.

45. Éva Bedecs, "A 'Nagyfák' sem nőnek az égig" [Even the "Great Trees" don't grow to reach the sky], *Magyar Ifjúság*, February 20, 1970, 4–5.

46. PSZL, f. 289, A Kommunista Ifjúsági Szövetség iratai [Documents of the Communist Youth League], cs. 8, ő.e. 282, 1, 5, Richárd Nagy, memorandum on

the measures taken in Budapest in order to put an end to hooliganism, November 30, 1959. The Budapest public prosecutor was of a similar opinion. He contended that "a great deal of what is published in the press is exaggerated" (BFL, f. XXV-60-b, Fővárosi Főügyészség [Budapest Municipal Public Prosecutor's Office], TÜK igazgatási iratok, 0017/61, 408).

47. Arcanum Digitális Tudománytár (Arcanum Digital Library), analysis, January 14, 2020, https://adt.arcanum.com/hu/. This is based on the analysis of how often the terms *hooligan* (huligán) and *youth gang* (galeri) were used in the digitized versions of the journals at https://adt.arcanum.com/hu/. The sample includes newspapers published in the highest number of copies, such as *Esti Hírlap, Magyar Nemzet, Népszabadság,* and *Népszava*; magazines like *Ifjúsági Magazin, Magyar Ifjúság,* and *Tükör*; and dailies published in the towns in regional Hungary, like *Fejér Megyei Hírlap* and *Hajdú-Bihar-Napló*. The Arcanum Digitális Tudománytár includes the digitized version of these newspapers and magazines, and the analysis is based on its contents.

48. "Felnőnek a gyerekek?" [Will the children grow up?], a series of debates, *Magyar Ifjúság*, May 13, 1961, 3; May 20, 1961, 3; May 27, 1961, 2; June 3, 1961, 3; June 10, 1961, 3; June 17, 1961, 3; June 24, 1961, 3.

49. See, for instance, *Magyar Ifjúság*, May 18, 1963, 5; Ferenc Gyulai, "A gondviselők" [The caregivers], *Magyar Ifjúság*, August 4, 1962, 4; P. K., "Néhány hiányzó dolog" [Some missing things], *Magyar Ifjúság*, January 28, 1961, 2.

50. For example, "Este a Csiliben" [One night in the "Csili" house of culture], *Magyar Ifjúság*, August 6, 1960, 2; "Helyeseljük és segítjük az oktatási reformot" [We approve and help the reform of education], *Magyar Ifjúság*, October 1, 1960, 2.

51. Arcanum Digitális Tudománytár (Arcanum Digital Library), analysis, January 14, 2020, https://adt.arcanum.com/hu/. This is based on the analysis of how often *Népszabadság* and *Magyar Ifjúság* mention the expression *ifjúsági probléma* (youth problems).

52. Interview with Éva Bedecs, February 4, 2005.

53. MNL OL, f. M-KS-288, ő.e. 36/1969/13, 57, Cultural Division of the Central Committee of the Hungarian Socialist Workers' Party.

54. Vincze, "Az ifjúság társadalmi beilleszkedésének problémái."

55. László Szabó, "Ki volt a feltaláló?" [Who was the inventor?], *Népszabadság*, October 30, 1960, 10.

56. For instance, BFL, f. XXV-44-b, PKKB, 22440/1968/587.

57. BFL, f. XXV-44-b, PKKB, 21699/1969/601, b. For instance, one could mention an article on the criminal case against the department head of the Cooperative Book Distribution Company and his associates (*Népszabadság*, May 25, 1969).

58. For instance, László Szabó, "Árt neki a tisztesség" [Decency does him harm], *Népszabadság*, August 30, 1964, 14.

59. Cf. S. Cohen, *Folk Devils and Moral Panics.*

60. BFL, f. XXV-60-b, Fővárosi Főügyészség [Budapest Municipal Public Prosecutor's Office], TÜK igazgatási iratok, 0017/61, 458, press report on the Gresham gang; László Diósdi, "Iskolakerülők," *Népszava*, October 4, 1960, 3.

61. Lőrincz, *A nagy fa árnyékában*, 44–60.

62. Press reports on the so-called hippie meetings: István Ivanics, "Hippik a körúton" [Hippies on the Grand Boulevard], *Magyar Ifjúság*, June 21, 1968, 3; András Simonffy, "Albérletek a dzsungelban" [Lodgings in the jungle], *Esti Hírlap*, November 14, 1969, 3. A recollection shared in the documentary film: Kresalek, *A vízüzemű Moszkvics.*

63. MNL OL, f. XIX-B-14, ORFK, 50-1025/1963, b. 437, detailed reports and plans for measures related to the gathering.

64. Ibid.

65. Szabó, *Kék fény*, 1st ed., 141.

66. Lőrincz, *A nagy fa árnyékában*, 114, 267.

67. BFL, f. XXV-60-b, Fővárosi Főügyészség [Budapest Municipal Public Prosecutor's Office], TÜK igazgatási iratok, 0017/61, 409, Budapest Police Headquarters, Political Investigation Division, among the gangs to be eliminated by May 31, February 22, 1961. Press report: H. E., "Bíróság elé kerül a Vidám Park-galeri" [The Amusement Park gang is going to court] *Esti Hírlap*, August 31, 1962, 1.

68. Tamáska, *Történeti riportok*, 83.

69. Tolnai, *Találkozás a galerivel.*

70. For instance, BFL, f. XXV-60-b, Fővárosi Főügyészség [Budapest Municipal Public Prosecutor's Office], TÜK igazgatási iratok, 205, 006/61, 228.

71. Speech held by János Kádár at the sitting on Csepel of the Budapest party activists, *Népszabadság*, September 26, 1979, quoted in Nemes, *Ismerkedés a csövesek világával*, 129.

72. The author of a feuilleton published in the section entitled "Aluljáró" (Underpass) of one of the 1963 issues of the periodical *Esti Hírlap* celebrates the underpass as a fantastic space of community life, although it was already seen, as the description confirms, as "erotically sultry" (*Esti Hírlap*, December 7, 1963, 8).

73. BFL, f. XXV-44-b, PKKB, b. 640, 9. B, 23598/1969, verdict of February 16, 1970.

74. *Népszabadság*, February 4, 1970, 9; "Kedden megkezdődött a 'Nagyfa' galeri bírósági tárgyalása" [On Tuesday, the court proceedings involving the "Great Tree Gang" began], *Népszabadság*, February 19, 1970, 9; "Elítélték a tüntető galeri tagjait" [The ostentatious members of the gang have been condemned], *Magyar Nemzet*, February 4, 1970, 9; "Hippiper a bíróságon" [Hippie trial before the court], *Magyar Nemzet*, February 17, 1970, 8; "A Nagyfa-galeri 'naívjai' Ítélet a hippiperben" [The "naïve" members of the Great Tree gang: verdict in the hippie trial], *Népszava*, February 4, 1970, 4; "Nagyfa sok

kicsi hippi" [The Great Tree is a bunch of little hippies], *Népszava,* February 17, 1970, 4; "Ítélet a Nagyfa galeri ügyében" [Verdict in the case of the Great Tree Gang], *Magyar Hírlap,* February 17, 1970, 8; Éva Bedecs, "A "Nagyfák" sem nőnek az égig" [Even the "Great Trees" don't grow to reach the sky], *Magyar Ifjúság,* February 20, 1970, 4–5.

75. Magyar Szocialista Munkáspárt [Hungarian Socialist Workers' Party], *A párt ifjúságpolitikájának,* 64, cited in Gazsó, "A hazai ifjúságkutatás fejlesztési programjáról," 104.

76. Ibid., 104–9.

77. According to the researchers at the Social Science Institute of the Central Committee of the Hungarian Socialist Workers' Party, the stratum of young unskilled workers "is recruited first and foremost from young people who do not finish elementary school. We have no reliable information on their circumstances" (MNL OL, f. M-KS-288, cs. 21, ő.e. 26, proposal concerning a mid-term research program on questions of youth policy, 1972–75 [1972], 201, cited in Pál, *Politikai döntéselőkészítés,* 232).

78. Császi, *Tévéerőszak és morális pánik,* 120.

SEVEN

# PROTEST IN A DIARY

IN AUGUST 1968, AN ARTICLE in *Ifjúsági Magazin,* one of the most popular periodicals of the socialist tabloid press in Hungary, offered the following characterization of Duck (Kacsa—mentioned in chaps. 1 and 2), who at the time was sixteen years old: "The Gellért Hill hermit. Lanky, awkward, his motions clumsy, never knows what to do with his hands. Has several days of beard stubble and curly hair dangling to the nape of his neck. He's 16 years old and his light-blue eyes persistently well with tears. Two sateen patches on his unbelievably dirty pair of jeans and eight real splotches, some of which are about to fall off. S. Zoltán lived on the hill for eight days."[1] Less than a year later, on July 8, 1969, Duck was one of the people at the front of the line in the infamous Hippie Stroll on the occasion of the death of Brian Jones. The article was based on documents from a police raid conducted as part of police efforts allegedly to protect the youth, and it gave Duck something of a special place among the group of young people, since it was not exactly a common occurrence for a newspaper article to be published focusing on a sixteen-year-old teenager.

Duck was one of the leading figures in the Hippie Stroll in the police documents, and in the trial that was launched against the gang he was sentenced to fifteen months in prison.[2] According to testimony given by several people who were not among the accused, he was at the head of the procession.[3] Several of the accused claimed that he had organized the march, though of course they may simply have wanted to put responsibility for the events on him.[4]

Why did the police decide to dub Duck one of the "leading figures" of the stroll and to what extent was his conduct any more noticeable or alarming than the conduct of the others? What made a young person come to be seen as

Figure 7.1. The front page of the article on Duck published in *Ifjúsági Magazin* [Youth magazine], the home of the "hermit" on Gellért Hill and the view from Gellért Hill, August 1, 1968 (*Ifjúsági Magazin*).

a rebel in Hungary of the late 1960s? How was Duck able to fashion an identity for himself as a hippie when the socialist tabloid press was the primary source on which he could draw for information of any kind concerning what was going on in the West? Did he really have any political views or stance at all, and how was this in any way related to the proceedings that were launched against him? In the months leading up to the momentous stroll, Duck kept a notebook that resembled a diary, and this notebook may offer answers to some of the questions I raise here.

In this chapter, I examine this notebook, which sheds light on Duck's perceptions of the group and the socialist world in which he lived, as a primary source. I put this source alongside the psychological report that was drawn up on Duck during the proceedings and consider the insights it yields both into his motives and the motives and perceptions of the authorities. I came across Duck's spiral notebook in the materials of the first legal action against the Great Tree Gang, while the psychological report was among the documents of the second legal action, which was launched by the police because of testimony he gave in a case involving a girl who had fled from an institution (an incident that is further detailed in the next chapter).[5]

In *Revolution on My Mind: Writing a Diary under Stalin,* Jochen Hellbeck examines diaries people kept under Stalin and shows how people internalized the Stalinist worldview, especially the idea of placing oneself into the historical narrative of the construction of socialism.[6] In this chapter, I examine Duck's diary as an example of the way a young person's search for identity was also shaped in no small part by the public discourses of the regime under which he lived. However, in this case, precisely the opposite seems to be true: Duck tried to construct a self that lay beyond the socialist discourses, so the public discourse merely offered subjects for him in his diary. In a sense, Duck is the opposite of Hellbeck's subjects, as he constructed his identity in the diary based on representations of villains under socialism. His diary also reveals how he attempted to fashion an identity for himself by borrowing from the tropes of the socialist ideology (consumer socialism, youth culture, revolt, religion, and so on) and working through his internal ideological demons. But in another sense, his notebook is not really a diary in the strictest sense of the term, as it was not written for him alone. The members of the group shared their notebooks.

In his youthful rebelliousness (at least as captured in his diary), Duck reflected on the struggle of the socialist system to present itself, in its propaganda, as a system that had created a more humane world than the capitalist system ever could. Meanwhile, he also regarded consumer socialism as selfish and narrow-minded, like the diarists who internalized the Stalinist worldview in Hellbeck's book. Also, the identity or identities Duck crafted of (and for) himself shifted from time to time.

Young people came into conflict with the police first and foremost. Their parents tended to be far more tolerant of their deeds and misdeeds. A teenager in Hungary in the late 1960s could relate to visions of rebellious youths and the various symbols of their rebellion precisely because the socialist propaganda presented youth rebellions in the West as rebellions against capitalism, and this interpretation reinforced the narrative according to which socialism was superior to capitalism. In the socialist propaganda, rebellion against consumer society was rebellion against capitalism, and to buttress this narrative, articles were published on youth culture that informed Hungarian young people about the student movements in the West. Meanwhile, as Patrick Patterson observes, consumerism "need not necessarily be grounded upon capitalist economic relations,"[7] thus its representation may vary from popular press articles to party reports. Accordingly, pro- or anticonsumerist discourses regarding the petty bourgeois mindset and refrigerator socialism and the stories about stars can exist at the same level of communication.

Duck's diary offers an example of how these articles and this discourse influence one young person's perception of himself. I argue that the social roles presented in the diary seem to have been taken almost directly from the socialist tabloid press and that the way Duck saw himself, as someone who was rebelling against the social system, may well have influenced his relationships with his peers. In order to be popular among the other members of the group, Duck tried to present himself as a "crazy hippie" in his diary, drawing his notions of what a hippie was from the articles published in Hungarian magazines on youth culture in the West, in particular articles that depicted hippies as outlaws and dropouts. His diary also offers an example of how the construction of a new social identity depended on the official image of Western youth cultures. Vowing to lead a life of poverty and eternal childishness, Duck was influenced by a popular narrative of the countercultural critique of socialist consumerism. He mixed this anticonsumerism with religious mysticism, also showing a marked inclination to posture as a martyr who suffered for others. He used the topos of a wandering, homeless hobo, an isolated, anticonsumer hermit, and a martyr who suffers at the hands of the adults around him. For him, his long hair and later his shaved head (he shaved his head in protest after having been insulted for having long hair) symbolized not only freedom but also his membership in a "counterculture." His idea of counterculture echoed the official stereotypes concerning Western youth subcultures. His narrative also was shaped by patterns established by the socialist tabloid press and television programs, both of which were strictly controlled by the state.

## THE DIARY OF A HERMIT

According to a report authored by sergeant László Szabó at the request of the police on Duck, his family background, and the circumstances in which he lived, Duck was born in Debrecen, a city in eastern Hungary, in 1952. His father was a mechanic and his mother a housewife who later took a position as a "kitchen worker." When Duck was two years old, the family moved to the inner city of Budapest, to an apartment on Lenin Boulevard that, as an apartment with one main room and a separate kitchen, at the time was considered a dwelling with all the modern conveniences. The other people who lived in the building, built at the turn of the century, contended that the members of Duck's family were not talkative and hardly greeted anyone. In 1964, Duck's mother and father divorced, and the breakup of his family left him troubled. He began to dress differently and his grades in school suffered. He lost weight, and he barely finished the eighth grade. He then began to work. He pursued training as a house painter's apprentice in an institute whose director was his mother's new husband, his stepfather. He did not even complete the first year, however, citing as an explanation his high blood pressure. He then took odd jobs as an unskilled laborer, for example at a leather works company, which is where he worked roughly up until the point at which he began keeping a diary.[8] On June 23, 1969, two weeks before the Hippie Stroll (and after he had begun to write in his notebook), he found a new job as a surveyor's assistant at the Budapest Geodesics and Cartography Institute, where he earned HUF 1,300 per month, about 60 percent of the average monthly salary at the time.[9] This workplace was very popular among young people who hung out around the Great Tree, not so much because of the salary one could make even if one did not have any particular skills or training but rather because of the relative liberty that the workers enjoyed. The work tended to be only occasional. It was important to have a job simply because the police at any time could compel young people to show their papers and prove that they had a job and were not committing the crime of avoiding work. Anyone who could not do so could be taken into custody.[10]

On the cover of Duck's notebook (of which the police took possession and which they quickly labeled "property of S. Zoltán"), one finds the following text in Duck's handwriting: "Lonely HOBO / WHO walks alone / Waits eternally for you alone / if you don't come / loneliness will kill him." Duck frequently plays in the text with lowercase and uppercase letters, mainly to emphasize parts of the text. The many spelling mistakes in the notebook are explained by the simple fact that his grades in the eighth year of elementary school suffered dramatically, presumably because of his parents' divorce. He had then begun training in a vocational school, where little emphasis was put on spelling.

The inscription on the cover of the notebook may have been added long after many of its pages had been scribbled full. The text on the first page, however, offers a good impression of Duck's perception of himself and the reader whom he envisioned might peruse his confessions: "This notebook was written / By a H e r m i t who lives here / among you don't even notice who he is? / he is DUCK / HE NEEDS ONLY 1 thing LOVE / Which he has not yet been given / COULD YOU LOVE ME? / I KNOW That you cannot!" The question raised in the penultimate line may have been addressed—as indeed the entire notebook may have been addressed—to Éva M. Éva's name and address are written underneath the lines cited here, presumably by Éva herself, at least judging by the change in the handwriting. The address was an apartment in Ferencváros (which, as noted in an earlier chapter, was a working-class neighborhood in an industrial area).

Duck made many appeals to Éva in his notebook, often referring to her as his reader. Sometimes, his observations and descriptions of everyday events are interspersed with bits of poetry and appeals to her: for instance, "Oh, you sweet girl, how much longer will fate keep me separate / from you? I have run out of tears, I await only / TOMORROW." Duck seems to have had difficulty deciding whether he preferred the role of a lonely troubadour, a hermit, a hippie, a hobo, or a madman. Éva is present in the text not only as the lyrical intended of his confessions. Sometimes, Duck emphasizes that specific passages were written directly to her: "I WROTE THIS FOR YOU <u>Saturday evening I give it to you!!</u> (underlined in the original)" (26).[11] Duck was suggesting with this that as soon as he could, he would give her the notebook. His assumption or hope that Éva might someday read his notebook explains the many rhetorical poses he strikes as a man be smitten and the many appeals he makes directly to her. Presumably, he wanted to ensure that she would take him seriously and even find him attractive.

Duck was not the only member of the group who kept a spiral notebook full of confessions with which, perhaps, he hoped to charm or perhaps seduce girls. He was friends with József H., or "Monk," as he was known by the other members of the group (he is also mentioned in chap. 2). Like Duck, Monk was also not one of the members of the group who had come from an institution. He was only a month younger than Duck, and neither of their families was originally from Budapest. Monk wrote poems in a spiral notebook, and Duck read these poems, as he mentioned in his testimony given to the police and as confirmed by other sources. They also seized the notebook with the brown cover, which included, alongside the poems, several drawings (two of which had stylized depictions of guitarist Béla Radics, who was the big star of the Youth Park) and somewhere in the middle a page full of scribblings in Duck's handwriting.[12] On the evening of the Hippie Stroll in the summer of 1969, Monk and Duck were apprehended together by the police. The authorities immediately took an interest in the poems Monk had written in his notebook because of their political content.

Monk and Duck met in the spring of 1969.[13] Monk began to write poems in part because of Duck's influence, for Duck, according to Monk, had spoken a great deal about how he wrote.[14] Though he wrote his notebook for his entire circle of friends, judging by the text, Duck seems to have regarded Éva as his intended reader, and he wrote to catch her attention. He may well have shared some of Monk's habits, however: for instance, always keeping the notebook on his person and giving it to others to read. But what identities and poses would be appealing to a girl, at least according to an adolescent who in 1969 was regarded by the organs of power as part of a counterculture?

The figure presented on the first page of Duck's notebook of a hermit who suffered from a lack of love was not Duck's invention. Rather, he borrowed the character from the description of him in the article printed in *Ifjúsági Magazin*, in which he was indeed described as a hermit.[15] Journalists at the time loved to use the testimony given by young people in the course of police raids when writing articles on the problems faced (and posed) by members of the younger generations. According to these portrayals, the police did not keep young people under constant surveillance. Rather, they protected them from lurking threats and dangers, and of course they protected respectable citizens from young people who had strayed down the path of hooliganism.

The subtitle of the first column of the article that was published in *Ifjúsági Magazin* about Duck was "The Hermit of Gellért Hill." The description of the boy in the article later shaped the aspects of his appearance that he himself emphasized in his notebook when crafting his identity: long hair, ripped blue jeans, and a ragged beard.[16] In other words, he seems, on the basis of his description of himself in his notebook, to have been pleased with this portrayal of him as a hermit who lived on the fringes of consumer society.

The author of the article writes as if he had done an interview with Duck, though in all likelihood, the two only spoke either in the police van disguised as a vegetable vendor[17] or in one of the cells of the youth protection police facility in Rómer Flóris Street, after Duck had been taken into custody. The article touches on the reasons Duck had for taking refuge in the woods on Gellért Hill, for instance in the following exchange: "My stepfather looks at me as if I were a leper, and my mother doesn't love me much either, and both of them are always calling me a moron. . . . everyone in the building, from the resident janitor on up, gives me a hard time because of my long hair.—Is that why you went to the hill?—Yes. I decided to leave after what my mom did to my pants.—What did she do?—After I got paid, I bought a new pair of jeans. My mom didn't like them, so she cut them to shreds." Duck's blue jeans and his long hair became important motifs in the scribblings in his notebook, in which he fashions his identity as a would-be hermit. The last question and last answer in the part of the article on Duck touched on subjects that became even more prominent elements of Duck's image of himself in the notebook: "And what did you do on the hill?—I told the guys that I would be there. They brought me a bottle of milk and two bread rolls every day.—But you can't live like that for long.—I didn't want to. I knew they would come looking for me soon and take me in. That's how I planned it. I want to end up in an institution. It won't be perfect either, cause I'm sensitive, and they'll make fun of me there too, but the people there will be strangers, not my mom and stepdad." The article foregrounds Duck's thirst for love and his conflicts with his mother and stepfather, topics about which Duck also wrote in his notebook. The portrayal of him offered in the article may well have prompted him to characterize himself as a "hobo" on the title page, a sort of lonely troubadour who "walks alone" and will soon die of loneliness if Éva does not come to him.

Peoples' images of hippies and hobos in Hungary in the late 1960s were varied and shifting. Clearly, impressions of hippie culture in the West were all secondhand, based either on newspaper articles or films, which is why people were able to arrive at their own relatively loose definitions of what it meant to be a hippie. In the course of the proceedings against the young people who hung out by the Great Tree, Lord Blondie offered an interesting explanation of the difference between a hippie and a hobo. To a question raised by Big Kennedy's attorney (who probably wanted to demonstrate to the court that the young people took little interest in politics and therefore should not be treated as political criminals), he replied, "in my view there is no socialism in Hungary yet. . . . If they were to assure me that I didn't have to work until I was 25 years old, I would pass my time with all kinds of foolery. If I didn't have to work all the time, I would pass my time with all kinds of nonsense. I would party all the time, dance, hang out with girls, go to the movies, listen to beat music, that's what I call a good time. Being a hippie and a hobo, shouldn't have to work." At this point in the exchange, Lord Blondie was probably asked what he meant by this, as, according to the minutes, he then made the following claim: "If you ask me, hippies fight, hobos don't fight. I imagine a hobo's a bozo."[18]

This distinction suggests that, at least in Lord Blondie's mind and quite probably in the minds of his peers at the Great Tree, the hobo was seen as a more peaceful, observant figure, in contrast with the hippie, and Duck may have found this image of the peaceful hobo more appealing than the poses struck by the other boys in the group, who were perhaps more physically domineering and who had been raised to a large extent in institutional settings. The image of the hippie in Hungary at the time, after all, was based on (frequently exaggerated) news reports of conflicts between hippies and the police in the United States, so it would be hardly surprising if it included an element of violence or aggression.

On May 15, 1969, not long before Duck began keeping his notebook and the teenagers who hung out by the Great Tree took their famous stroll, there was a clash in the United States in California between protesters in People's Park in Berkeley and the authorities. Governor Ronald Reagan ordered police and even the National Guard to take control of the park, which legally was university property but which was being used (largely with the university's consent) as a refuge for the homeless and a site for public protests. In the clashes that ensued, hundreds were injured and one man (James Rector) was killed by gunfire. The confrontations, which were caught on television cameras and broadcast by stations all over the world (including in Eastern Europe), became a symbolic event of the new Left.[19]

The socialist press made plenty of room in its reporting for news of the student movements in the West and the clashes and confrontations between young people and the police. In February 1969, *Népszabadság* started a series of articles on the student movements, and every week the paper had news concerning students agitating for reforms in the West.[20] The criticisms of capitalism voiced by young people were useful to the regime in its efforts to paint socialism as a more humane system. And of course, while the organs of the socialist power expressed compassion and support for the rebellious critics of the system in the West (since they were, in principle, fighting against capitalism), rebellious young people back home were characterized simply as deviants and hoodlums.

Characterizations of hippies and hobos in the Hungarian press also tended to suggest that young people who aped these Western lifestyle trends were "psychiatrically troubled," so Duck's description of himself as a "bozo" may have given him slightly more credibility. The author of an article that was published in *Magyar Ifjúság* in the wake of a 1968 police report cites the later widely discredited American psychiatrist Jules Masserman: "Hippies are in fact psychiatric cases. Many of them are not just vagrants and parasites, but, as we would call them, sociopaths or psychopaths. Some of them end up in mental institutions."[21] In Duck's case, Masserman's rather categorical contention was true at least in one sense. While he was not permanently institutionalized, in the course of the proceedings he was given mental health treatment.

The article in *Ifjúsági Magazin* had a strong influence on Duck's image of himself. This was due in part to the fact that the article ascribed various characteristics to him that were popular among the teenagers who hung out around the Great Tree but also simply because having an article printed about you in the newspaper can make any boy popular among his or her peers. In February 1970, an informant who went by the codename Kertész (or "Gardener") noted a similar phenomenon in a report submitted to Imre Seres, who was overseeing the surveillance of the Great Tree Gang.[22]

Duck did not date any of the entries in his notebook, with the exception of "Duck 1969," with which the notebook comes to an end. Any hypotheses concerning dating must be based on the actual contents of his notes. Next to this one date, he drew a picture of a boy with long hair, presumably himself. This would suggest that he drew the picture soon after he began keeping the notebook, since in early June (when, based on the contents of the entries, he was regularly writing in it), he shaved his head as a rebellious gesture.[23] He must have begun writing in the notebook sometime in early June 1969, and he must have finished before the eventual stroll, since there are no references to the events of that night in it whatsoever. There is also no mention of Brian Jones's death, in contrast with the notebook kept by Monk (who did mention Jones's passing). Thus, the notebook covers a period of time of roughly one month. One can also conclude that Duck began writing in the notebook in early June on the basis of a poem by Monk that he copied on the sixth page. In the course of the trial against the Great Tree kids, it caught the attention of and was used by the police, the prosecution, and, later, the journalists who wrote on the proceedings.

The poem by Monk that Duck copied into his notebook, "My Mother's Corpse Is For Sale," can be read as an adolescent's (not terribly imaginative) imitation of "With a Pure Heart" (available in several English translations), a poem by famous Hungarian poet Attila József.[24] Though József was a prominent figure in the regime's literary canon, Monk's poem was seen by the police as critical of the system:

> The snow falls in large flakes /
> My mother's corpse is up for sale /
> I'll sell it cause I'm cold /
> I'll sell it, buy a coat. //
>
> And people will rebuke me /
> Oh, you cruel child, cruelly /
> Your own mother you sell? /
> How do you have the gall! /
> Yes I'll sell her, I'm alive today, and them, they're all old and gray.[25]

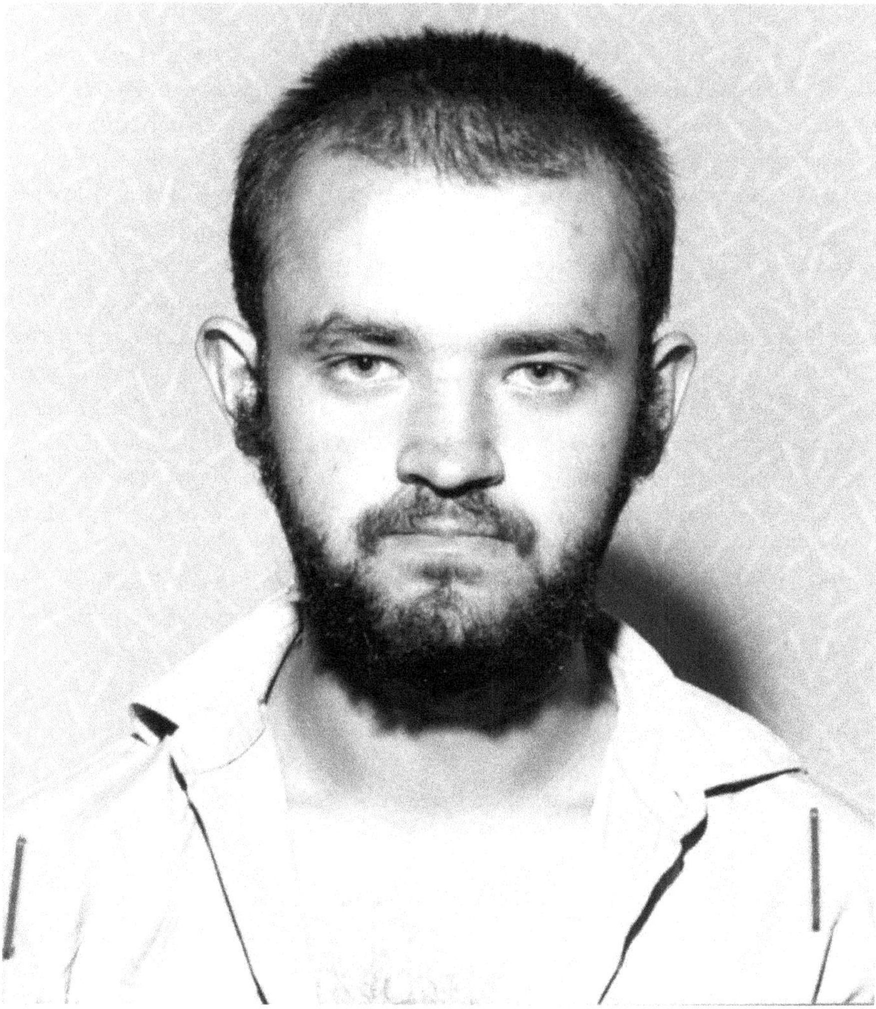

Figure 7.2. Duck after the stroll (HU BFL XXV-44-b 21201/1471).

In the course of the trial, Monk offered the following account of the inspiration (as it were) for the poem: "this one time one of the guys was cold, and this other guy told him to sell his mom's corpse and use the money to buy a coat. That's how my poem came to be."[26] Bedecs makes mention of the poem in her article in *Magyar Ifjúság* on the trial against the Great Tree Gang, as if, along with the police, she too (or the tabloid press, of which she was a representative) believed in the political power of poetry. As her article makes clear, she was given not only the indictment in the case, but also the kids' notebooks, which she characterized as "oppositional in their political content."[27] Duck wrote the following lines at the beginning of Monk's blue notebook: "Perhaps I will live to see / flowers cover the Earth / and there won't be any more / barbers or hairdressers."

Before the proceedings began in January and February, Monk spent two months in pretrial detention because of written evidence brought against him (the poems)—more than any of the other accused. His father, noting his poor health, asked on several occasions that his son be released until the trial began (eight of the ten accused were released). Géza Kelemen, the leading attorney for the prosecution, rejected these requests on the grounds that the accused might attempt to flee. Furthermore, Monk was named as the primary accused, not Big Kennedy (who at this point had not yet spent any time in foster institutions). Monk's father died before the trial began, and his mother suffered a nervous breakdown. When the proceedings began, the prosecutor felt sorry for Monk, who initially was not even able to give testimony because he had been so shaken by the events, and the prosecution asked that the boy immediately be released from custody.[28]

The court regarded four of Monk's poems as political in their content. The first stanza of one of these poems, the poem entitled "My Dear Land," became quite popular among the members of the Great Tree group after the trial:

> Slavery has broken you /
> Hungary, my dear land /
> A red curse above our heads /
> We will break it, hippie lads.

During the trial, Duck claimed that, although he had read Monk's poems, he had told Monk not to write about politics, since it would get him into trouble. The court accepted this as a fact.[29] It seems quite possible and even likely that, though the police seized Duck's notebook, they did not read it terribly thoroughly, since they make no mention in the various documents concerning the case of the fact that Duck copied Monk's poem and that he often wrote comments in Monk's notebooks (both the old one with the brown cover and the newer one with the blue cover). This was, of course, to Duck's advantage, since, had they read his notebook more closely, they might well have brought similar charges of political agitation against him too.

## RELIGION VERSUS CONSUMERISM

After the portrayal of the hermit on the first page of the notebook, on the second page Duck offers a critical assessment, from his perspective as a (would-be) hermit, of human vanities, so-called consumer socialism, and the world of shop window displays (described in chap. 4):

> God gave man reason, but not so that we would kill one another and keep our money in the national savings bank. What do they manage to accomplish with it? They live better, perhaps. You office worm! Hey, don't hide! I want to talk about you. Tell me, do you know how many slices of bread and butter your wife packed up for you today? You don't speak up, you just caress your Trabant, you got a good deal with it! And now the weekend is coming. You need it, cause otherwise the police will write you up! Gather up the money, your kid needs a stereo.

Duck borrowed from the arguments and ideas he found in the press at the time, which, as a consequence of the regime's pronatalist demographic policy, were expressive of a critical attitude toward refrigerator socialism and took a profamily view of the "kid or car" debate. Essentially, the stance of the government was that birth rates were dropping because people were more inclined to spend their disposable income on consumer goods rather than start families. This view harmonized well with the official portrayal of hippies as people who were critical of capitalist consumer society, which in the communist propaganda proved that socialism led to the emergence of a better, healthier society than capitalism. The so-called "debate," which at times was framed with simple oppositions (the self-standing home versus residential apartment buildings, the kid or the car), attributed political meanings to patterns of consumerism, and people would use these arguments when justifying their own lifestyle choices.[30] Critics of consumer society in Hungary used these arguments, and they also reflected on and even borrowed from the goals of the anti–consumer society student movements in the West.

Duck, however, linked the critique of consumer society with religious belief (based on a puritan image of religion that rejected consumerist behavior), and the open espousal of religious belief could also have been seen as a form of rebellion against the official norms of the day. During the first round of proceedings in his case, he explicitly identified himself as someone who was religious: "One of the members of the Rolling Stones had just died, Brian Jones, whom we considered a member of the family. We wanted to go to the Basilica to hold a mass for the dead. I figured we would pray in silence. As it so happens, I am religious, and I was given a religious upbringing."[31] Neither the report on Duck's family background by sergeant Szabó nor the two psychiatric evaluations of him made any mention of his religious beliefs, though both placed great emphasis on the importance of uncovering principles of childrearing that constituted deviations from socialist norms. An evaluation of Duck that was written by the personnel manager in his workplace in the spring of 1969 suggests that his insistence on his religiousness may well have been little more than a gesture of defiance or rebelliousness: “He claims to be religious, though neither of his parents is.”[32]

Duck’s notebook contains numerous criticisms of consumer society, which are expressed for the most part in the form of reproaches addressed to the observed or imagined figures of street life in the big city. Adopting the pose of the puritanical hermit, he depicts himself as someone who has the task of showing avid consumers the meaninglessness of their lives through the counterexample of his life as an ascetic: “as evening falls, you hurry, worn out, your boyfriend is waiting, shows you his new Volkswagen. And then you see me on the bench, me, and I am laughing without any cares!” (3–4, underlined in the original).

On the next page, Duck compares his sufferings with the Passion of Christ. In the narrative he crafts, religion plays a central role, which was not unusual at all in the narratives of social rebellion among young people of his generation: “The tower of the basilica gestures to me, I know that only Jesus Christ loves me. He was the one just man on this earth, and yet they stoned him nonetheless, spat on him, nailed him to the cross. I know that someday I too will suffer this fate, because I am incapable of lying. You can see this if you read what I write. They kick me too, spit on me too, what can I do about it” (5). It would be an exaggeration to characterize Duck as a religious activist, but he does include a puritan image of religion as a central element of his protest against the consumer socialist society in which he lived.[33]

## LONG HAIR AND PARENTS

In order to strengthen the image of himself as a martyr, Duck recounts the trials he endured one day because of his long hair. He was sitting as he often did on the bank of the Danube River, on this occasion surrounded by friends. As if to set the mood, he writes, “the water was murmuring, and I was meditating on the waves.” He notes that his mother had been complaining about his long hair for years: “Zoli, when are you going to go to the barber?” And when he was near the Western Train Station, a policeman had stopped him “because I was ruining the image of the city.” The policeman had said, “Windbreaker, blue jeans, let’s see your ID!” According to Duck’s narrative, someone in the crowd had shouted, “If I were a policeman, I would tear out his hair!” When the story ends, Duck is in tears: “The policeman gave me back my ID. You can go, he said, but his gaze pauses, a pair of blue eyes (my eyes) are welling with tears, what did you do that for, cop? His cheeks blush, LOVE has not yet died in him!" But Duck then finds himself embroiled in conflict again because of his hair. "There's a dirty tavern nearby," and the people in the tavern are jeering at Duck because of his long hair: "lots of drunk people in the tavern who are suffering from schizophrenia, I can hear THEIR TALK: Fag! Mary! Suck it!" According to Duck's account, the only reason he didn't bother with the people in the tavern was that "YOUR KIDS ARE WAITING FOR YOU BACK HOME, BUT YOU ROT IN THE TAVERN!!!" (5–7). His use of capital letters for parts of this passage may well reflect the very personal nature of this protest, and as earlier cited excerpts from the article published in *Ifjúsági Magazin* suggest, he may well have felt neglected by his parents.

According to the report on the circumstances of Duck's family, when his parents divorced in 1964 (when Duck was twelve years old), they dragged him into the conflict between them. His father noticed that his mother and their tenant "were taking part in couple's amusements. Several times, when he came home from work and found that his wife was not there, he set out with his son Zoltán to search for her, and he found her every time in one of the coffee bars in the area with F. [who later became Duck's stepfather]."[34] This observation, like the aforementioned passages in the *Ifjúsági Magazin* article, also suggests that Duck's reproach concerning children waiting at home while their parents pass time in a tavern was motived in part by memories of difficult moments of his childhood.

In Duck's narrative, his long hair becomes almost a symbol of his thirst for love and the failure of those around him to understand him. For instance, in one passage he writes, "I tell empty sheets of paper what I feel!! What a long-haired kid feels in the world of 'adults'! No one will ever understand me, except this notebook" (8). Alongside his long hair as a symbol of his nonconformity and the persecution he suffered (or felt he suffered) because of it, Duck also wrote about his inner struggles, which of course were important elements of his self-fashioned identity as a hermit or hobo. He wrote the following lines in his notebook and in Monk's notebook: "Life wouldn't be bad if people had brains in their heads, didn't just look at my hair and pants, but also my inner world" (8). In Monk's notebook, these lines are found on the first page of text after Monk's drawings, arguably in a prominent spot. Beneath this (and beside Duck's nickname), Duck wrote the word "Beatles" in his handwriting, as if the lines were a quote from one of the band's songs. Duck also wrote the following lines on the first page of Monk's blue notebook: "Perhaps I will live to see flowers cover the Earth and there won't be any more barbers or hairdressers" (9).

Duck returns many times to the issue of his hair and the barbershop, but he never loses sight, as it were, of his intended reader, Éva. On the next page of the notebook, his pose shifts a bit from that of the martyr persecuted as a nonconformist to that of a martyr for love. He even casts himself in the role of the fool who loses his mind because of love: "Dreams do not come, I plead, give them back / and together with them, my mind!" (10). The notebook contains several passages in which Duck strikes this pose: "If I should die, my friends, then let my gravestone say: / LOVE put him in his grave!" (11)

According to the psychological assessment done at the request of the authorities, the acts committed by Duck, including his participation in the stroll, could be explained by the absence of a father figure, though according to the background report on his family, it was his father who would set out with Duck to find the boy's mother when she was absent. Nonetheless, the psychologist arrived at the following conclusion: "The fact that the father abandoned the family when the boy was 14 years old [*sic*; Duck was twelve] because of an affair with a woman further damaged the development of his personality, i.e. he left precisely when, for a boy, the form of childrearing in which the father plays a strong role is a fundamental force in shaping personality."[35] According to the psychologist, Duck had difficulty accepting his stepfather, and this was why he had wanted to leave home. According to the report on Duck's family circumstances, his stepfather found Duck's mother's approach to childrearing too permissive and accommodating. He had been stricter with the boy, and Duck had rebelled against this.[36]

The bureaucrats (whether the psychologist who prepared the assessment of Duck's emotional state or the police responsible for his interrogation) characterized the sixteen-year-old boy as an adolescent who was rebelling either against his father or his stepfather. The important thing was to find the causes of his behavior, which was considered deviant, not in the society in which he was living at the time but rather in his childhood. As part of this narrative, the ridicule and exclusion he allegedly suffered as a child because of his weight problem provided a convenient explanation for why he had become, according to the psychologist's assessment, a "young man of sound mind but repeatedly and seriously damaged emotionally."

Immediately after the passages in Duck's notebook in which he writes about his fondness for pâté, one finds lines of poetry about how he has shaved his head: "My bald head shines, a beard on my chin / And lots of people ask me, woe, what have you done? / Should I answer to you, you rotten people / who know nothing about how I feel? / It's not my appearance that matters, take heed! / what's inside determines how a man is / outside" (12). Other remarks by Duck concerning his decision to shave his head are found not in his notebook, but rather in Monk's brown notebook. The remarks suggest that conflicts had arisen between Duck and several of the other members of the group who hung around the Great Tree. This was hardly the only source in which one finds signs of such conflicts. In his later testimony, Big Kennedy contended that on the day of the Hippie Stroll, he had wanted to beat up Duck and his pals. Indeed, when Duck and his group had approached Kennedy and his clique the day before, coming from the bank of the Danube, Kennedy had thought they were coming to start a fight. It only later turned out that Duck was coming to invite them to march in memory of Brian Jones.[37] According to Kennedy, he was never terribly close to Duck. He had been friends, rather, with Lord Blondie and other boys who had spent time in institutions.[38] The children who grew up in homes had disagreements with the children who grew up in institutions, and they probably also had different subgroups because of their different social backgrounds and the differing degrees to which they had some parental support.

The following lines, penned by Duck in Monk's brown notebook soon after he shaved his head, offer his perception of the other members of the group: "Youth Park, what is it? A locked ward for madmen, that's what! / I loathe the long-haired heads, though my hair once / dangled to my shoulders. I loathe you, you peasant / long-haired kids! / You steal, you cheat, and you're / the beautiful ones? I don't believe you! / You're a bunch / of young criminals, you deserve to have the police flip your papers [Duck uses a slang term in Hungarian that meant check your identity papers]." Thus, Duck distanced himself from the other young people who hung out around the Great Tree, many of whom had come from various institutions.

According to László Szabó, the author of the report on Duck's family life, the so-called residents' committee in the building in which the family lived (in other words, their neighbors) wrote a "polite letter in which they called the parents' attention" to the boy's eccentric behavior, "and they also offered to help rear the child if the parents so desired." In all likelihood, one of the members of the committee spoke to Szabó, as the report contains the following detail: "The mother aggressively rejected this well-intentioned offer in a letter, objecting angrily to the notion that the residents' committee would interfere in family affairs."[39]

After having sheared his locks, Duck again struck the pose in his notebook of love's fool. He seems also to have felt that with this dramatic gesture (cutting his hair), he had clearly demonstrated that he was not a member of the group. It was then that he began to favor the pose of the madman: "YOU who read these lines do not think / that I am INSANE, I only T h i n k / There is always some MADNESS in love, but / there is always some REASON in MADNESS" (13).

After having cut his hair, Duck addresses not only his reader but also himself, asking who would ever bother to read his scribblings: "I began a new page, but why? Tell me Zoli (Duck), who understands you? It's nighttime, the city is quiet, I am walking through a park and I can feel that I am cold! . . . But who could love 1 vagrant who wanders the streets at night? Perhaps YOU! Or no? My reader, do you not understand me? I am going now, because a policeman is coming! Finally, he's gone" (14). The typical style of a diary, in which the author reacts to and comments on the small tremors of everyday life, is interspersed with exclamations and proclamations that often resemble rallying cries and mantras. And though Duck had parted with his long hair, he still closes the notebook with statements that echo the rallying cries of hippies (and thus reaffirm his attachment to this image): "Beds not bombs!" (he wrote these words under the love poems, 13), "pick flowers instead of bombing bowers!" (this appeal is found under one of the passages in which he addresses his reader and himself, 14).

According to the minutes of her interrogation, Duck's mother told József Pogácsás that her son was "an individual very susceptible to influence, I think he acts without thinking." Of course, she may well simply have been trying to save her son by offering mitigating circumstances, but she insisted that he was lonely and dangerously eager to fit in: "He never developed a fixed group of friends. He would often bring different people up to the apartment, almost every day, and introduce them as his friends, but then they never came by again. Not a single person has come looking for him since he was taken into custody [July 8, 1969]. Since he never had any permanent friends, he tried to buddy up with others, and to get them to accept him, he would do anything they suggested."[40]

Duck's mother played an active role in her son's defense. She did not accept the public defender. Unlike most of the other Great Tree young people who were brought before the court, Duck was represented not by the public defender but rather by hired counsel.[41] After he was arrested, his mother immediately began to claim that her son was crazy and that was why he had organized the infamous stroll. Presumably, she wanted this claim to be part of her son's defense so that he would be declared of unsound mind and unable to stand trial. A workplace evaluation that was written about Duck one week after he was arrested shows traces of his mother's efforts to convince the courts that her son was not of sound mind. According to the assessment, between October 19, 1968, and May 31, 1969, Duck had worked assiduously and conscientiously at the leather works company: "He was respectful to everyone and polite in his behavior. His appearance was striking because of his long hair and beard. Though the subject was broached several times, he did not change this, and then later he cut his hair off entirely." Mrs. Paul Faragó, the personnel manager who wrote the apparently well-intentioned assessment, concluded the evaluation, however, with the following observation: "According to his mother, he is a little bit mentally handicapped."[42]

Eight days later, in his report on Duck and his family life, László Szabó built on this conversation with the boy's mother. He accepted, perhaps naively, the mother's characterization of her son as mentally handicapped, and he offered a simple, linear explanation of the boy's fondness of various aberrant poses (for instance the hermit) as a consequence of the unusual circumstances of his parents:

> A young dreamer, a boy who longs for quiet and a confused sense of peace that is swirling vaguely within him, family peace and peace that embraces all of humanity. That has drawn him away on several occasions, several days away from his family, into the hills, to a little stream, the bank of a rivulet, where he could be alone, somewhere quiet, waiting for the peace that eluded him. This is an indication of some depression, which is also suggested by his mother's statement that he was born in the breech position. It would be preferable to have this examined by a physician.[43]

## POSING AS THE MADMAN: COUNTER-IDENTITY AND PSYCHIATRIC EVALUATIONS

A day after the report on Duck's family was completed, a psychologist also met with and interrogated him, although Duck later had no memory of this. It is possible that Duck did not remember the psychologist simply because the psychologist asked questions that were very similar to the questions asked by the police who interrogated him, and the police, who obviously were not on patrol, were dressed in civilian clothes, not uniforms. Thus, the psychologist hardly stood out among the group of people who besieged the boy with questions. It was the nineteenth day since Duck had been taken into custody, thus it is hardly surprising that the psychologist characterized him as anxious, adding that "in our assessment, he is in need of psychotherapeutic treatment" (of the young men who were taken into custody, Duck was the only one who, according to the psychologist, needed this "treatment"). The psychologist explained Duck's conduct as a consequence of childhood experiences. In all likelihood, he concluded that Duck had suffered from personality disorders as a child on the basis of the conversation he had with Duck's mother. In the course of this conversation, Duck's mother had revealed that in fact he had not been delivered in breech position. Rather,

> the embryo had created difficulties for the mother during the pregnancy, but at birth he was delivered in the normal position. . . . Until he turned seven, he wet his bed at night and sometimes peed in his pants during the day. At roughly one year of age, he suffered a blow to the nape of his neck when he fell. At four years of age, he pulled a gravestone onto himself in the cemetery. Neither of the two accidents caused him to lose consciousness. Earlier, he had talked and walked in his sleep without this being deliberate behavior. He was treated for high blood pressure and abnormal heart function.

According to the psychologist, these issues explained "the extremity in the development of the boy's personality," one additional factor in which, in his assessment, was the fact that Duck had been born left-handed but had been encouraged to learn to use his right hand instead.[44]

In the first court case, Duck's mother failed in her efforts to have her son declared incompetent to stand trial. The attorney for the defense simply asked that the court take into consideration, when determining the sentence, that the accused's "nerves have been strained since his parents' divorce."[45] In its sentence, the court explained Duck's vagrancy as a consequence of his parents' divorce, not his alleged mental incompetence or traumatic childhood experiences. The section of the court's ruling containing a description of the circumstances of his family essentially accepted the contentions made in the report submitted by László Szabó. Thus, according to the sentence, "the stepfather tried to compensate for the mother's conduct with strictness, Zoltán S. therefore often fled his mother and his stepfather and lived as a vagrant."[46] Judge Miklós Horányi, however, did not take this earlier offense into consideration as an aggravating circumstance. Duck's mental and emotional state, however, was also not mentioned as a mitigating circumstance.

Duck's notebook does not create the impression of a mentally incompetent adolescent, except perhaps as a pose. According to the testimony given by his peers, however, he was quite capable of doing foolish things. For instance, in his response to a question raised by his attorney, Monk made the following claim: "Duck was at the head of the procession, and he led us, he knows lots of children's songs, and he was singing them up front, we sang them in the back. I saw lots of guys who I thought were from the workers' quarters, they looked to me like people who did hard physical work, they were very tone-setting in the political exclamations."[47]

Duck often closes his musings in his notebook with comments that suggest that his embrace of the role of the madman was simply part of an adolescent's attempts to craft an identity for himself. "Only a madman could have written this," he comments, for instance (18). "Some of them eat cherries, some of them travel on [tram] number six! Where? WHY? Don't close the notebook! Hey! I am perfectly normal, just alone, alas. . . . Be normal? I try, but I can't manage to be a serious KID" (24). Duck had had experience with the institutional system for people with emotional disorders when his parents had divorced. In 1963, he had been sent to the Central Children's Mental Ward for examination because of restless sleep patterns and a tendency to awaken suddenly in the night,[48] and between 1966 and the start of the legal proceedings against him, he was being treated continuously with the drug Rausedyl.[49] Rausedyl was being widely used at the time in clinical experiments and to treat high blood pressure caused by stress, but it was later taken out of circulation because of its harmful side effects. As a sedative, it also tended to induce sleep as well as migraines,[50] and the fact that Duck was taking it may well explain why he fell asleep, from time to time, under unusual circumstances, for instance during the proceedings in court.[51]

As he continues ever more emphatically to strike this pose, he also offers a new interpretation of his decision to cut his hair. With his bald head and long beard, he comes to resemble (or at least to see himself as) an eccentric hermit: "shoe size 44, 80 kilograms, and bearded! Bald, furthermore! I'm lying down now and my stomach hurts. I ate a lot of cherries. What's your opinion? Thanks, you're right" (23).

Having found a role that seemed to work for him, Duck continued to pose as a hermit tormented by love until the end of his notebook. Whatever genre he happens to adopt from this point on in the larger narrative (vision, poem, or confession), he almost exclusively addresses Éva, even (for instance) when writing about how he adored Mick Jagger: "You like the Beatles, I dig the Rolling [Stones]. Who understands this? I do, and you?" (29–30). Duck prepared for his rendezvous on Sunday by writing, this time about his love of nature, and perhaps to impress the girl, he poses for a moment as a new leader: "Zenith of the Youth Park! If I go up, I feel like I am stepping into a cave of sin! I have cut ties with you, you fake hippies! Now I am selective with my friends, won't miss more rows, I know! I plead with you, true beatniks, stand by me, you'll do better, believe me!" (31).

The comments written on Monday (after his rendezvous on Saturday, Duck began marking the days) suggest that he had not in the meantime made any progress with the girl: "I'm sitting on the bed, chewing my nails, and yet, not like it's gonna give me any advice, so what then?" (37). Duck goes down into the streets (according to the narrative in the notebook), where he watches passers-by, for instance old people and a woman carrying her child in her arms (37–38). It starts to rain, and Duck offers a dramatic description: "Winds wuther, rains fall, the trees shake, the brooks babble. Just a few people on the streets, and they too are scurrying off" (39).

The penultimate entry in the notebook (followed by some jottings which may well have been written earlier) and also the longest single text is a verse that was clearly intended to be read as a kind of visionary poem. Given the contents and the place (Duck did not note the date), he probably began writing it Monday afternoon, the (rainy) day after his Sunday meeting. The title, "Pamir, Roof of the World, Here, Down Here, That Is," was written in a narrow strip above the lines of the poem itself, which suggests that it was penned only after Duck wrote the poem (usually, Duck left plenty of space between the title of his poems and the poems themselves). He names his sources of inspiration, Allen Ginsberg and Cream, in the poem. As a man who had acquired symbolic status as the poet of youthful rebellion, Ginsberg was a useful prop for Duck, as was the progressive rock music of the late 1960s. In the vision, Ginsberg's doctrines are rolling away in a rusty stroller while Cream's song NSU plays in the background. As Duck's confession made clear, he did not know English well enough to understand the text of the Cream song. Among the Great Tree group, he did not play the role of translator either, although he bragged about going to the English embassy.

Eventually, Duck's mother succeeded in her well-intentioned efforts to have her son declared mentally incompetent. This was not easy for her to do, but once she had persuaded the authorities to take this step, Duck himself protested in vain against the decision. The visionary poem (allegedly inspired in part by Ginsberg) thus came to be regarded as an important piece of evidence from the perspective of the boy's mental state. After the court of the first instance reached its verdict, according to the testimony given by several witnesses, Duck became more fearful and anxious, which is hardly surprising, since he had been sentenced at a relatively young, vulnerable age to fifteen months in prison. Until the court of the second instance reached its decision, Duck was released from custody, but new charges (mentioned at the beginning of this chapter) were brought against him because of his alleged involvement in the case of a girl who had escaped from an institution.

On March 5, 1970, a girl with the nickname Ancsa Hippie and friends of hers who hung out by the Great Tree tried to help one of Ancsa's friends escape from a girls' foster institution, but they were caught by the police.[52] In order to prevail on the police to release her from custody, Ancsa gave detailed testimony concerning a hippie procession that had been planned for May 1. She may well have invented the whole thing to secure her own release. On the basis of her testimony, an investigation was launched to prevent the protest under the code name "May-ers."[53] Because of the investigation, accusations of political agitation were brought against the people who had taken part in the attempt to free the girl from the foster care institution and the people "who were going to take part in the planned procession," including Duck. This time, Duck was sentenced to eight months in prison. Because of the verdict against him, the pardon he had been granted in the first case (which meant he would only have had to serve half his sentence) was rendered invalid. Thus, he had to spend a total of two years and one month in a workplace for juvenile delinquents. In practice, this meant the prison in the Juvenile Law Enforcement Institute in the city of Tököl.[54]

Duck was arrested on March 24, 1970, and on April 2, Pogácsás, who already knew the boy well, let him speak with his mother. On April 7, Pogácsás interrogated Duck, who by that time had been in pretrial custody for two weeks. Pogácsás questioned Duck's mother on April 10, and this was a turning point in the case. She seems to have managed to convince Pogácsás that her son was mentally incompetent. It is also possible, however, that Pogácsás simply let the boy go, since by this point Duck was more cooperative with the authorities and clearly had been frightened by the measures taken against him.[55]

After the interrogation, Pogácsás ordered a psychiatric examination,[56] and before the examination had been done he again interrogated Duck. After Duck had spent a month in pretrial custody, he went to his psychiatric examination knowing full well that the results of the exam would determine whether or not he would be released. Thus, it is not surprising that, as the doctors noted, "during the examination—primarily at the beginning of the examination—he is very tense, initially his whole body is shaking, his facial expression is one of terror, sometimes he starts to cry for no reason. Calming words heighten his anxiety, he protests and claims that he is not afraid, and he becomes increasingly exasperated."[57] The narrative of the diagnosis is clearly structured by the intention to present Duck's musings, anxieties, and behavior as consequences of childhood traumas.

As far as the psychologist was concerned, Duck's experiences in prison were also symptoms of his disorder: "Sometimes in the cell he has an unusual feeling, as if 'the walls were pushing in on him,' as if he were pressed between the walls. He feels this pressure and squeezing physically too, in that his head hurts and then he feels the squeezing in his chest." Duck seems to have been familiar enough with the pose of the mentally disturbed man to know that he also had to claim to hallucinate: "These days in general he has problems with his hearing, because his ears are often ringing. But this is not just ringing, but rather a sound resembling the ring of a telephone. This began when, on the occasion of the interrogation, the phone rang, and then he went back to his cell and ever since then he has heard the continuous sound of a phone ringing." Duck's blood pressure during the examination was 155/100, which is a very high reading for a person his age, but of course it may have been high because of the stress he was under.

According to the assessment, "at the moment, he suffers from a serious degree of so-called anxiety nervous disorder, which has found expression in the development of a seriously ill—schizoid—personality." And the referral he was given three days earlier, which had been stamped by the neurologist, noted that he had been given treatment in the mental ward "because of anxious neurosis and unsteady blood pressure"; for this reason, he had been referred to the metal ward in the hospital, but he ignored the referral. The doctors finally reached a decision that, ultimately, was favorable to Duck, at least as far as his prison sentence was concerned: "he requires treatment in hospital and therefore, if he should be released, the area Mental Health Care Institute should be informed." That day, the decision was reached to release Duck, because, according to the explanation given, due to "Zoltán S.'s debility,[58] his scope of action is seriously limited in recognition of the danger he poses to society."[59]

After Duck was released, the authorities immediately began to subject him to treatment in the mental ward of a hospital until the proceedings in the court of second instance began, where his defense attorney asked that he be exempted of the charges brought against him.[60] On May 4, his mother sent a letter to the court requesting that it also take into consideration the fact that, since 1963, she had been getting oncological treatment and that her cancer could not be treated by surgery: "I live from day to day and I [ask] very kindly that the Court please not lock my child up, at least not while I am still alive, which alas will not be long."[61] The court of the second instance regarded the "limited state of his mental condition, which has been determined by medical experts," as a mitigating circumstance.[62] Even the attorney who appealed the ruling acknowledged that Duck suffered from an "underdeveloped mental capacity."[63] This assessment of Duck as "insane," however, did not save him from the labor to which he was sentenced in the Juvenile Law Enforcement Institute in Tököl, since the pardon he was effectively granted was nullified by the second trial, so he had to spend his sentence in Tököl.

Because of the stroll and his arrest, Duck enjoyed considerable prestige among his peers. For instance, Big Kennedy claimed in his testimony given in the autumn of 1969 that Duck had taught him ditties and mantras: "Stop the world, I want to get off, build a separate island, for I despise people."[64] Though Duck's friends seem to have believed that he was at least a bit mad, he nonetheless probably continued to become more and more popular. According to the boy who went by the nickname "Lekvár," or "Jam," "Duck got forced medical treatment 'cause allegedly he was the intellectual leader here, they put it all on him. They shocked him, etc. They put a strong persecution complex in him. He didn't even dare meet with his best friends."[65]

## CONCLUSION

The notebook offers no clear conclusion to the love story of Duck and Éva. At least a week passed between the last entry in the notebook and the afternoon of the Hippie Stroll on which Duck went to the Great Tree and suggested to the other members of the group that they pay tribute to the memory of Brian Jones.

The last comments in the notebook suggest that his attempts to win her heart failed. At the very least, it is difficult to imagine that he wrote the remarks with the intention of passing them on to her to impress her, as they are expressive of puerile misogyny. "Man is a being rank 1," he writes, "animal is a being rank 2 / woman is a being rank 3." And he also offers an admittedly less poetic version of François Villon's lament: "Virgins! Where are you now? / where is 1 girl who has preserved her purity?" (51)

If one were to regard these remarks as the concluding passages of the entire notebook, it would of course be tempting to imagine that Duck had ended up an embittered boy who had been disappointed and disillusioned by his precious Éva. Of course, it would be prudent to keep in mind how many times he changed genres and poses in this relatively short assortment of writings. The notebook is neither a heroic epic nor a diary, nor even is it simply a book of poems. It is, rather, a hodgepodge of genres, each of which offered Duck an opportunity to dabble with new styles and try out new identities.

Duck become a figure of great prestige among his peers, though admittedly not quite in the manner he had originally envisioned in his notebook. Indeed, he had even won the respect of some of the authorities. It would be an oversimplification, however, to characterize his behavior as youthful rebellion, since the conflicts within his family were of an entirely different nature (with the exception, perhaps, of his mother's disapproval of his long hair). It is hardly uncommon for an attitude or pose created by the cultural discourses and codes in one country to be interpreted differently in another culture. In American culture, the notion of the hippie was associated with withdrawal from conventional society and criticism of consumer culture. In the city of Lvov in western Ukraine, however, it became a symbol of the national and regional rebellion against Soviet rule.[66]

The Hungarian hippies were hardly seen by their parents in the same light as they were seen by the police, the courts, or the press. Duck internalized the regime's ideas about hippies and other antiregime elements, and his adoption of the "madman" identity was also an internalized aspect of his vision of himself. Duck struck the pose of the "madman hippie," both in his narrative portraits of himself in the notebook and in front of the authorities in the course of his trial. While in the case of the notebook, presumably he chose this role in the hopes of standing out among his peers and catching Éva's eye, in the case of the poses he struck in court, he did so in the hopes of being shown mercy. By donning this role and others, however, Duck seems not so much to have been rebelling against his family as he was striving to win acknowledgment and defend himself from the whims of a punitive system.

Based on various sources, one hardly has the impression that Duck was insane or even mentally incompetent. At most, he simply chose, from among the various identities that were part of the culture of his time, the role of the visionary soothsayer of a gang (even though the very notion of the gang was a concept propagated by the organs of power under the socialist regime). An element of madness was simply one of the defining features of this figure. He then tried to use this "madness" as part of his defense. He came into genuine conflict, however, not with his parents but with the police.[67] But the authorities (the police, the prosecutor's office, the court, and the doctors) strove to explain his acts as consequences of childhood traumas, as they needed to buttress the image of the state as an entity that had a positive influence on the family and, indeed, even stepped in when the family needed assistance. They used elements of the youth countercultures that emerged in the wake of the war in these efforts, much as they used theories of socialist education and the teachings and institutions of the science of psychoanalysis.

There are no further sources on the Éva who plays such a prominent role in Duck's notebook, and the proceedings that were launched against the young people involved in the stroll were in fact launched almost entirely against boys. The documents produced in the course of the proceedings offer almost no insight into the roles played by the girls in the group. The girl who went by the nickname Ancsa Hippie is the only girl on which there are several written documents. In the next chapter, I consider her fate, the roles of the girls who were part of these groups of young people, and the ways social gender roles are discernible in their stories.

## NOTES

1. Sándor Hankóczi, "A Kiskanál és a Duna" [The Teaspoon and the Danube], *Ifjúsági Magazin*, August 1968, 13–17.

2. BFL, f. XXV-44-b, PKKB, b. 640. 9. B. 23598/1969, verdict, February 16, 1970.

3. For instance, the testimony given by József S. and Erzsébet Sz (BFL, f. XXV-44-b, PKKB, f. 640. D, 21201/1971, József H. and associate, 14, FK (fiatalkorú [juvenile (under 18)], 30963 dossier, combined with 9.B. 23598/1969, József H. and associate, 31–32, 37–39). The testimony given by Erzsébet Sz. is questionable since her sibling was involved in the case. According to the testimony given by Péter Bognár, who had reported the kids to the police, Duck had been the person among them "who had arranged the rows and had urged them to keep up." He gave this testimony roughly ten weeks after the event on the basis of a photograph (ibid., 47).

4. The testimony given by Lajos Sz., or "Marcsello" (who was interrogated as a witness), also suggests this. Though according to several testimonies he was at the head of the procession, he was not found guilty of any wrongdoing (BFL, f. XXV-44-b, PKKB, f. 640. D, 21201/1971, József H. and associate, 41–42).

5. A size A4 spiral notebook with a brown cover and with notes and text on fifty-one pages (BFL, f. XXV-44-b, PKKB, b. 640, 21201/1971, included in the materials of the investigation as evidence).

6. See Hellbeck, *Revolution on My Mind*, 4–5.

7. Patterson, *Bought and Sold*, 57.

8. According to Duck's testimony, he worked there until June 2, 1969, but according to the workplace assessment, he only worked there until May 31.

9. ÁSZTL, 3.1.9, V-158094/1, Sz. Gyula és társai [Gyula Sz. and his associates], 57, report on the family circumstances of Duck, July 26, 1969; BFL, f. XXV-44-b, PKKB, f. 640. b. 21201/1971, József H. and associate, 14, FK, 30963 dossier, combined 9.B.23598/1969, József H. and associate, 205–11. For the data regarding the average salary in 1969, see Központi Statisztikai Hivatal, *Gazdaságilag aktívak bruttó átlagkeresete*.

10. Criminal idleness had been punishable by law since 1913. In 1950, the notion was changed according to the Soviet model (Kocsis, "Büntessük-e a közveszélyes munkakerülést?"). When they apprehended the Great Tree kids, the police usually justified their acts with the claim that the young people did not have registered places of employment.

11. I use parenthesis in the main text of this chapter and the footnotes to indicate the page numbers on which citations from Duck's notebook can be found.

12. The two spiral notebooks that were seized from Monk's belongings are among the evidence in the materials of the investigation against the Great Tree Gang in the first round of proceedings. These personal sources ended up in the archives because they were considered official documents (and used as evidence in the trial) (BFL, f. XXV-44-b, PKKB, b. 641, 21201/1971).

13. BFL, f. XXV-44-b, PKKB, Gyula Sz. and associates, minutes of the proceedings, February 4, 1970, 9; ibid., 54.468/1969/7, sz. indictment, 4.

14. Ibid., minutes of the proceedings, February 4, 1970, 14.

15. Sándor Hankóczi, "A Kiskanál és a Duna" [The Teaspoon and the Danube], *Ifjúsági Magazin*, August 13–17, 1968.

16. *Ifjúsági Magazin*, August 14, 1968, 13–17.

17. According to Bedecs, this van was used at the time by the police in the raids conducted as part of their alleged efforts to protect young people (interview with Éva Bedecs, February 4, 2005).

18. BFL, f. XXV-44-b, PKKB, b. 640, 9. B. 23598/1969, Gyula Sz. and associates, minutes of the proceedings, testimony given by Lord Blondie, February 3, 1970, 11.

19. Katsiaficas, *Imagination of the New Left*, 124. On the relationship between the hippie movement and the new left-wing ideology, see Marcuse, *New Left and the 1960s*.

20. "Diákmozgalmak Nyugaton" [Student movements in the West], *Népszabadság*, February 4, 1969, 6; February 12, 1969, 6. For instance, "There were intense clashes in Berkeley in California," *Népszabadság*, February 6, 1969, 2; *Népszabadság*, February 19, 1969, 6.

21. Ivanics István, "Hippik a körúton" [Hippies on the boulevard], *Magyar Ifjúság*, June 21, 1968, 3.

22. ÁSZTL, O-13708, "Májusiak" [May-ers], February 13, 1970, 31–32.

23. Duck writes about this on the twelfth page of the notebook, but the psychological assessment of him that was done one year later also offers an account of the event. According to the testimony he gave on July 9, 1969, the day after the stroll, when he was being placed (i.e., incarcerated) in the Division for the Protection of Adolescents and Children of the Budapest Police Headquarters, he had cut off his hair one month earlier (ÁSZTL, V-158094/1, Sz. Gyula és társai [Gyula Sz. and his associates], 57).

24. "Tiszta szívvel" [With a pure heart], Babelmatrix, accessed June 11, 2020, https://www.babelmatrix.org/works/hu/J%C3%B3zsef_Attila-1905/Tiszta_sz%C3%ADvvel/en/1793-With_a_pure_heart.

25. The poem, the line divisions of which are reproduced here in the English translation, is on the sixth page of the notebook.

26. BFL, f. XXV-44-b, PKKB, b. 640, 9. B. 23598/1969, minutes of the proceedings, February 4, 1970, 15.

27. Éva Bedecs, "A 'Nagyfák' sem nőnek az égig" [Even the "Great Trees" don't grow to reach the sky], *Magyar Ifjúság*, February 20, 1970, 4–5.

28. BFL, f. XXV-44-b, PKKB, f. 640. D, 21201/1971, József H. and associate, verdict in the first instance, 14–15.

29. Ibid., 16.

30. For a summary of these quasi debates, see Pótó, "A kommunizmus ígérete," 26–29; Mink, "Kesudió."

31. BFL, f. XXV-44-b, PKKB, Gyula Sz. and associates, minutes of the proceedings, February 4, 1970, 7.

32. Ibid., workplace assessment.

33. See Apor, Clifford, and Townson, "Faith," 211.

34. BFL, f. XXV-44-b, PKKB, f. 640. D, 21201/1971, József H. and associate, József H. and associate, report on the family circumstances, July 26, 1969, 205.

35. BFL, f. XXV-44-b, PKKB, b. 616, 21054/70, psychiatric examination, July 27, 1969, 242–47.

36. BFL, f. XXV-44-b, PKKB, f. 640. D, 21201/1971, József H. and associate, report on the family circumstances. July 26, 1969, 207.

37. BFL, f. XXV-44-b, PKKB, b. 640, 9. B. 23598/1969, testimony given by Gyula Sz. in the course of the examination. October 22, 1969, 69–73.

38. Interview with Gyula Sz., nickname "Big Kennedy," March 24, 2009.

39. BFL, f. XXV-44-b, PKKB, b. 640, 9. B. 23598/1969, report on the family circumstances, July 26, 1969, 209.

40. BFL, f. XXV-44-b, PKKB, b. 616, 21054/70, 237, minutes of the hearing of witnesses, April 10, 1970.

41. "Zoltán S.'s mother asked me not even to inform the public defense attorney, because she would not allow the public defender to represent her son. She would find an attorney and send the letter of authorization to the Prosecutor's Office." BFL, f. XXV-44-b, PKKB, f. 640. D, 21201/1971, József H. and associate (memorandum, September 30, 1969, 57).

42. Ibid., workplace assessment for the division for the Protection of Adolescents and Children of the Budapest Police Headquarters, July 16, 1969, 217.

43. Ibid., report on the family circumstances,. July 26, 1969, 209.

44. Ibid., psychiatric examination of Zoltán S. July 27, 1969, 173–75.

45. BFL, f. XXV-44-b, PKKB, Gyula Sz. and associates, minutes of the proceedings, VIII. r. defense attorney for the accused Zoltán S. Gyula Sz. and associates, minutes of the proceedings, February 16, 1970, 2.

46. BFL, f. XXV-44-b, PKKB, b. 640, 9. B. 23598/1969, 7, Gyula Sz. and associates, verdict in the first instance. The reasoning here is similar to the reasoning found in the report on the circumstances of Duck's family (. BFL,

f. XXV-44-b, PKKB, f. 640. D, 21201/1971, József H. and associate, report on the family circumstances, July 26, 1969, 207).

47. BFL, f. XXV-44-b, PKKB, Gyula Sz. and associates, minutes of the proceedings, minutes of the proceedings, testimony given József H., February 6, 1970, 8.

48. BFL, f. XXV-44-b, PKKB, f. 640. D, 21201/1971, József H. and associate, psychological examination, July 27, 1969, 173.

49. BFL, f. XXV-44-b, PKKB, 616. d, 21054/1970, Jenő S. and associate, psychiatric report and Opinion, April 23, 1970, 246.

50. Iványi, "Gondok a magasvérnyomás-betegség kezelésében."

51. BFL, f. XXV-44-b, PKKB, 23598/1969, Gyula Sz. and associates, petition submitted by Defense Attorney Zoltán Glück, April 16, 1970.

52. BFL, f. XXV-44-b, PKKB, b. 616, 21054/1970, Imre E. and associates. I touch on the girl's attempted escape in detail in the chapter on Ancsa Hippie.

53. ÁSZTL, O-13708, "Májusiak" [May-ers], 4–5.

54. BFL, f. XXV-44-b, PKKB, b. 616, 21054/1970, Imre E. and associates, verdict, September 23, 1970, 6.

55. BFL, f. XXV-44-b1, PKKB, f. XXV-41, 616. d, 21054/1970, Jenő S. and associate, minutes of the hearing of witness Mrs. János F., April 10, 1969. 235–37.

56. Ibid., 244–45.

57. BFL, f. XXV-44-b, PKKB, 616. d, 21054/1970, Jenő S. and associate, psychiatric report and opinion, April 23, 1970, 246–51.

58. The passage in the Hungarian text contains both grammatical and spelling mistakes, which perhaps is a sign of the lack of attention to detail in these kinds of cases.

59. BFL, f. XXV-44-b, PKKB, 616. d, 21054/1970, Jenő S. and associate, 267–68. In all likelihood, Pogácsás wrote the word *debilitas*, misspelled in the original Hungarian and translated here as "debility" in the text. However, this term is a bit inappropriate, given its derogatory tone, in this official document. This suggests that the text was probably written by Pogácsás.

60. BFL, f. XXV-44-b, PKKB, b. 640, 9. B. 23598/1969, Gyula Sz. and associates, minutes of the proceedings, May 15, 1970.

61. Ibid., letter by Mrs. János F. May 4, 1970.

62. BFL, f. XXV-44-b, PKKB, Budapest Court as the Court of Second Instance verdict number 1330/1970/44, May 25, 1970, 7; BFL, f. XXV-44-b, PKKB, b. 616, 21054/1970, Imre E. and associates.

63. BFL, f. XXV-44-b, PKKB, b. 616, 21054/1970, Imre E. and associates, VIII. 10.601/1970, appeal, July 15, 1970.

64. BFL, f. XXV-44-b, PKKB, b. 641, 21201/1971, Gyula Sz. and associates, 221-Bü-144/69. B, dossier 75, testimony of Gyula Sz., October 22, 1969, Gyula Sz. and associates.

65. Recollections of Jam in the film Kresalek, *A vízüzemű Moszkvics utasai.*

66. Risch, "Soviet 'Flower Children.'"

67. In the case of the boys who had been in institutes (for instance, Big Kennedy, Lord Blondie, Prince, and Doxa), the idea that they were rebelling against their families can hardly be raised as an explanation of their conduct, since their families had essentially given up on them (which is why they were in institutions).

EIGHT

# GIRL IN THE GANG

"AND THEN SHE SAID THAT, as a fan of the OMEGA band, she took part regularly in the band's events, where she met with the members of the gang. As she said, in the institution they were given a chance to go out three times a week. Of late, she has only taken advantage of the chance to leave on Sundays." These remarks, a negative characterization of Anna R., are from notes taken by policeman István Bereczki in Budapest on March 3, 1970, four days before Anna's seventeenth birthday. The text seems credible, given that Anna, whose friends usually referred to her as "Anna Hippie" or "Ancsa Hippie" (a Hungarian diminutive, similar to Annie; as this is the name she was known by among her friends, I use the diminutive in this text), did not go to church on Sundays but rather to rock concerts.[1] She was called into the Political Division of the Budapest Police Headquarters because the police sought to establish a "social contact"—in other words, a secret informant—with the members of the Great Tree Gang who were not in jail in early 1970.

Why were the police interested in a girl who was barely seventeen years of age? Why was the policeman investigating the case able to get along so well with the girl's father, at least on the basis of the records of their conversations? In this chapter, I examine how the communist political police coded and decoded the conflicts between parents and their children in the case of the family of one teenage girl and how a family dispute acquired political meaning. I argue that the rebellion of a teenage girl against her parents and their norms could be interpreted officially also as a revolt against the socialist system. However, this case acquired political significance only because of the intervention of the political police.

According to the police report, Bereczki sought out Ancsa because of her broad network of social ties and because in the trial of one of the ringleaders of the gang, "Indian" (András F.), she had been summoned as a witness on February 25 and had proven compliant when giving testimony. This was why the investigating officer advised that the police "concern themselves with her." The officer in the Political Division regarded Ancsa as sincere, so he suggested that they take advantage of her network of relationships. Three days after Bereczki's report, his boss, police lieutenant József Fülöp, wrote, "Close ties must be kept with her. She must be interrogated and reared, later she can be recruited [as an informer]."[2] The next day Ancsa spent her birthday in jail under remand.

Appearances notwithstanding, Fülöp's desire to, in his words, "rear" Ancsa was not the reason why she was held. Others had already tried to rear her, although when they had had to report on their efforts to the police or the public prosecutor, they had always emphasized their failure to influence her and their own blamelessness. Ancsa was constantly running away, from her parents, from the reformatory school, from the gang, and from the police. The linking of the struggle against mass culture and antifascist discourse, which was a kind of mobilizing force for communist parties in Eastern Europe for decades,[3] acquired new meaning in the police accounts of Ancsa's story.

Six weeks later, after Easter (which Ancsa also spent under remand), her father was called in to give testimony in his daughter's case. Police lieutenant József Pogácsás was an old acquaintance of the youths who hung out at the Great Tree. According to Pogácsás, the police were investigating Ancsa in connection with a criminal case against Jenő S. (referred to as "Midget") and his associates on the suspicion of incitement. The interrogation was held on April 23 in room 14 of the police headquarters in Lajos Tolnai Street, which was infamous for the use of brutal interrogation techniques. Ancsa, who on the basis of her earlier testimony had been entirely broken, had already been interrogated in the same room a month earlier. Pogácsás indicated that as a close relative, her father, who was probably appropriately frightened, was not obliged to give evidence against his daughter but was obliged to describe her character, the conditions in which she had been raised, and her intellectual development. He did as he was asked. He contended that he had learned of Ancsa's case in the course of the interrogation, and so he recounted what he knew of Ancsa's life and relationships to Pogácsás, who was curious to hear every detail.[4]

What role could a teenage girl play in these processes? Women and girls are rarely mentioned in police reports on gangs. During the period in which the police and public relations campaigns against the so-called Hungarian youth gangs (galerik) were underway (roughly between 1960 and 1975), women never constituted more than 20 percent of the gangs under surveillance in the course of any given police investigation, and there were some gangs that did not have any female members at all. The documents make mention of one "girls gang," which was identified as a gang simply because the wardens in a girls' foster institution claimed to have discovered a group among the residents in the institution that was organized according to a principles that resembled the police concept of a gang.[5]

According to the secondary literature, youth subcultures for women offered a kind of liberation from traditional norms (represented by family) but also conformity through socialization to the norms of a youth subculture.[6] This was a highly important starting point for the personal identifications of girls, so for Ancsa the "imagined gang'" could have meant a new way of not merely finding symbolic expression but also representing independence from her family.

In the public discourses of the 1960s, what functions did the depictions of young women and teenage girls who were described for various reasons by the police or the media as gang members actually have? Why was Ancsa regarded as "rebellious"? What kinds of gender stereotypes did they use when characterizing her and why? How did the existing images affect the ways in which she was identified (including by herself)? In order to understand her motivations better, one should begin by learning a bit about her family.

## PARENTING NORMS

Ancsa's father, Richárd R., who was forty when the police investigation began, was born to a "working-class family" in Pesterzsébet, which was a working-class town, and since 1950 a district of Budapest inhabited mostly by industrial workers. On March 7, 1953, two days after the death of Stalin, Richárd and his wife Anna's daughter, named after her mother, was born. According to his daughter, Richárd did not simply content himself with the prospect of spending the rest of his life next to the milling cutter. First, he became a technical inspector;[7] then, according to the official presentence report, he became a draughtsman in a factory.[8] While he made a decent living given the conditions at the time, nonetheless he struggled, unsuccessfully, to climb the ladder at his workplace. His monthly salary of HUF 2,200 (the average salary at the time) was just over half his wife's salary; she was working at the time as a chief accountant at a new "cooperative of service providers" for HUF 4,000 a month.[9] When Ancsa was ten years old, her brother was born. He was named after his father. When she was taken into custody, he was in kindergarten.

Richárd would go to kindergarten in the afternoons to get his son, since his shift lasted from 6:00 a.m. to 2:00 p.m. His wife only had to be at work from 8:00 a.m. until 4:00 p.m., but according to the presentence report, she often came home at 7:00 or 8:00 p.m. According to Mrs. József Nagy, the author of the presentence report (sergeant of the Juvenile and Children's Welfare Division of the Budapest Police Headquarters), "she paid little attention to her children, referring to the stresses of her job and her long shifts, as well as her distant workplace." It took her more than an hour to get to her workplace, which was in the town of Szentendre, on the western bank of the Danube to the north of Budapest. Sergeant Nagy looked more leniently on the older Richárd than she did the younger: "[the father] signed his absentee notes from school and the reprimands. The child took advantage of this, saying that his dad would take care of the problems that arose because of his various misdeeds."[10] Nagy reproached the mother for devoting herself more to her work than to her children. While this contention must have been based on little more than hearsay, given the expectations placed on women, it constituted a particularly harsh condemnation. In contrast, the father won praise for spending time with the children, regardless of how this time was spent. When Nagy learned of Richárd's habit of drinking to excess, she attributed it to exaggerated submissiveness. According to Nagy's portrayal of the family, the untraditional division of labor was one of the reasons why the girl had strayed down the wrong path. In principle, the socialist state supported women's emancipation and the entry of women into the workforce, but according to this police report, the fact that a mother worked overtime had a destructive effect on the family. According to Lynne Haney, "all sorts of men voiced such complaints in this period" and "also blamed their wives' work lives for general marital tensions and childrearing difficulties."[11]

By the time Ancsa was placed under remand, the family lived in Angyalföld, a working-class district in Budapest mentioned in earlier chapters that had been inundated with the housing projects characteristic of the Eastern Bloc. On the seventh floor of a cooperative building, they had a three-bedroom apartment equipped with all the amenities available at the time. The parents had a combined salary of more than HUF 6,000 a month, much more than the average, and their apartment contained multiuse furniture and household appliances. Nagy, who spoke with other residents in the building, discovered that they were relatively withdrawn people; they befriended no one and did little more than exchange perfunctory greetings. Apparently, they quarreled a great deal. According to Nagy and the residents of the building, they often argued because the father frequently drank to excess. The rumors about their behavior and the father's drinking habits, not to mention the daughter's practice of running away, suggest that the conflicts may have led to violence. This, of course, does not mean that such things didn't come to pass among their neighbors too, but the police did not have to draw up reports on them.

According to Jenő S., Pogácsás launched the investigation into Ancsa and her family, during which Ancsa was placed under remand out of spite, because proceedings against the members of the gang at the beginning of February had not gone as he had expected them to.[12] Richárd told Pogácsás that until August 1969, his daughter had lived with her parents, and he mentioned that they had enrolled her in the Árpád Grammar school in Óbuda; however, their efforts notwithstanding, he emphasized, the girl's fate was in her hands. According to the record, he noted that "she failed three subjects, so she abandoned her grammar school studies, and since she wanted to study to be a hairdresser, I let her pursue that."

According to both her father and the hairdressers' cooperative, Ancsa completed her training with zeal, and no objections were raised to her work as a trainee.[13] Her father contended that the fact that she had worked in alternating shifts had led to her ruin, since it had been impossible to supervise her in the afternoons. According to this logic, childrearing is a matter of continual oversight. But they could not supervise Ancsa's every minute, "so she was more likely to mix with an undesirable group of people." And an "undesirable group of people," in the assessment of Pogácsás and Ancsa's father, could ruin everything.

According to her father, Ancsa had gradually slipped out of her parents' control: "in the winter of 1968–69, it happened on occasion, though still only sporadically, that she would be gone for 8 to 10 hours at a time without telling anyone. Sometimes she didn't spend the night at home. When we called her to account, she gave unacceptable explanations." Richárd also found it incomprehensible that when he attempted to be stricter, he encountered more resistance.

On Easter Monday 1969, Ancsa vanished for five days. Her father reported her disappearance to the police and the police issued a warrant for her arrest. Richárd explained to Pogácsás that he had taken her back into the family home in part because she had threatened to commit suicide if he didn't. According to Richárd, in June, at the beginning of the summer vacation, he again had needed to report her missing to the police. Eight days later, the police had found her and returned her to her father. He recounted the most recent incident to Pogácsás, omitting, however, some of the less savory details: "In June 1969 she again disappeared, and she was taken into custody roughly three weeks later in Siófok. She had spent the three weeks at Lake Balaton in the company of other youths her age. Because of her disappearances, at my request she was admitted to the girls' reformatory school at 25 Villám Street in the 8th district of Budapest on August 1, 1969." None of the people involved in the investigation showed any surprise or outrage at Richárd's response to his daughter's conduct, a response prompted by anger and shame. It does not seem to have occurred to anyone that Ancsa might have learned aggressive patterns of behavior at home, before beginning to hang out with the gang.

Magda Berkó, one of the instructors in the reformatory school, noted in her assessment of the family that Richárd had failed to mention important details to Pogácsás: "On July 10, 1969, Ancsa had broken into her parents' apartment in their absence, forced open locked cabinets, and sold stolen items to the pawnshop. . . . She had sexual relations with the boys in the group and got a sexually transmitted disease."[14] Ancsa later confessed that she had taken a bottle of spirits and a silver cup from her parents.[15] The family dispute slipped out from under the control of the family itself and from then on became part of the bureaucratic process.

According to Nagy's presentence report, the father gave up on his daughter when the police physician determined that she did indeed have a sexually transmitted disease.[16] According to the decision regarding her admittance to the reformatory school, dated July 30, 1969, "the parents refused to take the youth back into their custody with the contention that, because of her repeated disappearances, they could not ensure her proper moral upbringing. Since the youth has completely slipped out from under parental control and her further upbringing is not ensured, for moral reasons it is necessary to place her in an institution."[17]

Richárd attempted to make excuses for his daughter to Pogácsás, assigning responsibility for her conduct to others while offering a positive portrayal of his intentions as a conscientious parent: "The child is very close to her father in nature, the relationship between me and my daughter was very understanding. This kind of good relationship could not develop between my daughter and my wife because of my wife's nervous temperament." Thus, Richárd also explained his daughter's conduct as a consequence, at least in part, of his wife's character. In the secondary literature on the social lives of youths, one of the typical distinctions that is drawn between the social lives of girls and boys is the contention that girls tend to form friendships at home, whereas boys form friendships away from home. Thus, if a girl makes friends on the street, this in and of itself can be deemed improper.[18]

As is often the case when the person in a relationship who is in control provides a characterization, Richárd (like most of the other people who sought to rear Ancsa) portrayed her as lacking independence and unable to make

Figure 8.1. Juvenile court: "Adults shall leave the room before discussing erotic details!" (*Ludas Matyi*, April 24, 1969).

decisions: "I wish to note that she is very susceptible to influence, whether good or bad." According to sergeant Nagy, "she committed criminal acts because her peers at the institution took the girl, who is very susceptible to influence, with them." It is conceivable that Ancsa's independent tendencies found expression in her continuous resistance to the harsh measures and behavior to which she was subjected. In other words, her rebellious gestures themselves can be seen as forms of resistance. The female roles she was given in the texts were also products of the stereotypes that circulated in the press at the time regarding girls who hung out in public spaces.

## ANCSA'S CASE: CHALLENGING GENDER ROLES?

What did it mean for a girl to be a hippie at that time? "'Cause on the street it's the height of falsehood, the whole 'it's a pleasure to be a textile worker, hauling crates is a joy' thing. So that's crap. I'm telling you, being a hippie, that's the real thing, you're only alive if you're enjoying life." This was the reply given by Vera Gy., a young girl who was hanging out in an underpass when, in 1969, she was asked to say what freedom meant to her by a journalist working for *Magyar Ifjúság*. "It means I don't have to go to school," she continued, "and don't have to work, because I am bored to death of both, that I can hang out with the guys when I feel like it. And don't look at me like that, don't think I mean what grownups always think we mean, 'cause they think we hippies are always sleeping with one another."[19]

Initially, Ancsa was brought to the police for questioning because she had taken part in an escape from an institution for girls that had been organized by gang members, but given the exigencies faced by the police, the simple conflict was soon transformed into a political issue. A special airing of *Blue Light* was held in which an account of her escape was given. Ancsa allegedly had been the leader of the hooligans, many of whom had been several years older than she: "The hooligans had rampaged through the rooms at the institution, breaking and shattering things as they went, lifting bedside tables into the air and throwing them to the ground, tearing articles of clothing, breaking open cabinets." As is often the case in accounts that are intended to provoke panic among the public, comparisons were drawn with natural disasters. According to the testimony of witnesses that was given in the course of the police investigation, however, the young boys had not rampaged through the rooms. Rather, they had behaved as if they had felt "at home," as if they had known many of the girls already. There is also no mention of anything resembling the description in the report of girls sprawling on the floor, beaten, their heads bleeding. By offering a depiction of the violence allegedly used by the youths, the police, who themselves resorted to violence, justified the measures they took.

The head of the reformatory school, Magda Berkó, who "worried" about Ancsa, requested the police's assistance in the interests of helping educate and raise the girls. According to her account, in which she presents herself as blameless (since Ancsa had been a "degenerate" child before coming to the school), she attempts to shift responsibility for the whole affair onto others by transforming Ancsa's story into a police story. The escapade provided a perfect pretext to turn the story of Ancsa's conflicts with her family and then at the reformatory school into a narrative of police intervention. In her account of Ancsa's story, contained in the characterization she provided for the police on May 6, the aforementioned Magda Berkó contends that Ancsa was simply impossible to instruct, as demonstrated by the fact that she had run away from home three times, broken into her parents' apartment, and had regularly run away from the reformatory school as well. She was not simply "bad"; she also corrupted others with her tales:

> She familiarized our children with the laws of the gang. "Frici was the boss, she was his lover, but there were completely different rules than any religion has ever had, etc." Our pupils refer to her as the "hippie," and the police do too.... She is completely uninhibited in her sex life, in accordance with the rules of the gang. She drinks to excess; she has presumably also used illegal drugs. In her torpor, she was in a state of complete ecstasy. She called this "hippie delirium." She had a very bad influence on the other pupils, who admired her, were amazed by her, and were scandalized by her too. For instance, Erzsébet L.[20]

Berkó makes no mention whatsoever of the possibility that others, in addition to Ancsa, might have played a role in her conduct. Ancsa is presented in the text as an adult who bears responsibility for all her acts. The principal instrument of instruction was punishment, which included confinement and isolation from the world outside.

Ancsa was first brought in for interrogation as a person of interest on March 23, 1970, one month before her father was questioned.[21] It was noted, as an identifying feature, that she had a tattoo on her right wrist that read, "LORD." This tattoo might have served as a means of expression for Ancsa of her place in society. "Lord" was a common nickname among her peers, but it is still possible that Ancsa got the tattoo because of her first boyfriend in the gang.

In the course of the interrogation, Pogácsás probably did not need to strike or yell at Ancsa to frighten her, as she had been in remand for more than two weeks. First, he made her tell them the story of her life; then he began to badger her with questions about the alleged hippie procession (the stroll). Ancsa's name came up as a potential candidate for recruitment because of the police's version of the procession story; however, later it proved more useful to fashion a witness out of her. The two weeks spent in remand at the Tolnai Street police headquarters were enough for Ancsa to resolve to save herself. She made the following statement to Pogácsás:

> As far as I recall, it was about a month ago that I met with Tibor K. and two guys I didn't know in the EMKE underpass. Erzsébet L. was with me too. Tibor K. said that they were organizing a procession for May 1, 1970. Tibor K. said that the members of the EMKE gang would march to Nagyfa with placards reading, "Long live EMKE!" There they would join the members of the Great Tree Gang. He also said that they were planning to do something in the summer like what the Lords [other members of the gang] had done, but not totally political.

Thus, Ancsa invented details about a new hippie march. It was very common for secret police to coerce testimony about arrestees' intentions (testimony that was then almost impossible to disprove) rather than past events (testimony that can be disproved). The relationship between Ancsa and her case officer was similar to the relationship between a teacher and a pupil, at least from the perspective of the testimony. She has taught to report what was expected from her.[22]

Pogácsás even asked Ancsa to come up with the texts that would be on the placards (based on the model of the official procession held every May 1) to make the whole story more believable: "placards have to be made for the procession with the following: 'Long live Kennedy, Love the Lord, We are waiting for your Return Lord Blondie and Big Kennedy, Make beds not bombs, Love live hippies, virginity is a luxury, Independence! Russians go home, Bread without work, Free love.'" The invented slogans were not merely intended to convey the official images that had been fashioned of the Great Tree Gang (led by Kennedy and Lord Blondie) but also to echo and reinforce characterizations of hippies and hippie mantras that were printed in the journals *Magyar Rendőr* and later *Magyar Ifjúság.* To serve the interests of the political subdivision, the slogans included the 1956 calls-to-arms as well, such as "Russians go home." Ancsa was inventive enough to include details such as who would get the boards and who would paint them (someone who, according to her, "can paint beautifully"). An attachment to Western mass culture was a simple financial conflict within the family, but at the reformatory school, it became a corrupting influence; at the police station, it acquired the dimensions of a political conflict.

At the trial, Ancsa's father explained that he had not allowed Ancsa to return to her parents' home because "she has a younger sibling, I will not take her home, I will turn her over to an institution, and there they will keep a tight hand on her."[23] The psychologist issued an expert's opinion on Ancsa after having met with only her father. Because of "transportation difficulties," the so-called psychological examination took place at the police station. The psychologist soon arrived at the opinion that all of Ancsa's problems stemmed "first and foremost from her mother's mistake, who it seems did not place due emphasis on the importance of the development of gentle, sensitive emotional contact with her daughter." The psychologist was the first person, however, to explain Ancsa's conduct not simply as a consequence of the influence of American culture and her gang member acquaintances but also of the fact that her parents had turned her away and had had her admitted to a state institution. The report noted, "The parents bear considerable responsibility for their child."[24]

In the indictment, the prosecuting attorney moved that Ancsa be sentenced to confinement at a disciplinary workplace.[25] On July 15, 1970, the court sentenced her to confinement for one year to be spent at a workplace for juvenile offenders for her participation in the alleged escape from the institution (though not a single girl had actually fled the institution). At the lawyer's request, on November 5, 1970, the court of second instance ordered Ancsa's release. Thus, in the end she spent six months in a reformatory school and eight months under remand or in prison. According to the petition, which bears her signature, the first argument in support of her release was simply that "the contention according to which, given my earlier conduct, there is a risk of recidivism is incorrect. My father has taken the necessary steps at the Court of Guardians to bring my stay at the reformatory school to an end."[26] Thus, Ancsa's father had agreed to take her back, but this is not why she was released from prison, much as her participation in the alleged escape from the institution was not why she was imprisoned in the first place. Rather, they released her because they needed her as an informant. The police sought to present the activities in which the groups of young people engaged not simply as occasional gatherings but rather as parts of a linear process leading toward a clear culmination. Thus, the police needed informants from the so-called gangs to be able to craft stories that provided causal explanations of one misdeed as the consequence of some earlier bad influence.

Ancsa was released because she gave testimony against her peers and became a police informant. After her release, Ancsa again "offered her assistance" to police sublieutenant István Bereczki, who classified her as a social contact.

As such, Ancsa was given neither a codename (in the texts she is referred to by her initials) nor any kind of allocation. She had to give oral testimony, usually against the important gang members who were being released at the same time she was: Big Kennedy and his narrower circle. Ancsa was valuable to the authorities because of her ties to Big Kennedy, since they saw this as a chance to transform the unconventional behavior of young people into a political issue. Also, the police were pressured to produce cases with political implications and overtones.

Following the second case, which was referred to by the codename "The May-ers," a third state security dossier was opened on the Great Tree Gang in the fall of 1971 by police major Imre Seres containing Ancsa's reports. Drawing on her accounts, Seres claimed, "We have information from many sources indicating that the members of the various gangs in the capital, together with university students, are planning a major anti-Soviet and anti-socialist protest on October 23, 1971, the 15th anniversary of the counterrevolution [the official name of the 1956 uprising against the Soviet rule]. Having taken into account that the police will be exercising larger than usual oversight, they are planning to conduct their disturbance of the peace not on October 23, but rather on October 6, the anniversary of the execution of the Martyrs of Arad" (the Martyrs of Arad were the thirteen Hungarian generals who had fought in the revolution and War of Independence of 1848–49 against the Habsburgs; they were executed in the city of Arad, today in Romania, on October 6, 1849). On the basis of Ancsa's reports, Seres considered Big Kennedy one of the principal instigators.[27]

Citing her parents' strict oversight, Ancsa told the police that she could only meet with the members of the gang to which she had once belonged on weekends.[28] In late January 1971, she submitted a report in which she recounted how she had met with Big Kennedy at a concert of the Vanderersz (Wanderers) band at the factory cultural center. According to the report, "he doesn't want to work, he is a believer in Western freedom of speech and hippie ideals" (as if this were new information).[29] In June 1971, roughly two years after the Hippie Stroll, she provided information that seemed important to Bereczki. She said that Big Kennedy had come to her apartment on several occasions looking for her: "He had neglected his appearance, he was disheveled. He does not have a job, he is not living at his registered address, he crashes at friends' places. . . . He is planning to get a group of guys and girls together and teach them to live according to hippie ideals. He asked me to help him get the group together, but I refused."[30]

The summary report on the case makes clear that the police had a new goal in mind. They needed a pretext to be able to increase their presence on March 15, 1972, when there would be a commemoration of the revolution of 1848–49.[31] Tremendous preparations were made by the organs of state security in the days leading up to March 15. Consequently, when the day came, there were many disturbances on which the Ministry of Interior prepared separate reports for the leaders of the communist party, and the case was discussed at a sitting of the Political Committee on April 6, 1972. Eighty-eight people were arrested.[32] From that year on, March 15 was regarded as a dangerous day from the perspective of state security.

## CONCLUSION

By that time, Ancsa had turned eighteen, and she no longer figured as a social contact in the third dossier. She was let go, as she had done her duty. In the meantime, however, as a consequence of the measures taken by the state security organs, the Great Tree Gang and its members had become symbols of national radicalism. As they had intended all along, the police were able to characterize the protest as a rowdy gathering of fascist hooligans that they had been able to prevent, thereby defending the property and safety of law-abiding citizens.

Even forty years later, Big Kennedy did not know that Ancsa had secretly reported on him. According to him, the authorities always tried to recruit people who had been in prison upon their release, so what had taken place in Ancsa's case may have been quite common. They had tried to recruit him as well, but he had not wanted to cooperate with the secret police; instead, he had been kept under police surveillance. This meant, for instance, that he had to report to the police once a month, and they would regularly search his domicile. Big Kennedy had run into Ancsa on the street a few years before I spoke with him of the reports she had made. They had embraced, and Ancsa had informed him that in the meantime she had married and had children. After Big Kennedy's release from prison, Ancsa had been the first person to inform against him, and it was in part because of her reports that he had ended up back in prison. He said he was not angry with her: "She must settle her accounts with herself. Ancsa must have had a reason, something that they used to force her. I'm sure she didn't submit reports because she wanted to, rather they forced her, and not everyone was able to withstand this."[33]

In the parlance of the state bureaucracy, Ancsa's rebellion against her parents and their norms was an indication of her fondness for mass culture, a conflict that could (only) be solved with the intervention of the police. As far as the police were concerned, the story was one of political struggle, while for the girl it was one of constant flight. Ancsa's case acquired political significance because of the intervention of the political police. The public discourse on mass culture, however, made other, divergent forms of expression of political participation possible. Society did not become apolitical. Rather, new political symbols emerged, such as rock music, hairstyles, and clothing, and even gender roles acquired new political significance.

According to the official discourse, consumer habits that were based on Western models (consumer habits that, in the 1960s, were increasingly accepted) spread among the youth circles first, especially among young consumers of popular culture, so this attraction to the culture of the West could be represented as a generational disease. The fight against the new consumer culture had numerous functions, one of the most important of which was to strengthen the discursive opposition between the socialist and capitalist value systems, collectivism and individualism, and the cultures of the younger and the older generations. With the acceptance of the new consumer habits, however, the youth cultures of the 1960s gradually came to harmonize with the new value system known as refrigerator socialism or consumer socialism, and later the notion of youth culture or subculture largely lost its significance as a form or threat of resistance or opposition. But at this point, a family conflict could still be represented as a political one, and a woman who in fact was fighting against the control of her father could be depicted as a lone warrior seeking to undermine the state and communism.

How did the various stories of the Great Tree Gang survive in collective cultural memory in Hungary? How did these stories begin to acquire new meanings and connotations, and how did these new interpretations of the stories touch the lives of the main actors in these narratives? How did these individuals perceive the events of 1969 and their roles in these events? In the next chapter, I offer answers to these questions.

## NOTES

1. ÁSZTL, O-13708, "Májusiak" [May-ers], the report of István Bereczki, police sublieutenant, March 3, 1970, 33–34.

2. Ibid., "Májusiak" [May-ers], 33–34.

3. "The early communist state before 1956 presented history in terms of the antifascist struggle; the recent past was the story of an ongoing and constant battle between communists and the forces of Fascism. After 1956,

the Kadár state retained this antifascist historical narrative but added a new element: the 1956 uprising was understood as the latest clash with reactionary 'counterrevolutionaries' who were intent on restoring Fascism to Hungary" (Mark, "Antifascism," 1210).

4. BFL, f. XXV-44-b, PKKB, 21054/70, b. 616, 351–52, police report on the interrogation of Richárd R., April 23, 1970.

5. Kó, Münnich, and Németh, "A magyarországi galeribűnözés néhány jellemzője," 162.

6. Campbell, *Girls in the Gang.*

7. BFL, f. XXV-44-b, PKKB, 21054/70, b. 616, 375–76, police report on the interrogation of Anna R., March 23, 1970.

8. Ibid., presentence report on Anna R., March 20, 1970.

9. For the data regarding the average salary in 1969, see Központi Statisztikai Hivatal, *Gazdaságilag aktívak bruttó átlagkeresete.*

10. Ibid.

11. Haney, *Inventing the Needy*, 49.

12. Interview with Jenő S., nickname "Midget," May 27 and June 31, 2006; interview with András Sz., nickname "Hobó," May 27, 2006.

13. BFL, f. XXV-44-b, PKKB, 21054/70, b. 616, 367, May 7, 1970.

14. Ibid., characterization of Anna R.

15. Ibid., police report on the attorney's interrogation of Anna R., April 9, 1970.

16. Ibid., presentence report, March 20, 1970.

17. Ibid., 21054/1970, Imre E. and associates, 225, resolution on temporary assignment to the Institute for the Protection of Youth, Siófok, July 30, 1969.

18. Mitterauer, *History of Youth*, 233.

19. Éva Bedecs, "Hippik. Made in Hungary," *Magyar Ifjúság*, December 12, 1969, 4–5.

20. BFL, f. XXV-44-b-1, PKKB, 21054/70, b. 616, Characterization given by Magda Berkó, 358–359.

21. BFL, f. XXV-44-b, PKKB, 21054/70, b. 616, 375–80, police report.

22. See Verdery, *Secrets and Truths*, 17.

23. BFL, f. XXV-44-b, PKKB, 21054/70, b. 616, official record of the court proceedings, July 9, 1970.

24. BFL, f. XXV-44-b, PKKB, 21054/1970, E. Imre E. and associates, expert opinion, March 28, 1970, 237–38.

25. Ibid., bill of indictment, April 17, 1970.

26. Ibid., petition to the district court, n.d.

27. ÁSZTL, O-14729, "Dunai" [Danubian], 5–6, proposal of Imre Seres; ibid., 184–85.

28. Ibid., 9, report, January 20, 1971.

29. Ibid., 10, report, February 9, 1971.
30. Ibid., 22, report, June 10, 1971.
31. Ibid., 202–15.
32. Tabajdi and Ungváry, *Elhallgatott múlt*, 364–67.
33. Interview with Gyula Sz., nickname "Big Kennedy," March 24, 2009.

NINE

# MEMORY

IN 2006, INDIAN, ONE OF the leading members of the Great Tree Gang, shared the following observation concerning the role of the younger generation in the collapse of socialism in Hungary:

> That I was part of a seething generation of young people, there is nothing unusual in that. There is only one noteworthy thing in that, that we realized that the party state or socialism leads nowhere. It's a dead end. Why doesn't it lead anywhere? Because it didn't have any ideology, the concept is rootless, without a homeland, without a nation. . . . The Hungarian young people at the time, and I am thinking of the beat generation too, and the students too at a certain level, contributed to a great extent to the collapse of the party state. In quotation marks: the way in which it collapsed. You needed the younger generation for that too, because there was a very deep chasm yawning between the adult social system at the time and the youth. They often raised the question, said that we were aping the West, though I insist even today that we never, ever aped it. To this day, we won't ape it. The Hungarian was always able and always prepared to form his own history. Perhaps these are big words, but still, it's true. In the end, what made the young people of the 1960s great? The fact that they had an ideology, a poet, a writer, and an ideologue. I could mention a few examples, from literature, for instance, Salinger, *Catcher in the Rye*. I read that stuff at the time.[1]

Like many of his peers at the time, Indian transformed the hippie identity into a nationalist and antisocialist identity, an identity connected, in his mind, with foreign (Anglo-American) influences. According to Indian's recollections, the Great Tree and the surrounding area were symbols of the younger generation's form of political resistance. At the same time, he seems to have accepted the notion of a chasm separating the younger generation and the older generation, an idea cultivated and promulgated by the media and the authorities. The practices of surveillance used by the party state and the various punishments it meted out seem to have influenced the attitudes of young people toward politics and their conception of their relationship to the state. They became considerably more active and also more radical when it came to political issues. The individuals who were punished by the state became more susceptible to the more radical ideologies in the panoply of nationalistic narratives, ideologies that were at times tinged by shades of fanaticism.

In this chapter, I examine how the story of the Great Tree Gang was later remembered by some of the people involved, how the whole affair reshaped the views of the people looking back on the events of their identity as a generation, and how it acquired meaning within larger political narratives. I argue that the measures taken by the police against the group made the young people involved more politically active, and, indeed, when these same people look back on the events, they recall them as expressions of the oppositional political views of their generation. In other words, in response to the measures taken by the police, the courts, and the press, young people who, until the authorities began to craft the story of the Great Tree Gang, for the most part were politically neutral or indifferent came to see their own life stories and the life story of their generation as narratives that were intricately intertwined with the political events and narratives of the day, and many of them even became radical nationalists. Accordingly, narratives created around the Great Tree case (and perhaps around hooliganism as a whole) generated a sense that the subculture was real and had political meanings.

Indian works today as the chairman of a fisherman's association and owns a large house in a suburb of Budapest where residences are comparatively expensive. To the extent that I could tell from the occasions on which we met, he still seems drawn to fashions that mark him as a nonconformist. His wardrobe includes all the accoutrements of various youth subcultures of the past several decades. For instance, he had a T-shirt with an image of Greater Hungary (Hungary according to its borders before the 1920 Treaty of Trianon, in which Hungary lost roughly two-thirds of its territory); a cross and high-heeled leather boots (fashions of the nationalist subcultures of the 1980s and 1990s); golden chains and golden bracelets (part of the hedonistic subculture of the 1980s, which mimicked styles associated with Italian fashion); leather pants[2] and a leather jacket (garments worn by the "leathers" and the "tramps," who became the new figures of menace in the 1970s[3]); long hair, a long beard, and pins (part of the hippie culture of his youth); and a broad-brimmed hat (popular among the so-called jampec boys or Hungarian teddy boys of the 1950s, mentioned in earlier chapters). During our conversations, when he spoke of issues of importance to him, the various positions he adopted, all of which were expressive of these identities, were tied to the kinds of "ideologies" associated with youth subcultures. The fate of the Hungarian nation is as important to him as material wealth is irrelevant. Sexual libertinism and American beatnik culture were both forms of cultural opposition to the regime, in his assessment. This transformation of the hippie into a sort of nationalist radical is hardly a phenomenon unique to Hungary or Central Europe. It can be observed in other territories of the former Soviet Union as well.[4]

For Indian, the notion of himself as a rebel became such an important part of his identity that, since the 1970s, he has always dwelt in his recollections of the period in question on his place as a member of the Great Tree Gang. His identity as a member of the gang was in fact given to him by László Szabó's television show *Blue Light*. Indian seems to have embraced it, even though he himself admitted in the course of our conversation that the interview he had done for the show at the time had been the product of compulsion: "they came into the prison with a camera and you had to talk."[5] Indian seemed so well suited for the role of soothsayer, however, that in the novel *Sírig tartsd a pofád* (Shut your face till the grave) by István Csörsz (published in 1983), which is structured as a collection of first-person narratives told by gang members, the most important character, Zord Khán, is based on him. The stories in the novels are presented as depictions of the rebellious youth of the 1970s.[6]

Indian is quite a storyteller, which explains in part why he was often asked to share his recollections. When talking with me, he explained his hippie identity and his attachment to Hungarian national identity as consequences of the fact that his family was originally from Transylvania.[7] He recounted the events of his past like a professional storyteller, using epithets and florid descriptions, as if he had told the tales hundreds of times already. For instance, one could cite his recollection of his arrest:

> What was it like when they arrested you?
>
> INDIAN: It happened like this. I'll tell you in detail, if you're interested. It happened one cold, snowy afternoon in January. We were drinking coke in restaurant called The Apostles, exceptionally, as it so happens, not in the "Jégbüfé" snack bar, cause that's right next to it.

Considering Indian's colorful style and the fact that he was able to craft a dramatic story out of anything (often with sexually suggestive overtones), it seems clear why both László Szabó and István Csörsz chose him as the primary storyteller for the tale of the Great Tree Gang. His stories, furthermore, tended to follow the narratives about youth subcultures that the reading public had already encountered in the press, and in this sense, like Duck, Indian fashioned his identity in part from the official press representations of youth cultures. Loafing, vagrancy, nationalism, orgies, destitution, and the ethics of the Kádár era were as natural elements of his stories as they were of the accounts given by "journalists." Yet he seemed a more credible source, in part simply because he was in prison and in part because his appearance and his speech style both resembled the images the reading public had of the members of the Great Tree Gang. Of course, rarely, if ever, mentioned in the accounts given by Indian himself and those given about him in the press is the fact that he was not apprehended by the police because of the Hippie Stroll. Rather, he was arrested on charges of rape, and the people who were convicted in the trial themselves said several times that Indian had not been a particularly important or prominent figure in the group, his characterizations of himself as a gang member notwithstanding. His lifestyle, thus, could be seen as a means of constructing a (mis) remembered past, as he seems, with his stories and his appearance, to strive even to the present day to embody the rebellious youth of the 1960s. In doing so, he may seek to obscure a part of the past that would be hard to confront openly.

I got Indian's telephone number from Jenő S., who, as noted earlier, was a member of the group who went by the nickname Midget. Midget ended up in prison under charges, based largely on the testimony given by Ancsa Hippie, of having taken part in planning a procession for May 1, 1970. (As noted in chap. 7, József Pogácsás had come up with the idea of the procession because it gave him a pretext to bring charges against the Great Tree Gang again.) Midget was also accused, on the basis of testimony allegedly given by several witnesses, of having recited a widely known antisemitic ditty in the EMKE underpass and having greeted the others "with a fascist salute."[8] Both Midget and the other gang member included on this indictment, Hobo (mentioned in chap. 1), had Jewish family backgrounds, so the accusations brought against them seems questionable, although their Jewish identity only became significant in the postsocialist period. As an opposite to Indian, today Midget no longer seeks, with his garb and lifestyle, to conjure the subculture that was allegedly characteristic of young people in the 1960s. He keeps an enormous custom motorcycle in a garage on the edge of the city. After our first meeting (to which the other interviewees invited him), I gave him my telephone number and the two of us agreed to meet on a street corner in a neighborhood of Budapest that has a bad reputation. I was to go to the street corner at a specific time and wait for him to call. In all likelihood, he took these precautions because, as someone who had already done time, he wasn't entirely convinced that I wasn't working for the police. For Midget, who wore a gold necklace with the star of David, his Jewish roots had been important to him when he had been compelled to go to soccer games with his friends where the Ferencváros team was playing, which was awkward and unpleasant for him, because nationalistic and antisemitic rhymes were often chanted at soccer games. In the course of our first conversation, in which Hobo and Gyula L. (who goes by the nickname Pharaoh) also took part, Hobo and Pharaoh were surprised to see how important Midget's Jewish identity had become for him.[9]

The door to the apartment where Midget and I met was next to the gate of a building that stood half in ruins. There were huge paintings on the wall and an enormous plasma television, and sitting in front of it was a woman in revealing clothing. At one point in our interview, Midget told her to leave because, he said, she had the television turned up too loud. Midget informed me that a few years after he had served his sentence as a political criminal, he was again brought before the courts on charges of pimping. He had been arrested numerous times for trying to cross the border illegally, and eventually he had been able to flee the country for West Germany, where he often managed to live off the money provided by relatives who lived there. At the end of the interview, Midget, who takes a passionate interest in astrology, told me what the typical characteristics of someone with my sign are as well as the typical characteristics of a few friends of mine, after I had given him their signs.

Before the meeting, I had promised to take him some of the state security memorandums on him. Midget seems to have had a close relationship with a teacher who was submitting reports on him to the authorities. I thought he would be amazed to learn that this teacher had informed on him, but when he read the reports (some of which were quite malicious, as the authorities would have expected them to be), he did not seem surprised in the slightest—not because he had suspected that his teacher was informing on him, but rather because, as he put it, "it was customary at the time."[10] Perhaps as a consequence of this, he treated the story of the Great Tree Gang with considerably more distance than the other members of the group with whom I spoke.[11] They all agreed that the whole thing, including the idea of gang leaders, had been invented by the police, while they (the young people involved) had hardly caused any serious fuss. The importance of the events as part of their formative years varied, however, depending on which of them I asked.

The case of Imre M., who went by the nickname "Jimmy," offers a good example of this. Jimmy was charged with having participated in the attempt to free one of the girls from the institution, and though the police used his testimony against the others in much the same way they used the testimony that had been given by Ancsa Hippie, he was not given a more lenient sentence (in the end, he spent sixteen months in prison). According to Jimmy,

> It was a bunch of invented bull. Just the fact that it was openly a gang, well if you ask me that means, it means literally a group of friends. And up by the Great Tree there really was this kind of intertwined group. So really you can't even say that there was a core, but seriously, a few people came up, we sat down, talked, chatted, left, or drank something, then moved on, something, so I don't know of anything explicitly like . . . let's go break in somewhere, or let's go do this or that, nothing like that came up there. . . . it was a totally peaceful kind of thing.

According to Jimmy, the first time the police took him into custody was after a soccer game in which the Ferencváros team had played, and it was because he and his friends had been waving Ferencváros flags and singing on the tram. For them, the Ferencváros soccer games were the best place for expressions of national sentiment (they had made the Ferencváros flags out of a Hungarian flag). "Almost everyone [all the members of the group] were Ferencváros fans," he claimed, which also meant that as soccer fans they expressed their national sentiments.[12]

After he was released from prison, Jimmy almost immediately got married and stopped hanging out with the group. When Jimmy met his girlfriend's mother, she informed him that she wouldn't let her daughter date him unless he cut his hair. In the wedding pictures, Jimmy is wearing a dress jacket and his hair is short.[13]

Pharaoh helped me get in touch with Jimmy and Hobo.[14] Jimmy and Hobo only agreed to meet with me after I informed them that I had already done interviews with other gang members. They both canceled the interview twice, perhaps anxious about conjuring their recollections of the past. Hobo, Pharaoh, and Jimmy knew one another from the Ferencváros soccer games. They spoke of this period of their youths as a time that had shaped the rest of their lives, in spite of the fact that before the interview they had not attributed much significance to these stories at all. The context of our meeting—namely, the fact that they were being interviewed—influenced the ways in which they remembered their pasts and the identities they presented to one another and to me. It seemed a bit as if, as once happened in the interrogation room, they again became members of the Great Tree Gang. Thus, symbolically at least, they accepted and embraced their identities as gang members, an identity that had been fashioned for them decades earlier by the authorities (the police, the courts, and the press), even if they always rejected the notion that their group of peers had been a tightly knit, hierarchically structured gang that had engaged in organized campaigns or committed planned political acts. They seemed to have the testimonies they gave in the course of the trial (the documents with which I presented them during the interview), and the books that had been published in the meantime about them helped them recall events that they otherwise had largely forgotten or remembered only vaguely (as they themselves noted). After they were released from prison, the only people who met regularly were Big Kennedy, Midget, and Midget's sister.[15] Sometimes some of the old members of the group would go to the Great Tree, but in all likelihood, the relatively loose ties between the members of the group, which was presented at the trial as an organized gang, frayed quickly.

When I went to the bar at which Hobo, Pharaoh, and I had agreed to meet for a second interview, Hobo was not there. Pharaoh did not find this surprising at all. He said he knew the bars Hobo tended to frequent and suggested we look for him. We did in the end find him. At the time, Hobo worked in a bar in Újpest (a working-class district in the northern part of Pest) as a bartender. Although he was given a relatively mild sentence compared to the others, of the people convicted of charges in the case brought against the Great Tree Gang, Hobo spent the most time in prison. He was sentenced to serve time in juvenile detention for his participation in the "May procession plan" and for hooliganism allegedly committed during the attempt to free a girl from one of the institutions (during the Ancsa incident; see chap. 8).

In the 1970s, charges were brought against him again for nonpolitical crimes. He got married and divorced, and he often made use of his remarkable strength by taking odd jobs (he was exceptionally strong), sometimes working at night. Like Midget, he was also accused of pimping, but he was not convicted. His life would have been completely different, in his opinion, if the police had not invented the Great Tree Gang, since then he would not have had a criminal record. He was given harsh sentences for nonpolitical crimes because the police had made the whole Great Tree affair into a political issue. In 1993, a few years after the communist state had fallen, he requested that the verdicts that had been passed against him be nullified and that he be given some compensation for the years he spent in prison. However, in Hungary, the secret service documents were not connected on the institutional level with the practice of dispensing justice retroactively; instead, the authorities usually based their decisions only on the original sentences and not the whole documentation of the process.[16] So, although the communist state in Hungary had fallen three years earlier (albeit with many functionaries and politicians remaining in their positions), the court nonetheless rejected his request. According to the judge in the case, during the stroll, Hobo had exhausted "all forms of expression of any kind of national, racial, and religious hatred that incites people to discrimination, hostility, and violence." When announcing his decision, the judge accepted the facts of the case as they had been presented in the 1970 court verdict and the verdict reached by the court in the case referred to by the codename "May-ers."[17]

Six months earlier (in the autumn of 1992), another judge in the same court had nullified the sentence given to Big Kennedy because of his alleged participation in the Hippie Stroll and had thrown into question the competence of the court that had dealt with the case at the time.[18] Big Kennedy had even been given so-called compensation coupons, one of which he once tried to give to a ticket checker on the public transportation system instead of paying the fine for having used public transportation without a ticket, but the ticket checker had not accepted it.[19] In 1993, the judge in Hobo's case took neither his Jewish background (in other words, the possibility that he had suffered discrimination as someone with Jewish roots) nor the circumstances under which verdicts were reached against him in his trials for political crimes into consideration. Other members of the group also wound up in prison after having served their sentences and having been released.

After he got out, Lord Blondie was called up to do compulsory military service. In February 1972, he got married, and according to his mother, his wife had a good influence on him. He promised, for instance, to work in his father-in-law's vegetable shop after completing his military service. As a soldier, Lord Blondie even joined the Communist Youth League. After he completed his military service, the league decided to act as his patron, and representatives of the league asked his mother to ask him to call them if he was on leave. Since he never called them, in the autumn of 1972, they tried to contact his wife. She was not at home because she was in the hospital giving birth to their daughter. His sibling told the representatives of the league who had been sent to his home that Lord Blondie was again being held in pretrial custody for insubordination in the military.[20] Big Kennedy often got together with him, and as far as he knows, though Lord Blondie was kept under police surveillance for a time, he was never sent back to prison. After his release from prison, he had the ÉSZ tattoo removed from his forehead. In the 1990s, he worked first as a security guard and then as a steeplejack.[21]

The mid-1970s was to some extent a period of "settling down" for the members of the Great Tree Gang. Some of the young men, who by that time were between twenty and twenty-five years old, got married for the first time and had their first children (for instance, Big Kennedy, Jimmy, Duck, Lord Blondie, and Pharaoh). For the most part, their marriages did not last long. I did not meet a single member of the one-time gang who had not divorced his first wife, and few of them had had long-lasting monogamous relationships later.

Three of the four youngest defendants (with the exception of Duck) went on to lead lives in which the Great Tree Gang played almost no significant role; it was only a short episode in their life. After his release from prison, Pressel (mentioned in chap. 1) seems to have broken his ties to the other members of the group. According to a report on his circumstances, he worked as a driver for the Budapest Municipal Waterworks, he never met with his old friends, and he formed a beat band with a group of new friends.[22] Monk, who had been convicted for his allegedly subversive poetry, quieted down a bit, as noted by his neighbors. They only had one complaint: after being released from prison, he again let his hair grow.[23] Meanwhile, according to his neighbors and his mother, Christ (also mentioned in chap. 1) never meets with his old friends, although other sources suggest that on occasion Big Kennedy would sleep at his place.[24] After he was released from prison, Little Kennedy married and was registered as an elevator repairman.[25] According to the Communist Youth League Committee for the Protection of Personal Interests, in most of the cases, the punishment meted out had the desired effect and the young people in question mended their ways. The stories of these four men seem to attest to that.[26]

Duck, who at one point contended that he had indeed been the one who had come up with the idea of the stroll, also got married and had one child, a daughter. By the time I began interviewing the former gang members, he had already passed away. His wife, Mária (whom he had divorced), contacted me because she had read something I had written about him. They had met in 1973 in a restaurant on the Buda side of the Danube River after a concert by a band called Mini.[27] Duck and his wife had gotten married in 1975, and their daughter had been born one year later. In the late 1970s, they had been given a temporary apartment by the government. Until then, they had lived with her parents.

According to his ex-wife, Mária, though he spent a great deal of time with his daughter when she was young, later Duck met quite often with his friends, among whom he stood out as a popular figure, with his striking appearance. He wore a bandana, having gone bald quite young, and he grew a long beard. He got a tattoo of the Kossuth coat-of-arms and a dragon. At the time, as a member of the one-time Great Tree Gang, he enjoyed some prestige even among university students or more educated young people. He loved to go on excursions, and he began to take an increasingly strong interest in Eastern philosophies.

According to his wife, "he devoured books" and liked to go to used bookstores, but she never once heard him sing (and she emphasized that she certainly never heard him sing "Erika," the German marching song mentioned in chapter 1, or any other marching song). The 1956 revolution and its commemorations were frequent topics of conversation for him. In the 1970s and 1980s, reports were filed on him by the state security forces, on several occasions by people who belonged to his narrow circle of friends. When a pulp novel by László L. Lőrinc (mentioned in the first chapter) was published in 1979, Duck was enraged by the characterization of the stroll in the novel as a "fascist protest."[28] The novel, of course, met the expectations of the censors, and it was intended to reflect and adhere to the position of the state security forces. He wanted to use the book as part of his appeal to West Germany to grant him political asylum, but he never actually got around to submitting it.[29]

Duck rarely spoke of the whole Great Tree affair. According to Mária, this was because he had suffered a tremendous shock at the time. When they went to the movies, he always preferred to sit directly next to the aisle to ensure that he would be able to leave easily if he wanted to. Because of his experiences in prison, he feared being confined. His ex-wife characterized him as someone who practiced what he preached: "there was no separation between word and deed." He was not a consumer, and he ridiculed people who followed the consumer lifestyle. In her assessment, his candor and honesty where his most admirable characteristics. True, Duck would sometimes vanish unannounced from one day to the next, but he never said that this was something he would not do. According to his ex-wife, "he lived in a given society, and in this society, there were many restrictions. A society doesn't need so many restrictions." Her memories of Duck are so intertwined with her memories of the Kádár era that it is hard for her to escape the impression that her ex-husband's fate was determined from the outset by the needs and mechanisms of the system. In her narrative of this past, Duck has become a kind of symbolic figure who must not be forgotten, in no small part because of her sense that the change of regimes that began in 1989 was never actually brought to completion.[30]

When the borders of Hungary were opened to the West, Duck went abroad more often, and for the most part during his travels, he simply slept outside. He went to Barcelona to see the works of Dalí and Gaudí and also to spend time in a warmer clime. According to Mária, "he did not think that there had been a change of regimes, because the same old comrades or their relatives or acquaintances were in leading positions who had been there before. This is one of the reasons why he went abroad. He wanted this country to be his homeland, but it could not become his homeland." Presumably, he was able

Figure 9.1. Duck in 2002.

to sell some of his drawings when he wasn't using drawing simply as a means of self-expression. Some of the drawings that were part of his bequest seem to borrow from Dalí's style. One of the most common motifs of his last drawings is the intertwined silhouettes of two people growing out of the knotted branch of a tree. He died in 2004 in Barcelona and was probably buried in a common grave. His daughter was informed of his passing by the Hungarian Ministry of Foreign Affairs, and she was sent his remaining belongings in a suitcase. These belongings included a sleeping bag, a small folding chair (on which he may have sat while doing drawings in the streets of the city to make money), a few sweaters, his passport, his public transportation pass, some tobacco, a drawing board and some drawings, an English-Hungarian dictionary, and a calendar. His wife thought he probably had been making money by doing drawings in the streets and had been sleeping outside in his sleeping bag. Even as a man no longer young, he kept notes as he had done as an adolescent—or at least the pages of the calendar, which had one page for every day of the year, are covered with notes in his handwriting. According to Mária, "I don't think he thought anyone would ever read them, or that he was trying to impress anyone. And there was one that was interesting, something was written like, 'Again a new year, again alone, again I will try.' Perhaps at the beginning of the calendar."[31]

Big Kennedy had a different fate, and not surprisingly, his memories of the Great Tree differed. His older daughter helped me get in contact with him, though this took some time. She said that he would go to the Great Tree almost every week, and though by the time she and I spoke I myself had explored the area several times, I had never run into him. We met for the first time by the tree. It was not difficult to recognize him, even several decades after the fateful summer of 1969. There was nothing particularly striking about the way he looked. The small tattoos on his fingers had faded with time, but he regarded the Great Tree as if it were a kind of native land to him: "I grew up here, I lived here, I slept here many, many times, I married a girl I met here, the police apprehended me here, everything happened here."[32] He invested the place with such profound significance not because of the interest I was taking in it as a historian but rather because even the minor details of his life story somehow tied him to this spot.

According to the account he gave me of his time in prison, he labored in a workshop alongside "class-enemy priests," who helped him find the psychological strength to weather his imprisonment at a mere nineteen years of age. He was incarcerated in the Budapest Penitentiary (Budapesti Gyűjtőfogház—today Budapesti Fegyház és Börtön). He lived here alongside other people who had been convicted of political crimes. The prison, which was built in 1896

Figure 9.2. One of the last drawings by Duck.

originally to hold eight hundred inmates, was for a long time the largest facility of its kind in Central Europe. After 1956, many of the people convicted of political crimes were incarcerated here, and many of the executions of political prisoners were held here. Lord Blondie also ended up in this prison, and when the two of them were placed in adjacent cells, they would communicate with each other by knocking on the wall. Big Kennedy characterized the place as strict, but because he had already spent time in the correctional institution in Aszód, he was more accustomed to confinement than his friends who had also been sentenced to serve time. He mentioned that on one occasion the members of the Bergendy band had come to the prison, the musicians whom he had once helped by carrying their speakers: "they found out which cell I was in and they pulled up in the neighboring cemetery in their car and played a song on the trumpet." He was often put in solitary confinement; however, because of the amnesty that was granted in 1970, his two-year prison sentence was cut in half, and in October, he was released on probation.

The political police tried to recruit him as an agent or informer, but he was not willing to work for them. He was again put under police surveillance (possibly because of his unwillingness to cooperate), and he was forbidden from going to the first district in Budapest (both the Youth Park and the Great Tree were in the first district). In the spring of 1971, he was imprisoned for thirty days on charges of criminal idleness, and that autumn, the police began to take him into custody regularly when important dates were approaching that might be occasions for political commemorations or protests. He lived off odd jobs. Though he was still under police surveillance, he nonetheless regularly went to the Great Tree, so the authorities prohibited him from coming into any part of the capital. He again began to live as a vagrant, since all his acquaintances lived in Budapest. In 1973, the police arrested him again. He was convicted of having repeatedly violated the conditions that had been set by the authorities and was forced to serve the remainder of his original sentence. He spent half of his last year in prison in the penitentiary in the castle in Veszprém, an old building with thick, damp walls. Even in the summer, the courtyard, where prisoners were able to get some fresh air, only got a few rays of sunshine. "They tried to bring me up right there," he noted, "and again I was beyond fixing." He was moved for the last six months of his sentence to the penitentiary in Sopronkőhida, one of the harshest prisons in the country. Because he was regarded as someone who might incite the other inmates to commit acts of defiance, he was not allowed to mix with the other prisoners.

> This was the toughest part of the country. But true, I only had half a year left there. They couldn't do anything with me. They didn't put me in with the

> confined group, where there are others, cause then something would happen in the confined group. They put me in a cell for two, and then I was the person responsible for the courtyard. I could move about as I pleased, I had a ribbon on my hand, and I had to sweep up alone. I was not allowed to go anywhere where the others were working. They always isolated me from the others.

In 1975, very soon after he was released, Big Kennedy got married. The wedding was held in the Church of Saint Anna on Batthyány Square, not far from the Great Tree. Several of his old friends from the gang attended the service. His wife had once lived in a building next to the Youth Park. The two of them moved to Kőbánya, a working-class neighborhood, where they were given a temporary apartment on Salgótarjáni Avenue. He knew that Fősped, the taxi and delivery company where his father worked, offered jobs with good pay, so he found a position there working as a delivery man who transported heavy machinery. His father had been stationed abroad by the company at the time, and when he returned, Big Kennedy was fired because "two family members cannot both be employed at a dangerous workplace." He and his wife had two daughters, one born in 1976 and the other in 1978. In 1978, he got a job doing loading work at a meat plant. The police continued to come to his home, for the most part at night, to search the premises. His daughters remember these searches, even though they were young at the time. In 1983, he and his wife divorced, and he found a new job. He also regularly met with old friends from the Great Tree. He contended that "my life didn't change much because of it [the divorce], I continued going to the Great Tree with the kids."

In the 1980s, he worked at the Construction and Mixed Industry Cooperative as a carpenter, his first position in his original trade. He said he had always wanted to work as a carpenter. Even back at the institution in Aszód he had studied carpentry. He has been working as a carpenter ever since. Today, for the most part, he restores antique furniture. He lived at several addresses in Budapest in the 1980s and had several longer and shorter relationships with romantic partners. Until 1989, the police continued to conduct searches of his homes and summon him to give accounts of his activities. In the 1990s, he worked for eighteen months in Istanbul restoring woodwork in the old bazaar, and he also worked for three years restoring the benches and doors of the St. Stephen's Basilica in Budapest. The priests with whom he had once been in prison helped him get this position. Since the late 1990s, he has lived with his current girlfriend, whom he refers to as his wife though they are not actually married.

He often has dreams about the area around the Great Tree and the church in the Tabán neighborhood, where he and his friends often hid from the police.

Figure 9.3. *Left to right*: Indian, Big Kennedy, and the author under the Great Tree, 2009.

He doesn't know why, but the police never went into the church in search of them. On one occasion, he sprained his ankle while running from them, and he ended up spending two nights in the church: "It's possible that the police didn't dare come in, but it's also possible that they didn't know that we were there. The others knew. The girls brought us food. And I got a lot of strength back in the day from the priests, in the prison years."[33] When the weather is nice, Big Kennedy often takes his granddaughter to the Great Tree. He is still attached to the place that to a large extent shaped his life.

None of the people who had been convicted in the case brought against members of the Great Tree Gang and with whom I did interviews spoke about the events of 1969 as if they had been part of some political protest or revolt. However, the events acquired political meaning for all of them when the authorities began to fashion the case against them, based on the notion of an organized gang. This became increasingly true as they aged, because the police continued trying to catch them in some act of political opposition, holding investigations and searching their homes even years later. By declaring them to be enemies of the state, the system seems to have made them more politically aware and politically active, in spite of the fact that originally they had sought to do little more than relax and enjoy themselves while listening to music near a concert space (the Youth Park) provided by the government. This outcome fits quite well with Stanley Cohen's suggestions regarding cycles of deviancy. In other words, once the media-state-society (here instead of the media, the police had a more important role) constructed a notion of so-called deviancy, subcultures were able to subscribe to it. This is what we saw in the case of Duck and what we see in the case of the Great Tree arrestees later in life in this chapter. However, the discursive production of so-called deviance (e.g., Duck reading about himself and trying to fashion himself into a hippie) and the criminological production of deviance (e.g., Big Kennedy and others being arrested because of their association with the group) were both important factors in producing the story about the Great Tree Gang and in creating this specific type of Eastern European moral panic.

## NOTES

1. Interview with András F., nickname "Indian," June 6, 2006.
2. Kőbányai, "Bőrnadrád és biztosítótű."
3. The notion of the tramp, which in the 1970s became the bogyman that replaced the hooligan of the 1960s, was also very much a product of media. Even in the texts in which this identity was crafted, however, these tramps did not constitute a homogenous group. See Kresalek, "Aluljáró nemzedék."
4. Pilkington, "Reconfiguring 'the West,'" 181; Risch, *Youth and Rock in the Soviet Bloc.*
5. Interview with András F., nickname "Indian," June 6, 2006.
6. Csörsz, *Sírig tartsd a pofád*, 1:115.
7. Transylvania is a historical region that today lies in central and western Romania. Until 1920, it was part of Hungary within the Austro-Hungarian monarchy. After the 1920 Treaty of Trianon, it became part of Romania.
8. ÁSZTL, O-13708, "Májusiak" [May-ers], 162, indictment, May 22, 1970.
9. Interview with András Sz., nickname "Hobó"; Gyula L., nickname "Fáraó" [Pharaoh]; and Jenő S., nickname "Midget," May 27, 2006. Pharaoh got his nickname from the 1966 Polish movie *Pharaoh* (*Faraon*), adapted from the eponymous novel by Polish writer Bolesław Prus and directed by Jerzy Kawalerowicz. Pharaoh claimed to have seen the film at least three times.
10. Compare with the legacy of the security state for personal relationships, as also described by Verdery, *My Life as a Spy*, 227–30.
11. Interview with Jenő S., nickname "Midget," June 31, 2006.
12. Interview with Imre M., nickname "Jimmy," May 26, 2006.
13. Ibid.

14. Interview with Gyula L., nickname "Fáraó" [Pharaoh], May 25, 2006.
15. ÁSZTL, O-14729, "Dunai" [Danubian], 9, report, January 20, 1971.
16. On the context of the compensations, see Stan, *Transitional Justice*.
17. Interview with András Sz., nickname "Hobó," May 27, 2006; and BFL, f. XXV-44-b, PKKB, b. 640, case against András Sz. for incitement, combined with case 9. B. 23598/1969, order of the Pest Central District Court in the case against András Sz., April 7, 1993; ibid., letter of support of the Hungarian Communist Youth League Committee for the Protection of Personal Interests in the case of András Sz., August 3, 1972.
18. Ibid., case against András Sz. for incitement, combined with case 9. B. 23598/1969, order of the Pest Central District Court in the case against Gyula Sz., October 7, 1992.
19. Interview with Gyula Sz., nickname "Big Kennedy," March 24, 2009.
20. BFL, f. XXV-44-b, PKKB, b. 640, letter of support of the Hungarian Communist Youth League Committee for the Protection of Personal Interests in the case of György D., October 5, 1972.
21. Interview with Gyula Sz., nickname "Big Kennedy," March 24, 2009.
22. BFL, f. XXV-44-b, PKKB, b. 640, letter of support of the Hungarian Communist Youth League Committee for the Protection of Personal Interests in the case of Attila Cs., June 15, 1972.
23. Ibid., in the case of József H., June 8, 1972.
24. Ibid., in the case of Imre H., July 27, 1972.
25. Ibid., in the case of László H., June 27, 1972.
26. Ibid., letter of support of the Hungarian Communist Youth League Committee for the Protection of Personal Interests in the case of the Members of the Great Tree Gang from 1972.
27. The band Mini, which was formed in 1968, performed in the Mini Club on the Bem Wharf. Today the site is home to the Buda Castle House of Culture.
28. Lőrinc L., *A nagy fa árnyékában*.
29. Interview with Mrs. Mária Zoltán S. (the widow of S. Zoltán, Duck), October 17, 2008.
30. See Sas H., *Közelmúlt: rendszerváltások, családtörténetek*.
31. Interview with Mrs. Mária Zoltán S. (the widow of S. Zoltán, Duck), October 17, 2008.
32. Interview with Gyula Sz., nickname "Big Kennedy," March 24, 2009.
33. Ibid.

# CONCLUSION

TOWARD THE END OF THE 1960s, the socialist system seemed as stable as it had a decade earlier. This stability was due in part to the shrewd practice by the Kádár regime of adopting a comparatively permissive approach to consumption and the private sphere of family life. This made socialism in the Hungary of the 1960s more acceptable and more bearable than it had been at the beginning of the 1950s. The creation of a kind of mass culture based largely on patterns of mass culture from the West was part of this strategy, as was the establishment of various places where young people could spend their leisure time.

The political police, the socialist media, and parents and youths (out of whom the discourse on mass culture in the 1960s made "teenagers") reflected in numerous ways on mass culture, which was seen as Western even in the political sense. The contention has often been made that society at the time simply turned away from politics, but this was not the case. Hungarian society did not become apolitical. Rather, politics and political participation were transferred into new fields.

It was not simply the state institutions (the police, organs of youth protection, and the press) but also young people, the majority of whom had been apolitical before they had been transformed into figures in this narrative, that took part in fashioning the official story of the Great Tree Gang. Because of the proceedings that were launched against them, however, they often found themselves drawn to radical nationalistic ideas, and the regime responded by labeling them fascists, using one of the key terms of the narrative with which the regime had always striven to acquire legitimacy (namely, the narrative according to which the Soviet army had freed the country and the region from fascism).[1]

The socialist system did not simply need compliant subjects. Rather, their ideal was the citizen who took part voluntarily in the construction of communism because he/she believed in it. In the interests of crafting this citizen, it was necessary to transform the system of political participation in the construction of communism in all spheres of cultural life, including youth and leisure time policy.

The reason for the creation of the story of the Great Tree Gang was that by the 1960s, Kádár and Khrushchev, along with many other leaders in the socialist countries of the Eastern Bloc, had to look for new sources of political legitimacy.[2] They had to do this in part because, in the fifteen years since the end of the war, the societies of these countries had undergone dramatic social transformations. These transformations included the challenges posed by rapid industrialization and the influx into the cities of people who earlier had worked in and lived off agriculture, but perhaps most importantly, the regimes had to address the fact that the earlier Stalinist cultural policies had lost all credibility. Furthermore, in the 1960s, a generation was coming of age that had been born after the war. Youth policy became a crucial issue in all the countries of the Eastern Bloc in the 1960s. The communists needed new mobilization tools to persuade the members of the younger generation that they could take part actively in the transformation of the world in which they lived. They launched several (mass) culture campaigns targeting young people, and they also initiated movements that allegedly were organized from below.

One of the primary functions of the story of the Great Tree Gang was to serve as a tool that the complex network of institutions through which the regime exerted power could use to instruct young people on modes of acceptable and unacceptable behavior. In doing so, it exerted a form of oversight over the socialization of young people and controlled images and ideas of youth in the public discourse. The characters in the story underwent a process of identification that was shaped by the distinctive features of the ruling order. The story embodied an expression of the official interpretation of the West and the new ethos of the consumer lifestyle but also, more narrowly, of 1956 and of the limits placed on the right to freedom of assembly. For members of society who accepted the limits of the new political system, experiences and perceptions of everyday life acquired new garb. In this new garb, the story of the Great Tree Gang was an element of the official discourse concerning antifascism and the "counterrevolution." For the generation that grew up in the 1960s, the attempts by the regime to transform the memory of the 1956 revolution, the creation of taboos, and the use of disciplinary measures against minors were everyday experiences.[3] Because of the efforts to shape the memory of 1956, the practices of everyday life—an everyday life that was interwoven with secrets and lies[4]—became cornerstones of the ruling order.

The state made its everyday use of violent measures (or repression) acceptable or at least palatable to the citizenry by making these measures less visible and by criminalizing people who allegedly had committed political crimes. In other words, someone accused by the state of a political crime (which the population might well not have regarded as a crime at all) was also depicted as a run-of-the-mill criminal guilty not only of crimes against the state or its ideology but also against society at large. This was true in the case of the proceedings launched against the Great Tree Gang, which essentially followed the model of repression used in the wake of 1956. As Attila Szakolczai notes, after 1956, "it was in the interests of the police to have as many cases as possible conclude with a recommendation for indictment, and this emphasis on quantity logically came at the cost of quality. Often, the cases did not in fact merit an indictment."[5] The repressive measures used by the authorities also contributed to the formation of identities, both among the people convicted for having taken part in the uprising in 1956 and among the young people who were branded hooligans. When the state institutions fashioned the official discourse concerning gangs in 1960, there were still people in prison who had been convicted for taking part in the revolution and who had been labeled fascist criminals by the state propaganda machine.

The state also needed young fascists to make its discourse concerning the antifascist ideology and the antifascist measures used by the regime plausible. But the hooligans and gangs were created not simply to serve as characters of sorts in the official discourse but also to make the acts of the various representatives of state power (for instance, the police) acceptable to the citizenry. One of the goals was to make people believe that they needed the police to maintain public order, the tabloid press to inform and entertain them, and newly available consumer goods so that they could keep up, as it were, with their neighbors. As people came to accept the institutions of power and indeed even came to use their services, everyday practices became new buttresses of the regime, as they embodied expressions of an acceptance at least of the status quo and of the state's hold on power. Attending concerts at the Youth Park, purchasing or saving up for a Trabant, or reading *Esti Hírlap* or *Magyar Ifjúság* were all gestures that involved participation in the ruling system.[6]

In the 1960s, the image of power changed. This was due in part to the fact that the institutions of power sought to use methods other than violence and force to prevail on the citizenry to accept their goals, even if they still were able to use violence at any time against anyone if necessary. In the 1960s, the police and the press of the socialist system were able to gain more credibility among the citizenry than they had enjoyed in the 1950s because the image of both had changed. With the emergence of the tabloid press, the new magazines and newspapers, which worked closely together with the police and met the expectations of the party, began to deal with topics that were considered popular and that they earlier had not covered.

The continual game of cat and mouse between the police and the younger generation was also in the direct interests of the police, as they were able to use it to prove that they were performing useful tasks that were essential to the maintenance of public order. When it came to the specific story of the Great Tree Gang, the police and the press did the casting to ensure that the narrative served as a clear illustration of the need for official youth policy and state institutions of youth protection. Because of the 1956 revolution and the government's insistence on tying allegedly deviant or subversive acts committed by young people in the late 1960s to the legacy of the revolution, youth policy and youth protection became primarily issues of public security. The distinctive or identifying characteristics of the young people who ended up in the focus of youth protection were hardly typical of all the various adolescent groups and youth subcultures in Hungary in the 1960s. However, through the various disciplinary measures that they used against the groups, the state institutions expressed a set of expectations that clearly applied to all members of the younger generation. They took care, when selecting individuals for the different roles in the story, to ensure that the tale would seem plausible to the wider public and would serve as a cautionary example. They also made sure it would meet the expectations of the propaganda machine, which characterized the state institutions as essential parts in a larger mechanism that safeguarded society from fascism and counterrevolutionaries.

In the construction of the story of the Great Tree Gang, the state security forces, the organs of youth protection, and the press all used prevalent stereotypes concerning the different spaces of the city and the people who inhabited these spaces. Gradually, the dangerous working-class young people were replaced by the hooligans and the lumpenproletariat by the gang. The state institutions sought, among the young people against whom proceedings were launched, figures who embodied these stereotypes. When they could not find an ideal embodiment of a given stock character, they emphasized elements of the individual's life story that suggested that his or her alleged rebellion against the state order or his or her membership in a gang had been an inevitable development. In the construction of these stories, the state institutions also borrowed stereotypes concerning rebellious young people in the West, which served to reinforce the notion that socialism was preferable to Western capitalism.

After 1956, violence, not fashion, became the defining characteristic of the allegedly rebellious members of the younger generation, who had been labeled the enemy, so the most important state organ, when it came to handling an adolescent exposed to the threat of corruption by his deviant peers, was the police. Thus, the most intense and everyday relationship young people purportedly at risk had with the organs of the state was their relationship with the police, and the police were able to exert a direct influence on the ways these young people expressed their shifting identities. In the meantime, the meanings of the urban spaces also changed. The inner city of Budapest became one of the most important symbolic spaces of the new socialist-consumerist ethos of Hungary of the 1960s, while the city periphery, the slums, and the housing projects being built in their stead became the new hotbeds of social problems in the official discourse. The city was divided in the public mind into two very separate worlds: the shop windows and foreign tourists of the inner city, which were clear proof of a burgeoning consumer culture supported by the socialist state institutions, and the slums and housing projects in the surrounding neighborhoods, which were increasingly distant from the glimmer and shimmer of the downtown area. Because of this increasingly stark contrast (which was both a matter of perception and reality), the tiniest flourish that threatened the jealously guarded order of the inner city caught the attention of the vigilant police, even, for instance, the presence of a beggar. In this context, the story of the Great Tree Gang was built in part out of and also strengthened prevalent stereotypes concerning the wild people who lived on the fringes of the city and who threatened at any moment to inundate the opulent streets of the downtown area. It was thus essential to punish these people when they threatened the public order not simply because it was in the interests of the party to maintain strict control over a society under its rule but also because it was important to protect the respectable citizenry, who came to support the measures taken by the authorities, allegedly in defense of their safety and interests.

The story of the Great Tree Gang adhered to the familiar plot line of the crime story, and it thus could easily be sold as a kind of consumer product—for instance, in the reports presented in the television show *Blue Light* or the crime novels that were based loosely on it. And, thus, a hierarchical power system was able to reinforce the pillars of its rule through the everyday (often consumer) practices of its respectable citizens. The policeman and the socialist-consumer citizen were on the same side in this story, both opposed to the hooligan and the gangs.

In the police documents, the young people who were interrogated only rarely offer any suggestion in their testimony that they were rebelling against their parents or against society. Nonetheless, the stereotypes concerning the youth revolt exerted such a strong influence on the police, prosecutors, judges, and authors of the media reports on the trial that the whole story of this casual group of friends and acquaintances was framed to suggest that the only real goal of the group had been to rebel. One has the impression, reading the documents, that the young people, who seem almost predestined to rise up against the social order, were going through a slow process of crafting their own conceptions of themselves when they found themselves compelled to accept the roles that the authorities were assigning to them. They only gradually came to see the story the police presented as a story about them, in which they were prominent characters. This process of accepting, at least in part, their place in a story constructed by the state was part of the everyday practices through which the Kádár regime maintained its hold on discourse and power, incorporating people who earlier had been peripheral to its narratives of revolution versus counterrevolution and socialism versus fascism into these narratives as prominent characters. Respectable citizens, in turn, also participated in this process by accepting their place in a story that had been created by the organs of power because doing so allowed them to assert their places in the social order.

Big Kennedy became the leader of the gang in the documents in which the story was created not because he had in fact been chosen by or was seen as a leader by the young people themselves but rather because the authors of these documents (namely, the police, who wrote the primary source) sought to portray the group as an organized hierarchy that needed a leader. As far as who ultimately became a main character and who played only a supporting role, this was decided by the police or simply by chance (e.g., by a coincidental factor, like the phone call made by Péter Bognár the night of the Hippie Stroll or the change in the weather).

From this perspective, in the Kádár era, personal decisions had as great a role in the processes of shaping an individual's identity as the discourse created by the organs of power. This discourse made it possible for people to decide, depending on the given situation, how the regime would shape their identities. In other words, practices that were gradually becoming parts of everyday life gave people the possibility to choose identities through their use of urban spaces and their consumer habits, but these identities themselves were shaped by the connotations of these spaces and habits, which were determined largely by the organs of the state. For in the end, the institutions that wrote the narratives in which young people were presented to the public determined how these young people were perceived by society. The narratives offered the young people identities from which they could chose, and they would have to accept the consequences of their choices. They could rise in the ranks of the Communist Youth League, or they could risk being stopped by the police after a concert and compelled to show their identity papers.

Thus, the system of everyday practices that reinforced the ruling order determined to a large extent the processes by which the individual formed his or her identity. Decisions that might at first seem personal in fact reflected official expectations. The border between the private and the public was blurred, as indeed was clear in the transformed language that the everyday practices that buttressed the ruling order followed. A given sentence had very different meanings depending on whether it was used in an informant's report, a court case, a newspaper article, a television show, or a diary. Statements made in private (for instance in a diary) were saturated with elements from the official discourse, even in the case of young people. One could mention, for instance, the emphasis Duck places in his notebook on the debate concerning refrigerator socialism: the debate was part of public and official fora at the time, but it also became a way that Duck expressed, in a private notebook, his critical view of consumer culture and thus fashioned his perception of himself.

For the children of communism, the regime may have set the borders, but they, too, took active part in the process through which these borders were continually reasserted and reinforced by making compromises in everyday life (either by choice or compulsion) with the expectations of the ruling order. The internalization of these expectations, of which the story of the Great Tree Gang is arguably an example, can be interpreted as a process of socialization during which apolitical young people grew into adults who often openly espoused very explicitly political views. The actors in this apolitical moment of youthful rebellion (the Hippie Stroll, which seems, in retrospect, to have been little more than a bit of youthful antics) became the protagonists in the story created about them by attributing political meaning to their acts, much as the institutions of the state had done. The story gave the impression that, even as early as the late 1960s, these young people were striving to bring down the system, which, in fact, was perhaps more stable than it had ever been (and which would survive for another twenty years). However, the failure of the political campaigns launched by the communist party targeting the younger generation and the construction of imagined subcultures out of groups of marginal and marginalized young people did, in fact, play an important part in the ultimate fall of the regime.

## NOTES

1. Cf. Mark, "Antifascism," 1210.
2. See, for example, Jones, *Dilemmas of De-Stalinization*; Reid, "Cold War in the Kitchen."
3. On the maintenance of 1956 as a taboo topic in the lives of the next generation, see Kőrősi and Molnár, *Carrying a Secret in My Heart*.
4. Cf. Feinberg, *Curtain of Lies*, 173–74.
5. Szakolczai, "Az 1956-os forradalmat követő megtorlás dimenziói," 89.
6. Cf. Apor, "Joy of Everyday Life."

# BIBLIOGRAPHY


## ARCHIVES

*Állambiztonsági Szolgálatok Történeti Levéltára (ÁSZTL) [Historical Archives of the Hungarian State Security]*

3.1. O (Objektum [Target]) and M (Munka [Work]) files.
3.1.2. M-16170. "Répási" [Répási].
3.1.2. M-41158. "Dejkó," [Dejkó].
3.1.5. O-10431. "Huligán" [Hooligan].
3.1.5. O-13575. "Tőröző" [Foiler].
3.1.5. O-13708. "Májusiak" [May-ers].
3.1.5. O-14729. "Dunai" [Danubian].
3.1.5. O-17638. "Csövesek" [Vagrants].
3.1.9. V-157854/1. V. János és társa [János V. and his associate].
3.1.9. V-158094/1-3. Sz. Gyula és társai [Gyula Sz. and his associates].

*Budapest Főváros Levéltára (BFL) [Budapest City Archives]*

f. XXIII-101-a. Budapest Főváros Tanács [Budapest City Council].
f. XXIII-102-a. Budapest Főváros Tanácsa Végrehajtó Bizottsága üléseinek jegyzőkönyvei [Minutes of the meetings of the Budapest City Council's Executive Committee].
f. XXIII-115-c. A Szociálpolitikai Csoport iratai [Social political group].
f. XXIV-1. Budapesti Rendőr-főkapitányság Központi irattára iratai (BRFK) [Documents of the Central Archive of the Budapest Police Headquarters].
f. XXV-44-b. Pesti Központi Kerületi Bíróság Iratai (PKKB) [Central Pest District Court]. Büntetőperes Iratok (BI) [Criminal trial documents].

f. XXV-60-b. Fővárosi Főügyészség [Budapest Municipal Public Prosecutor's Office]. Titkos ügykezelésű (TÜK) igazgatási iratok [Administrative documents of classified cases].
f. XXXV-1-a-4. Az MSZMP Budapesti Végrehajtó Bizottsága jegyzőkönyvei, 1957–1989 [Sittings of the Budapest Executive Council of the Hungarian Socialist Workers' Party, 1957–1989].

*Magyar Nemzeti Levéltár Országos Levéltára (MNL OL)*
*[Hungarian National Archives]*

f. XIX-B-1-Z. Belügyminisztérium (BM) Kollégium [Panel of the Ministry of Interior].
f. XIX-B-14. Országos Rendőr Főkapitányság (ORFK) [National Police Headquarters].
f. M-KS-288. Magyar Szocialista Munkáspárt (MSZMP) iratai [Documents of the Hungarian Socialist Workers' Party]

*Politikatörténeti és Szakszervezeti Levéltár (PSZL)*
*[Political History and Trade Union Archives]*

f. 35. Az MSZMP Budapesti Bizottsága Archívuma (BBA) [Archive of the Budapest Committee of the Hungarian Socialist Workers' Party].
f. 289. A Kommunista Ifjúsági Szövetség iratai [Documents of the Communist Youth League].

## INTERVIEWS

*(Presented in alphabetical order by surname or nickname)*
Interview with Éva Bedecs, February 4, 2005, by the author.
Interview with Gyula Sz., nickname "Big Kennedy," March 24, 2009, by the author.
Interview with Gyula L., nickname "Fáraó" [Pharaoh], May 15, May 25, and May 27, 2006, by the author.
Interview with András Sz., nickname "Hobó," May 27, 2006, by the author.
Interview with András F., nickname "Indian," June 6, 2006, by the author.
Interview with Imre M., nickname "Jimmy," May 26, 2006, by the author.
Interview with "Törpe" [Midget], May 27, and June 31, 2006, by the author.
Interview with Aurél Molnár, November 1995, by Eszter Zsófia Tóth and the author.
Interview with Mrs. Mária Zoltán S. (the widow of S. Zoltán, Duck), October 17, 2008, by the author.

## PRINT MEDIA

*Esti Hírlap* [Evening post], 1956– (1952–56: *Esti Budapest* [Budapest evening post])
*Ifjúsági Magazin* [Youth magazine], 1965–

*Magyar Ifjúság* [Hungarian youth], 1957– (1951–56: *Szabad Ifjúság* [Free youth])
*Magyar Rendőr* [Hungarian policemen], 1947–90
*Népszabadság* [People's liberty], 1956– (1944–56: *Szabad Nép* [Free people])
*Nők Lapja* [Women's magazine], 1951–62
*Szolnok Megyei Néplap* [Szolnok County herald], 1968

## PRINT SOURCES

*A párt ifjúságpolitikájának néhány kérdése* [Some questions concerning the party's youth policy]. Budapest: Kossuth Könyvkiadó, 1970.

Apor, Péter. *Fabricating Authenticity in Soviet Hungary: The Afterlife of the First Hungarian Soviet Republic in the Age of State Socialism*. London: Anthem Press, 2015.

———. "The Joy of Everyday Life: Microhistory and the History of Everyday Life in the Socialist." *East Central Europe* 34, no. 1 (2007): 185–218.

Apor, Péter, Rebecca Clifford, and Nigel Townson. "Faith." In *Europe's 1968: Voices of Protest*, edited by Robert Gildea, James Mark, and Anette Warring, 211–38. Oxford: Oxford University Press, 2013.

Balázs, Magdolna. "Az Ifipark" [The youth park]. *Budapesti Negyed* 2, no. 1 (1994): 137–50.

Balina, Marina R. "'It's Grand to Be an Orphan!': Crafting Happy Citizens in Soviet Children's Literature of the 1920s." In *Petrified Utopia*, edited by Marina Balina and Evgeny Dobrenko, 99–114. London: Anthem Press, 2009.

Barthes, Roland. *Camera Lucida: Reflections on Photography*. New York: Hill and Wang, 1980.

Bauman, Zygmunt. *Liquid Modernity*. Cambridge: Blackwell, 2000.

Benda, Gyula. "Budapest társadalma 1945–1970" [Society of Budapest 1945–1970]. In *Magyar társadalomtörténeti olvasókönyv 1944–től napjainkig* [Hungarian social history reader from 1944 to today], edited by Tibor Valuch, 211–44. Budapest: Osiris, 2004.

Berger, Peter L., and Thomas Luckmann. *The Social Construction of Reality*. Garden City, NY: Doubleday, 1966.

Bernstein, Seth. *Raised under Stalin: Young Communists and the Defense of Socialism*. Ithaca, NY: Cornell University Press, 2017.

Berszinski, Sabine. *Modernisierung im Nationalsozialismus? Eine soziologische Kategorie und Entwicklungen im deutschen Schlager, 1933–45* [Modernization under national socialism? A sociological category and developments in German Schlager, 1933–45]. MA thesis, Albert-Ludwigs-Universität zu Freiburg [Albert Ludwig University of Freiburg], 2000.

Bittner, Egon. *The Function of the Police in Modern Society: A Review of Background Factors, Current Practices, and Possible Role Models*. Chevy Chase, MD: National Institute of Mental Health, 1970.

Bodor, Endre. "Hozzászólás Szabó László 'A rendőrség és a sajtó' című cikkéhez" [Reflections on the article entitled "The police and the press," by László Szabó]. *Belügyi Szemle* 2, no. 1 (1964): 98–103.
Bottoni, Stefano. *Long Awaited West: Eastern Europe since 1944*. Bloomington: Indiana University Press, 2017.
Bren, Paulina. *The Greengrocer and His TV: The Culture of Communism after the 1968 Prague Spring*. Ithaca, NY: Cornell University Press, 2010.
Bren, Paulina, and Mary Neuburger, eds. *Communism Unwrapped: Consumption in Cold War Eastern Europe*. Oxford: Oxford University Press, 2012.
Campbell, Anne. *The Girls in the Gang: A Report from New York City*. New York: B. Blackwell, 1984.
Charone, Barbara. *Keith Richards: Life as a Rolling Stone*. Garden City, NY: Doubleday, 1982.
Chibnall, Steve. *Law and Order News: An Analysis of Crime Reporting in the British Press*. London: Tavistock, 1977.
Chih Lin, Ann. *Reform in the Making: The Implementation of Social Policy in Prison*. Princeton, NJ: Princeton University Press, 2000.
Clark, Roland. *Holy Legionary Youth: Fascist Activism in Interwar Romania*. Ithaca, NY: Cornell University Press, 2015.
Clifford, Rebeca, Robert Gildea, and James Mark. "Awakenings." In *Europe's 1968: Voices of Revolt*, edited by Robert Gildea, James Mark, and Anette Warring, 21–45. Oxford: Oxford University Press, 2013.
Cohen, Albert K. *Delinquent Boys: The Culture of the Gang*. New York: Free Press, 1955.
Cohen, Phil. *Subcultural Conflict and Working Class Community*. Birmingham: Centre for Contemporary Cultural Studies, University of Birmingham, 1972.
Cohen, Stanley. *Folk Devils and Moral Panics. The Creation of the Mods and Rockers*. London: MacGibbon and Kee, 1972.
Cohn, Edward. *The High Title of a Communist: Postwar Party Discipline and the Values of the Soviet Regime*. DeKalb: Northern Illinois University Press, 2015.
Császi, Lajos. *Tévéerőszak és morális pánik* [Violence in TV and moral panic]. Budapest: Új Mandátum, 2003.
Cseh, Gergő Bendegúz, Melinda Kalmár, and Edit Pór, eds. *Zárt, bizalmas, számozott: Tájékoztatáspolitika és cenzúra 1956–1963 (Dokumentumok)* [Closed, confidential, numbered: Information policy and censorship (Documents)]. Budapest: Osiris, 1999.
Csörsz, István. *Sírig tartsd a pofád* [Shut your face until the grave]. Vols. 1–2. Budapest: Magvető, 1983.
David-Fox, Michael. *Showcasing the Great Experiment: Cultural Diplomacy and Western Visitors to the Soviet Union, 1921–1941*. Oxford: Oxford University Press, 2012.

Dupcsik, Csaba. *A magyarországi cigányok/romák a hétköznapi és a tudományos diskurzusok tükrében* [The Hungarian Gypsies/Roma in the mirror of the everyday and scholarly discourses]. Budapest: MTA TK Szociológiai Intézet, 2018.

Edele, Mark. "Strange Young Men in Stalin's Moscow: The Birth and Life of the Stiliagi, 1945–1953." *Jahrbücher für Geschichte Osteuropas: Neue Folge* 50, no. 1 (2002): 37–61.

Ellwood, William N. *Rhetoric in the War on Drugs: The Triumphs and Tragedies of Public Relations.* Westport, CT: Praeger, 1994.

Eörsi, László. *Corvinisták, 1956: A VIII. kerület fegyveres csoportjai* [Corvinists, 1956: The armed groups of district VIII]. Budapest: 1956-os Intézet, 2001.

Fehérváry, Krisztina. *Politics in Color and Concrete: Socialist Materialities and the Middle Class in Hungary.* Bloomington: Indiana University Press, 2013.

Feinberg, Melissa. *Curtain of Lies: The Battle over Truth in Stalinist Eastern Europe.* Oxford: Oxford University Press, 2017.

Feitl, István, Sándor Horváth, György Majtényi, and Zsófia Eszter Tóth, eds. *A Magyar Szocialista Munkáspárt Központi Bizottsága Titkárságának jegyzőkönyvei, 1957. július 1.–december 31.* [Record books of the Office of the Central Committee of the Hungarian Socialist Workers' Party, July 1–December 31, 1957]. Budapest: Napvilág, 2000.

Fekete, Gyula. *Éljünk magunknak? A "Nők Lapja" vitájának anyagából* [Shall we live for ourselves? From the writings of the Women's Magazine debate]. Budapest: Szépirodalmi, 1972.

Fishman, Mark. *Manufacturing the News.* Austin: University of Texas Press, 1980.

Fitzpatrick, Sheila. Introduction to *Stalinism: New Directions,* edited by Sheila Fitzpatrick, 1–14. London: Routledge, 2000.

Fürst, Juliane. *Stalin's Last Generation: Soviet Post-War Youth and the Emergence of Mature Socialism.* Oxford: Oxford University Press, 2010.

Gazsó, Ferenc. "A hazai ifjúságkutatás fejlesztési programjáról" [On the Hungarian development program for youth research]. *Szociológia* 3, no. 1 (1974): 104–12.

Germuska, Pál. *Odacsap a munkásököl? A Munkásőrség 1989-ben* [The worker's fist strikes? The Workers' Militia in 1989]. In *Kádárizmus: Mélyfúrások,* évkönyv 16 [Kádárism: Deep drilling, almanac], edited by János Tischler, 439–80. Budapest: 1956-os Intézet, 2009.

Gieseke, Jens. *The History of the Stasi: East Germany's Secret Police, 1945–1990.* Translated from the German by David Burnett. New York: Berghahn, 2014.

Gilburd, Eleonory. *To See Paris and Die: The Soviet Lives of Western Culture.* Cambridge, MA: Harvard University Press, 2018.

Gillis, John R. *Youth and History: Tradition and Change in European Age Relations, 1770–Present.* New York: Academic Press, 1974.

Ginzberg, Eli, ed. *Values and Ideals of American Youth*. New York: Columbia University Press, 1961.

Glaeser, Andreas. *Political Epistemics: The Secret Police, the Opposition, and the End of East German Socialism*. Chicago: University of Chicago Press, 2011.

Gorsuch, Anne E. *Youth in Revolutionary Russia: Enthusiasts, Bohemians, Delinquents*. Bloomington: Indiana University Press, 2000.

Green, Rachel F. "'There Will Not Be Orphans among Us': Soviet Orphanages, Foster Care, and Adoption, 1941–1956." PhD dissertation, University of Chicago, 2006.

Gyáni, Gábor. *Az utca és a szalon: Társadalmi térhasználat Budapesten 1870–1940* [The street and the salon: Social uses of space in Budapest, 1870–1940]. Budapest: Új Mandátum, 1999.

Gyuris, György. *A Tiszatáj fél évszázada 1947–1997* [Half-century of Tiszatáj]. Szeged: NKA Irodalmi és Könyvkiadási Szakmai Kollégiuma, 1997.

H. Sas, Judit. *Közelmúlt: Rendszerváltások, családtörténetek* [The recent past: Changes of regime, family histories]. Budapest: Új Mandátum Könyvkiadó, 2003.

Hall, Stuart, and Tony Jefferson, eds. *Resistance through Rituals: Youth Subcultures in Post-War Britain*. London: Routledge, 1991 [1975].

Hanák, Katalin. *Társadalom és gyermekvédelem* [Society and youth protection]. Budapest: Akadémiai Kiadó, [1978] 1983.

Haney, Lynne. *Inventing the Needy: Gender and the Politics of Welfare in Hungary*. Berkeley: University of California Press, 2002.

Harrison, Martin. *Young Meteors: British Photojournalism, 1957–1965*. London: Jonathan Cape, 1998.

Harsányi, István. *Fiúk könyve* [Boys' book]. Budapest: Gondolat, 1963.

Havas, Ottóné, György Elkán, and Gyula Gayer G. *Gyermek- és ifjúságvédelem* [Children and youth protection]. Budapest: Közgazdasági és Jogi Könyvkiadó, 1962.

Hellbeck, Jochen. *Revolution on My Mind: Writing a Diary under Stalin*. Cambridge, MA: Harvard University Press, 2006.

Hernon, Ian. *Riot!: Civil Insurrection from Peterloo to the Present Day*. London: Pluto, 2006.

*Horthy Miklós táborában*. Budapest: Nemzetek Európája Kiadó, 2001. CD.

Horváth, Sándor. *Két emelet boldogság: Mindennanpi szociálpolitika Budapesten a Kádár-korban* [Two-story happiness: Everyday social policy in Budapest in the Kádár era]. Budapest: Napvilág, 2012.

———. *Stalinism Reloaded: Everyday Life in Stalin-City, Hungary*. Bloomington: Indiana University Press, 2017.

Hunt, Arnold. "'Moral Panic' and Moral Language in the Media." *British Journal of Sociology* 48, no. 4 (December 1997): 629–47.

Huszár, Tibor. *Fiatalkorú bűnözők* [Juvenile delinquents]. Budapest: Tankönyvkiadó, 1964.

———, ed. *Kedves, jó Kádár elvtárs!: Válogatás Kádár János levelezéséből, 1954–1989.* [Dear, kind comrade Kádár!: Selections from the correspondence of János Kádár, 1954–1989]. Budapest: Osiris, 2002.

Iványi, János. "Gondok a magasvérnyomás-betegség kezelésében" [Problems in the treatment of hypertension]. *Békés Megyei Népújság* 43, no. 114 (May 14, 1988): 10.

Janssen, Wiebke. *Halbstarke in der DDR: Verfolgung und Kriminalisierung einer Jugendkultur* [The "half-strongs" in the GDR: Surveillance and criminalization of a youth culture]. Berlin: Links, 2010.

Jessen, Ralph. *Polizei im Industrierevier: Modernisierung und Herrschaftspraxis im westfälischen Ruhrgebiet 1848–1914* [Police in the industrial zone: Modernization and practices of rule in the Westphalian Ruhrgebiet, 1848–1914]. Göttingen: Vandenhoeck & Ruprecht, 1991.

Jobs, Richard I. *Riding the New Wave: Youth and the Rejuvenation of France after the Second World War.* Stanford: Stanford University Press, 2007.

Jones, Polly, ed. *The Dilemmas of De-Stalinization: Negotiating Cultural and Social Change in the Khrushchev Era*. London: Routledge, 2006.

Junes, Tom. *Student Politics in Communist Poland: Generations of Consent and Dissent*. Lanham, MD: Lexington Books, 2015.

Kádár, János. *Válogatott beszédek és cikkek 1957–1974* [Selected speeches and articles, 1957–1974]. Budapest: Kossuth Könyvkiadó, 1975.

Katona, Katalin. *Ifjúságunk problémái* [Problems of our youth]. Budapest: Gondolat, 1967.

Katsiaficas, George. *The Imagination of the New Left: A Global Analysis of 1968.* Boston, MA: South End Press, 1987.

Katz, Jack. "What Makes Crime 'News'?" *Media, Culture and Society* 9, no. 1 (1987): 47–75.

Keleti, Márton, dir. *Dalolva szép az élet*. 1950; Budapest: Magyar Filmgyártó Nemzeti Vállalat [Hungarian National Film Production Enterprise] / Hunnia Filmstúdió [Hunnia Studio], Magyar Nemzeti Filmarchívum [Hungarian National Film Archives]. Record no. HF 763.

Kelly, Catriona. *Children's World: Growing Up in Russia, 1890–1991.* New Haven, CT: Yale University Press, 2007.

Kende, Péter. "Mi történt a magyar társadalommal 1956 után?" [What happened to Hungarian society after 1956?]. In *Évkönyv 11: Magyarország a jelenkorban* [Almanac 11: Hungary in the modern era], edited by Éva Standeisky and János M. Rainer, 9–17. Budapest: 1956-os Intézet, 2003.

Kengyel, Miklós. *Magyar polgári eljárásjog* [The Hungarian civil procedure law]. Budapest: Osiris, 2013.

Kenkmann, Alfons. "The Subculture of Young Urban Workers in Germany 1930–1950: The Example of the Blasen, the Meuten and the Edelweißpiraten in Rhineland and Westphalia, 1930–50." In Schildt and Detlef, *European Cities*, 43–56.

———. *Wilde Jugend: Lebenswelt großstädtischer Jugendlicher zwischen Weltwirtschaftskrise, Nationalsozialismus und Währungsreform* [Wild youth: Lifeworld of big-city youths between the Great Depression, national socialism, and the currency reform]. Essen: Klartext, 2002.

Kenyeres, István. "A Superman hippik és a tanácstalan rendőrök A Budapesti Rendőr-főkapitányság és a hippik 1968-ban" [The Superman hippies and the baffled police: The Budapest Police Headquarters and the hippies in 1968]. *Archivnet* 1, no. 4 (2001). Accessed November 12, 2019. http://www.archivnet.hu/hetkoznapok/a_superman_hippik_es_a_tanacstalan_rendorok.html?oldal=2.

Kiss, Dávid. "A munkásőrség megalakítása" [The formation of the Workers' Militia]. *Múltunk* 54, no. 3 (2009): 238–77.

Kó, József, Iván Münnich, and Zsolt Németh. "A magyarországi galeribűnözés néhány jellemzője" [Some distinctive features of gang-related crime in Hungary]. *Kriminológiai és Kriminalisztikai évkönyv: Kriminológiai és Kriminalisztikai Tanulmányok* [Criminological and criminalistical almanac: Criminological and criminalistical studies], 32 (1995): 156–72.

Kőbányai, János. *A margón* [On the margin]. Budapest: Szépirodalmi Könyvkiadó, 1986.

———. "Bőrnadrág és biztosítótű" [Leather pants and safety pin]. *Mozgó Világ* 5, no. 2 (1979): 64–76.

Kocsis, Piroska. "Büntessük-e a közveszélyes munkakerülést?" [Should we punish criminal idleness?]. *Archívnet* 13, no 6. Accessed June 11, 2020. http://www.archivnet.hu/politika/buntessuke_a_kozveszelyes_munkakerulest.html.

Konrád, György. *The Case Worker.* New York: Penguin, 1987. Originally published as *A látogató*, Budapest: Magvető, 1969.

Kőrősi, Zsuzsanna, and Adrienn Molnár. *Carrying a Secret in My Heart. . . : Children of the Victims of the Reprisal after the Hungarian Revolution in 1956: An Oral History.* Budapest: CEU Press, 2003.

Kotalik, Matej. *Rowdytum im Staatssozialismus: Ein Feindbild aus der Sowjetunion* [Hooliganism under state socialism: An enemy image from the Soviet Union]. Berlin: Christoph Links, 2019.

Kotkin, Stephen. *Armageddon Averted: The Soviet collapse, 1970–2000.* Oxford: Oxford University Press, 2001.

Központi Statisztikai Hivatal. *Gazdaságilag aktívak bruttó átlagkeresete* [The average gross earnings of economically active people]. Accessed June 13, 2018. http://www.ksh.hu/docs/hun/xstadat/xstadat_hosszu/h_qli001.html.

Kresalek, Gábor. "Aluljáró nemzedék" [The underpass generation]. *Törökfürdő* 7, no. 3 (1999): 14–17. Accessed June 7, 2021. c3.hu/~torokfurdo/kresalek.htm.

Kresalek, Gábor, dir. *A vízüzemű Moszkvics utasai*. 2000; Budapest: Fórum Film Alapítvány [Forum Film Foundation].

Kucherenko, Olga. *Little Soldiers: How Soviet Children Went to War, 1941–1945*. Oxford: Oxford University Press, 2011.

Kuhr, Corinna. "Children of 'Enemies of the People' as Victims of the Great Purges." *Cahiers Du Monde Russe* 39, nos. 1–2 (1998): 209–20.

Kürti, László. *Youth and the State in Hungary: Capitalism, Communism and Class*. London: Pluto Press, 2002.

Lampland, Martha. *The Value of Labor: The Science of Commodification in Hungary, 1920–1956*. Chicago: University of Chicago Press, 2016.

LaPierre, Brian. *Hooligans in Khrushchev's Russia*. Madison: University of Wisconsin Press, 2012.

Lebow, Katherine. "Kontra Kultura: Leisure and Youthful Rebellion in Stalinist Poland." In *Pleasures in Socialism: Leisure and Luxury in the Eastern Bloc*, edited by David Crowley and Susan E. Reid, 71–92. Evanston: Northwestern University Press, 2010.

———. *Unfinished Utopia: Nowa Huta, Stalinism, and Polish Society, 1949–56*. Ithaca, NY: Cornell University Press, 2013.

Lindenberger, Thomas. *Aufklären, zersetzen, liquidieren* [Reconnoiter, break up, liquidate]*: Policing Juvenile Rowdytum in East Germany, 1956–1968; Policing Juvenile Rowdytum in East Germany, 1956–1968*. Paper at the annual German Studied Association (GSA) conference, Arlington, Virginia, October 4–7. 2001.

———. *Straßenpolitik: Zur Sozialgeschichte der öffentlichen Ordnung in Berlin, 1900–1914* [Street politics: A social history of public order in Berlin, 1900–1914]. Bonn: Dietz Verlag J. H. W. Nachf, 1995.

———. *Volkspolizei: Herrschaftspraxis und öffentliche Ordnung im SED Staat 1952–1968*. [The people's police: Practice of rule and public order in the Socialist Unity Party State, 1952–1968]. Cologne: Böhlau, 2003.

Lőrincz, László L. *A nagy fa árnyékában* [In the shadow of the great tree]. Budapest: Kozmosz Könyvek, 1979.

Lüdtke, Alf. *"Gemeinwohl", Polizei und "Festungspraxis": Innere Verwaltung und staatliche Gewaltsamkeit in Preußen, 1815–50* ["Common welfare," the police, and "stronghold practice": Internal administration and state violence on Prussia, 1815–50]. Göttingen: Vandenhoeck & Ruprecht, 1982.

———. *Police and State in Prussia, 1815–1850*. Cambridge: Cambridge University Press; Paris: Editions de la Maison des sciences de l'homme, 1989.

Lynch, Kevin. *The Image of the City*. Cambridge, MA: MIT Press, 1960.

Maase, Kaspar. *Was macht Populärkultur politisch?* [What makes popular culture political?]. Wiesbaden: VS Verlag für Sozialwissenschaften, 2010.

Magyar Szocialista Munkáspárt. Központi Bizottság [Hungarian Socialist Workers' Party. Central Committee]. *A párt ifjúságpolitikájának néhány kérdése* [Some questions on the youth policy of the party]. Budapest: Kossuth, 1970.

Majtényi, György, and Balázs Majtényi. *A Contemporary History of Exclusion: The Roma Issue in Hungary from 1945 to 2015*. Budapest: Central European University Press, 2016.

Marcuse, Herbert. *The New Left and the 1960s*. London: Routledge, 2005.

Mark, James. "Antifascism, the 1956 Revolution and the Politics of Communist Autobiographies in Hungary 1944–2000." *Europe-Asia Studies* 58, no. 8 (2006): 1209–240.

Mark, James, Robert Gildea, and Anette Warring, eds. *Europe's 1968: Voices of Revolt*. Oxford: Oxford University Press, 2013.

Markó, György. *Egy zendülő a kelefről: A Moszkva téri galeri 1966–1968* [A kelef rebel: The Moscow Square gang, 1966–1968]. Budapest: H&T Kiadó, 2006.

Mazurek, Malgorzata, and Matthew Hilton. "Consumerism, Solidarity and Communism: Consumer Protection and the Consumer Movement in Poland." *Journal of Contemporary History* 42, no. 2 (2007): 315–43.

McRobbie, Angela, and Sarah Thornton. "Rethinking 'Moral Panic' for Multi-mediated Social Worlds." *British Journal of Sociology* 46, no. 4 (1995): 559–74.

McWilliams, John C. *The 1960s Cultural Revolution*. Westport, CT: Greenwood Press, 2000.

Mejstrik, Alexander. "Urban Youth, National-Socialist Education and Specialized Fun: the Making of the Vienna Schlurfs, 1941–1944." In Schildt and Detlef, *European Cities*, 57–79.

Middendorff, Wolf. *New Forms of Juvenile Delinquency: Their Origin, Prevention and Treatment*. Reproduced from typewritten copy. Presented to the Second United Nations Congress on the Prevention of Crime and the Treatment of Offenders, London, August 8–20, 1960. New York: United Nations, Department of Economic and Social Affairs, 1960.

Minisztertanács: Tájékoztatási Hivatal [Council of Ministers: Information Office]. *Ellenforradalmi erők a magyar októberi eseményekben* [Counterrevolutionary forces in the October events in Hungary]. Budapest: Minisztertanács: Tájékoztatási Hivatal [Council of Ministers: Information Office], 1957.

———. *Nagy Imre és bűntársai ellenforradalmi összeesküvése* [The counterrevolutionary conspiracy of Imre Nagy and his accessories]. Budapest: Minisztertanács: Tájékoztatási Hivatal [Council of Ministers: Information Office], 1958.

Mink, András. "Kesudió" [The cashew nut]. *Beszélő* 3, no. 7–8 (1998): 116–125.

Mitterauer, Michael. *A History of Youth*. Oxford Cambridge, MA: B. Blackwell, 1992.

Molnár, József. *Galeribűnözés: Antiszociális fiatalkori csoportok, a fiatalkori csoportos bűnözés* [Gang-related crime: Antisocial youth groups, group-related crime among minors]. Budapest: Közgazdasági és Jogi Könyvkiadó, 1971.

Müller, Rolf. *Politikai rendőrség a Rákosi-korszakban* [*Political police in the Rákosi era*]. Budapest: Jaffa, 2012.

Nagy-Csere, Áron. "Az ellenség neve: 'huligán'" [The enemy's name is "hooligan"]. In *A politikai diktatúra társadalmiasítása: Nyelv, erőszak, kollaboráció, ellenálllás, alkalmazkodás* [The socialization of the political dictatorship], edited by József Ö. Kovács and Gergely Kunt, 125–34. Miskolc: Miskolci Egyetem Bölcsészettudományi Kar Történettudományi Intézet Új- és Jelenkori Magyar Történeti Tanszék, 2009.

Nemes, Péter. *Ismerkedés a csövesek világával* [Introduction to the life of the vagrants]. Budapest: Tankönyvkiadó, 1984.

Neuberger, Joan. *Hooliganism: Crime, Culture, and Power in St. Petersburg, 1900–1914*. Berkeley: University of California Press, 1993.

Ómolnár, Miklós. *R. B. kapitány avagy pengék és halak* [Captain Béla Radics or blades and fishes]. Budapest: Ifjúsági Rendező Iroda, 1986.

Osgerby, Bill. *Youth in Britain since 1945*. Oxford: Blackwell, 1998.

Pál, Zoltán. *Politikai döntéselőkészítés és valóságismeret a Kádár-korban: Az MSZMP KB Társadalomtudományi Intézete (1966–1989)* [Political decision preparations and knowledge of reality in the Kádár era: The Social Science Institute of the Political Committee of the Hungarian Socialist Workers' Party]. PhD dissertation, Eötvös Loránd University, Budapest, 2018.

Patterson, Patrick Hyder. *Bought and Sold: Living and Losing the Good Life in Socialist Yugoslavia*. Ithaca, NY: Cornell University Press, 2011.

Pearson, Geoffrey. *Hooligan: A History of Respectable Fears*. London: Macmillan, 1983.

Péteri, György. "Nylon Curtain—Transnational and Transsystemic Tendencies in the Cultural Life of State-Socialist Russia and East-Central Europe." *Slavonica* 10, no. 2 (2004): 113–23.

Pető, Andrea. *Nőhistóriák: A politizáló magyar nők történetéből, 1945–1951* [Women's histories: From the history of Hungarian women involved in politics, 1945–1951]. Budapest: Seneca, 1998.

Pilkington, Hillary. "Reconfiguring 'the West': Style and Music in Russian Youth, Cultural Practice." In *Looking West? Cultural Globalization and Russian Youth Cultures*, edited by Hillary Pilkington, Elena Omel'chenko, Moya Flynn, Ul'iana Bliudina, and Elena Starkova, 165–200. University Park: Pennsylvania State University Press, 2002.

Pittaway, Mark. *The Workers' State: Industrial Labor and the Making of Socialist Hungary,* 1944–1958. Pittsburgh: University of Pittsburgh Press, 2012.

Poiger, Uta G. *Jazz, Rock, and Rebels: Cold War Politics and American Culture in a Divided Germany*. Berkeley: University of California Press, 2000.

Pótó, János. "A kommunizmus ígérete: Sajtóviták az 1960-as években" [The promise of communism: Press debates in the 1960s]. *História* 8, no. 5–6 (1986): 26–29.

*Prevention of Juvenile Delinquency: First United Nations Congress on the Prevention of Crime and the Treatment of Offenders*. Geneva, August 22–September 3, 1955. New York: United Nations, Department of Economic and Social Affairs, 1956.

Rácz, József. "Semmittevés: Lakótelep és szegénynegyed-mentalitás" [Idleness: The housing project and the slum mentality]. *Szociológiai Szemle* 6, no. 2 (1996): 81–93.

Rainer M., János, and Vaceslav Sereda, eds. *Bevezetés a kádárizmusba* [Introduction to Kádárism]. Budapest: 1956-os Intézet, 2011.

———. *Döntés a Kremlben, 1956: A szovjet pártelnökség vitái Magyarországról* [Decision in the Kremlin, 1956: The debates of the Soviet party presidium concerning Hungary]. Budapest: 1956-os Intézet, 1996.

———. *Jelentések hálójában: Antall József és az állambiztonság emberei, 1957–1989* [In the web of reports: József Antall and the people of the state security, 1957–1989]. Budapest: 1956-os Intézet, 2008.

Rehák, Géza. "'Szállodaiparunk és idegenforgalmunk fejlesztése tárgyában soron kívül teendő intézkedések', avagy a Kádár-korszak turizmusának első lépései" ["Measures to be taken as a priority in the development of our hotel industry and our tourist industry," or the first steps of the tourism of the Kádár era]. *Debreceni Szemle* 15, no. 3 (2007): 331–47.

Reid, Susan E. "Cold War in the Kitchen: Gender and De-Stalinization of Consumer Taste in the Soviet Union under Khrushchev." *Slavic Review* 61, no. 2 (Summer 2002): 211–52.

———. "The Khrushchev Kitchen: Domesticating the Scientific-Technological Revolution." *Journal of Contemporary History* 40, no. 2 (2005): 289–316.

Reid, Susan E., and David Crowley, eds. *Style and Socialism: Modernity and Material Culture in Post-War Eastern Europe*. Oxford: Berg, 2000.

Révész, Sándor. "Számtükör: A Központi Statisztikai Hivatal 1957-es és 1968-as Statisztikai évkönyvének adatai alapján" [Statistical report on the basis of the data in the 1957 and 1968 statistical almanacs of the Central Statistical Office]. In *Beszélő évek, 1957–1968: A Kádár-korszak története, Első rész* [Telling years, 1957–1968: The history of the Kádár era, part 1], 600–11. Budapest: Beszélő politikai és kulturális folyóirat, 2000.

Risch, William Jay. Introduction to *Youth and Rock in the Soviet Bloc: Youth Cultures, Music, and the State in Russia and Eastern Europe*, edited by William Jay Risch, 1–23. Lanham, MD: Lexington Books, 2015.

———. "Soviet 'Flower Children': Hippies and the Youth Counter-culture in 1970s L'viv." *Journal of Contemporary History* 40, no. 3 (2005): 565–84.

———, ed. *Youth and Rock in the Soviet Bloc: Youth Cultures, Music, and the State in Russia and Eastern Europe*. Lanham, MD: Lexington Books, 2015.

Riskó, Géza. *Diszkó A.B.C.D.* Budapest: Hungaria Sport, 1989.

Roudakova, Natalia. *Losing Pravda: Ethics and the Press in Post-Truth Russia*. Cambridge: Cambridge University Press, 2017.

Rubin, Eli. *Synthetic Socialism: Plastics & Dictatorship in the German Democratic Republic*. Chapel Hill: University of North Carolina Press, 2008.

Schildt, Axel, and Detlef Siegfried, eds. *European Cities, Youth and the Public Sphere in the Twentieth Century*. Aldershot, UK: Ashgate, 2005.

Sebők, János, ed. *Volt egyszer egy Ifipark* [Once upon a time there was a youth park]. Budapest: Lapkiadó, 1984.

Shearer, David R. *Policing Stalin's Socialism: Repression and Social Order in the Soviet Union, 1924–1953*. Yale University Press, 2009.

Shelley, Louise I. *Policing Soviet Society: The Evolution of State Control*. London: Routledge, 2004.

Siegfried, Detlef. "'Don't Trust Anyone Older Than 30?' Voices of Conflict and Consensus between Generations in 1960s West Germany." *Journal of Contemporary History* 40, no. 4 (2005): 727–44.

Solomon, Howard M. "Stigma and Western Culture: A Historical Approach." In *The Dilemma of Difference: A Multidisciplinary View of Stigma*, edited by Stephen Ainlay, Gaylene Becker, and Lerita M. Coleman, 59–76. New York: Plenum, 1986.

Solomon, Peter. *Soviet Criminal Justice under Stalin*. Cambridge: Cambridge University Press, 1997.

Springhall, John. *Youth, Popular Culture and Moral Panics: Penny Gaffs to Gangsta-Rap, 1830–1996*. New York: St. Martin's Press, 1998.

Stan, Lavinia, ed. *Transitional Justice in Eastern Europe and the Former Soviet Union: Reckoning with the Communist Past*. London: Routledge, 2009.

Szabó, László. "A rendőrség és a sajtó" [The police and the press]. *Belügyi Szemle*, no. 9 (1963): 16–25.

———. *Kék fény* [Blue light]. Budapest: MRT–Minerva, 1972.

———. *Kék fény* [Blue light]. 2nd ed., expanded. Budapest: Táncsics Könyvkiadó, 1981.

Szakolczai, Attila. "A fegyveres erőszakszervek restaurálása 1956–1957 fordulóján" [The restoration of armed organ of violence on the anniversary of 1956–1957]. In *Évkönyv 7., 1999: Magyarország a jelenkorban* [Almanac 7, 1999: Hungary in the modern era], edited by János Rainer M. and Éva Standeisky, 18–60. Budapest: 1956-os Intézet, 1999.

———. "Az 1956-os forradalmat követő megtorlás dimenziói" [The dimensions of the repression in the wake of the 1956 revolution]. In *Megtorlások évszázada: Politikai terror és erőszak a huszadik századi Magyarországon* [The century of repressions: Political terror and violence in twentieth-century Hungary], edited by Cecília Szederjesi, 75–90. Budapest: 1956-os Intézet–Nógrád Megyei Levéltár, 2008.

Szamos, Rudolf. *Barakkváros* [Barrack city]. Budapest: Kossuth Kiadó, 1960.

Szendrei, János. *Romák a rendészeti források tükrében* [Roma in the mirror of the police sources]. PhD dissertation, Zrínyi Miklós Nemzetvédelmi Egyetem [Miklós Zrínyi Military University], 2011.

Szőnyei, Tamás. *Nyilvántartottak: Titkos szolgák a magyar rock körül, 1960–1990* [People on whom records were kept: Secret servants around Hungarian rock, 1960–1990]. Budapest: Magyar Narancs–Tihanyi-Rév Kiadó, 2005.

Tabajdi, Gábor, and Krisztián Ungváry. *Elhallgatott múlt: A pártállam és a belügy; A politikai rendőrség működése Magyarországon, 1956–1990* [The past fallen silent: The party state and internal affairs; The functioning of the political police in Hungary, 1956–1990]. Budapest: 1956-os Intézet, 2008.

Takács, Róbert. "Sajtóirányítás és újságírói öncenzúra az 1980-as években" [Press control and self-censorship of journalist in the 1980s]. *Médiakutató* 6, no. 1 (2005): 55–70.

Takács, Tibor. "Az ügynökhálózat társadalomtörténeti kutatása" [The study of the network of agents from the perspective of the social sciences]. In *Az ügynök arcai: Mindennapi kollaboráció és ügynökkérdés* [The faces of agents: Everyday collaboration and the agent question], edited by Sándor Horváth, 107–28. Budapest: Libri, 2014.

Tamáska, Péter. *Történeti riportok* [Historical reports], 2004. Accessed June 11, 2018. http://mek.oszk.hu/01500/01530/01530.pdf.

Tantner, Anton. *"Schlurfs": Annäherungen an einen subkulturellen Stil Wiener Arbeiterjugendlicher* ["Schlurfs": Getting closer to a subcultural style of working Viennese adolescents]. Morrisville: Lulu, 2007.

Tarján G., Gábor. "A Budapesti Rendőr-főkapitányság 'mindennapjai' 1957–58-ban" [The "everyday lives" of the Budapest Police Headquarters in 1957–1958]. In *1956 szilánkjai: Tudományos konferencia, 2006, november 15.* [The shards of 1956: Scholarly conference, November 15, 2006], edited by Katalin Molnár, 29–54. Budapest: Rendőrtiszti Főiskola Büntetés-végrehajtási Tanszék, Társadalomtudományi Tanszék, 2007.

Tauber, István, and Zoltán Ferencz. "A fiatalkorú cigány bűnelkövetők cselekményeinek sajátosságai" [Peculiarities of the crimes committed by "young gypsies"]. *Belügyi Szemle* 18, no. 11 (1980): 95–101.

Thompson, Kenneth. *Moral Panics*. London: Routledge, 1998.

Thrasher, Frederic M. *The Gang: A Study of 1.313 Gangs in Chicago*. Chicago: University of Chicago Press, 1927.

Tolnai, Kálmán. *A Mohikán-galeri* [The Mohican gang]. Budapest: Táncsics, 1975.

———. *Találkozás a galerivel*. Számvetés. [A meeting with the gang. Account]. 2nd edition of *A Mohikán-galeri*, with the illustrations of Gyula Lengyel. Budapest: Népszava, 1984.

Tuchman, Gay. *Making News: A Study in the Construction of Reality*. New York: Free Press, 1978.

———. "Making News by Doing Work: Routinizing the Unexpected." *American Journal of Sociology* 79, no. 1 (July 1973): 110–51.

Varga, Balázs. "Várostérkép: Az ötvenes-hatvanas évek magyar filmjeinek Budapest-képe" [City map: The image of Budapest in the Hungarian films of the 1950s and 1960s]. In *A mesterség iskolája: Tanulmányok Bácskai Vera 70; születésnapjára* [The school of the trade: Essays on the occasion of the 70th birthday of Vera Bácskai], edited by Zsombor Bódy, Mónika Mátay, and Árpád Tóth, 502–16. Budapest: Osiris, 2000.

Varga, Krisztián. "Politikai vagy köztörvényes? Márász Sándor és társai vizsgálati anyagából" [According to political or common law? Investigation against Sándor Márász] *Betekintő*, 1, no. 1. (2007). Accessed June 7, 2020. https://betekinto.hu/sites/default/files/betekinto-szamok/2007_1_varga_k.pdf.

Verdery, Katherine. *My Life as a Spy: Investigations in a Secret Police File*. Durham, NC: Duke University Press, 2018.

———. *Secrets and Truths: Ethnography in the Archive of Romania's Secret Police.* Budapest: CEU Press, 2014.

Vincze, Béla. "Az ifjúság társadalmi beilleszkedésének problémái" [The problems of fitting in socially among the youth]. *Belügyi Szemle* 3, no. 4 (1965): 54–58.

Weiner, Amir. *Making Sense of War: The Second World War and the Fate of the Bolshevik Revolution*. Princeton, NJ: Princeton University Press, 2001.

Wolf, Thomas. *Die Entstehung des BND: Aufbau, Finanzierung und Kontrolle* [The emergence of the Federal Intelligence Service: Structure, financing, and control]. Berlin: Ch. Links, 2018.

Wolfe, Thomas C. *Governing Soviet Journalism: The Press and the Socialist Person after Stalin*. Bloomington: Indiana University Press, 2005.

Wyman, Bill. *Rolling with the Stones*. New York: Dorling Kindersley, 2002.

Yurchak, Alexei. *Everything Was Forever, Until It Was No More: The Last Soviet Generation*. Princeton, NJ: Princeton University Press, 2006.

Zahra, Tara *Kidnapped Souls: National Indifference and the Battle for Children in the Bohemian Lands*. Ithaca, NY: Cornell University Press, 2008.

———. *The Lost Children: Reconstructing Europe's Families after World War II*. Cambridge, MA: Harvard University Press, 2011.

Zezina, M. R. "The System of Social Protection for Orphaned Children in the USSR." *Russian Social Science Review* 42, no. 3 (2001): 44–63.

# INDEX

SÁNDOR HORVÁTH is Senior Research Fellow and Head of the Department for Contemporary History at the Institute of History in the Research Centre for the Humanities at the Hungarian Academy of Sciences. He is author of *Stalinism Reloaded: Everyday Life in Stalin-City, Hungary* (2017) and founding editor of the *Hungarian Historical Review.*

Lightning Source UK Ltd.
Milton Keynes UK
UKHW010953280122
397775UK00002B/36

9 780253 059734